The WHIPPET

Bo Bengtson

Bengtson, Bo
The Whippet

Published by MIP Publishing
P.O. Box 50632
Montecito, California 93150

Second revised and enlarged edition.
First edition published by David & Charles, England, 1985
ISBN# 0-9617204-6-8

Manufactured in the United States of America

Book & Jacket Design:
Terry Bickmore, White Raven Design

Illustrations:
Gail Trower

Printing:
Chroma Litho

To Leader, Flush, Ettan, Squirrel, Beebe,
Angel, Betsy and all the other whippets
which have brightened my days
for more than thirty years.

Table of Contents

A reflection of her heritage: Ch. Whippoorwill Bohem Aria (Ch. Hardknott Maestro of Bohem - Ch. Whippoorwill Precious Gem), the daughter of an English sire and an American dam—a combination which has produced outstanding results for several decades. Aria, shown at eight years of age, is the dam of twelve titled offspring in the show ring, field and obedience and has descendants in Europe and Australia as well as North and South America. Owned by the author.

Acknowledgements

Almost a decade has passed since my book The Whippet was published by David & Charles in England. It met with a favorable reception among whippet fanciers around the world and sold out within a couple of years. Since the original publishers were not planning a second edition they generously returned the publishing rights to me, and I was delighted when MIP Publishing, which has already published several beautiful dog books, expressed an interest in printing a revised edition.

Revising a book, I quickly learned, is almost more work than writing a new one: so much has happened in the last decade that the manuscript had to be gone over with a fine-tooth comb and changed in more places than I could have imagined. In addition, with a new cover, a new layout and mostly new photographs, it has a totally different look than the original book. I am greatly indebted to MIP's Steve Eltinge for help and encouragement in every respect; it certainly helps when the publisher is also a dog lover, a dog show judge and a dog photographer!

Compressing a hundred years of whippet world history into one volume means that you have to leave out too many great dogs and condense lifetime achievements of influential breeders into a passing phrase. If you ask a hundred whippet fanciers what's the most important omission from a book like this one, there will most likely be a hundred different answers. What's important to one person seems utterly uninteresting to another, and we are all more subjective in our judgments than we'd like to think. Pity the poor author who is trying to balance his own ignorance and prejudices against the hundreds of thousands of pieces of factual information unearthed during years of research through kennel club records from all over the world.

This is simply my selection, from the photos and facts available, of dogs which appear to have exerted a particularly strong influence, as winners or producers, or which otherwise illustrate a particular bloodline, trend or feature which seemed worth representing. No photograph was included or discarded without considerable soul-searching, although I admit that a few were included simply because I just couldn't resist them. So sue me.

When I started writing this book I did not foresee that I would need help from so many different quarters. I had to go to many sources for information and am grateful for all the help that was so willingly given, often at short notice, with the original manuscript and the revised version.

My thanks to Mrs. M.B. Garrish and to the late Mrs. "Poppy" Martin in England for generously sharing their recollections as well as old photographs and clippings; to Harry Whimpanny for providing more photographs than I could use; to Mrs. Hilda Meek for sending information about the top racing dogs and to both Mrs. I.H. Lowe and Col. E.G. Walsh for details about coursing in England. Also my thanks to the editors of Dog World in England for letting me copy hundreds of pages from old stud books and magazines, and particularly to Simon Parsons for checking up The Kennel Club stud records of British sires.

In the United States my thanks go to Mrs. Roberta Vesley, past librarian of the American Kennel Club, for providing copies of whippet articles printed in the AKC Gazette over several decades; to Mr. and Mrs. Charles Billings for lending me a large number of old records and pedigrees, to Mrs. W. Potter Wear and Mrs. M.P. Newcombe for sharing valuable information and old photographs; to Barbara Koch, Merril Woolf, Vicky Clarke, David Rosenstock, Mary Beth Arthur, Fern Lockrem, Elizabeth Blalock, Don Papin and the late Betz Leone for information about the "working" whippet, to Barbara Parsons for show statistics, and to many others for help with photographs.

Several people helped with information from their own countries, notably Linda Buchholz and Pat Miller in Canada, Karen Mesavage from France, Thomas Münch from Germany, Espen Engh from Norway, Magnus Hagstedt from Sweden and Lee Pieterse from Australia.

Thanks also to American Whippet Club president Cathy Gaidos for reading through parts of the manuscript and making valuable suggestions, and to AWC for giving me free access to the club library (not too difficult in practice, since it is in my care anyway). Having access to the Sighthound Review computer records of top sires and dams didn´t hurt. Finally my thanks to Paul Lepiane and Fran Reisman for endless patience and support during the production of this book, and to the dogs for putting up with too many missed squirrel hunts in the park.

Any mistakes in the information assembled must be attributed to the author and not to the contributors.

B.B.
Santa Barbara, California
May 1994

Introduction

There are already thousands of dog books, even quite a number on whippets, so why write one more? Basically because it seemed to me that so far no book has shown how the whippet evolved into the elegant, affectionate and useful dog it is today, nor how, from the breed's relatively humble beginnings in England less than a century ago, it has become known and appreciated the world over.

One thing I knew when setting out to write this book. This was not going to be one of those how-to breed books which use valuable space on the general care which is basically the same for every breed of dog. These matters are already admirably and extensively treated in many general dog books. What has concerned me here has been matters which pertain especially to the whippet: its history, its breed standard, its modern development, its many different uses. Although breeding and showing are the activities which—beyond simple "pet" ownership—attract the highest number of whippet fanciers, it seemed important to me to include at least the basics about the history of racing and coursing as well.

I hope the reader will be able to share in my fascination for these little dogs. If the book can convey just a small portion of all the pleasure which whippets have given me over many years, then its purpose will have been served.

Chapter 1

Liking Whippets

The first time I saw a whippet I decided that I would never have a dog like that. It was a skinny, shivering mousy-looking little thing, not at all like the cute cocker puppy we had at home. I must have been all of ten years old and knew that when I grew up I wanted a *real* dog ...

Not so many years later I got involved with dogs—but not in whippets: the memory of that first encounter still lingered. By then there were a few whippets, in my native Sweden, which didn´t look like that first one. There were some colorful Tinribs dogs from England, the attractive black-and-white Ch. Bojars Bettina, and an imported bitch named Ch. Chanctonbury Hi Fi, the first brindle-and-white whippet I had seen.

But it was in England that I became hooked for life. In 1961 I saw a young dog during a visit to the famous Windsor championship show which even to my untrained eye was something out of the ordinary. That dog was Laguna Ligonier, then not yet a champion. I wish I could say that I realized immediately what a pivotal part Ligonier would play in the breed´s future, but that wouldn´t be true; I just thought he was an incredibly beautiful dog and wanted a whippet just like that. Later of course I followed his career with a certain amount of vicarious pleasure; he became a world-famous stud dog, and since the 1970s a high percentage of whippet pedigrees all over the world go back to Ligonier over and over again.

That experience at ringside in England triggered my own involvement in the breed and spawned an interest which has been a constant source of fascination for over thirty years. All my first whippets were closely related to Ligonier—or "Kim" as I came to know him—and they were also closely related to the top whippets in America of that time. Through frequent visits to England in the 1960s and 1970s, living in Australia for a year and in the United States for almost fifteen, I eventually learned to appreciate the qualities of many different bloodlines. Talking to older breeders, reading everything in sight and doing my own research into the largely unexplored past of the breed turned out to be an absorbing, nearly full-time hobby.

Later I was lucky enough to judge whippets in several different parts of the world, which helped to develop a keen awareness of a need for more international cooperation within the breed. It was during these travels that the idea for a breed chronicle was born, one that was slightly more detailed than anything written before but also more international in scope. All whippets are related, and it ought to be useful as well as interesting for breed fanciers everywhere to know more about their dogs´ relatives not only in their own time and place, but also in the past and in other countries.

Since 1961 I have always owned whippets, usually several at a time. (They are rather like peanuts—if you start having them it´s difficult to stop...) Eventually I learned to like even the miserable-looking little creatures which resemble that first whippet I saw. One lesson which whippets teach you is the danger of judging anything by its surface; some of the most insignificant-looking dogs I have known have had hearts like lions!

For someone who likes all dogs it can sometimes be tempting to stray on to bigger, more glamorous, more immediately impressive breeds—but once you get down to it, it´s almost impossible not to get another whippet instead. There just isn´t a sweeter, smarter or more sensible breed anywhere.

Whippets can develop peculiar tastes: the author´s dogs love the fat, juicy hibiscus buds and will go to great lengths to reach them on the higher branches.

Two top dual purpose American whippets in the 1980s, Marial´s Memphis and Marial´s Padneyhill Illusion — both champions in the show ring and recipients of the Award of Racing Merit. Many whippets compete in different fields but few can be so successful that they win official titles in more than one activity.

Chapter 2

Your Whippet Puppy

So you have decided to get a whippet. This in itself shows a certain independence of mind, for the whippet is not everybody's choice, and it is difficult to see it ever becoming one of the really big breeds numerically. In recent years there has been much talk of over-popularity, especially in the U.S., but there isn't much real evidence for this. Usually not more than 2,000* whippet puppies are registered per year in each of the two biggest whippet countries, England and the United States, and those figures do not place the whippet even close to the most popular breeds. Although the whippet breed deserves all the recognition which may come its way, most fanciers are content to keep it a well-guarded secret; the problems which go along with too much popularity can do a great deal of damage, and the day when we see whippet puppies regularly displayed for sale in the pet stores will be a sad one.

The total world population of the breed is difficult to estimate, but it is probably between 20,000 and 30,000 individuals. Once someone gets hooked on whippets he or she tends to stay so forever. A few people like the graceful look of the whippet right away, but gradual acceptance is more usual—starting with a grudging admission that those skinny little dogs aren't so bad when you get to know them. From this there are just a few steps to the realization that whippets have a charm all their own, and to the final decision to get one for yourself. And then one more, and another ... The family member who was the least enthusiastic in the early stages is often the one who ends up letting the whippet sleep in the bed (not on it—whippets like to sleep under the sheets, down by the feet) and makes the biggest fuss over it.

If you have a friend with a whippet you like, it should be easy to find one for yourself. Track down the breeder of that dog and inquire if anyone is planning a litter from similar bloodlines. Don't expect that a puppy will be sitting there waiting for you: the whippet is not a commercially viable breed and most breeders raise very few litters, preferably only when they

*1993 figures: U.S. 1,958 registrations, UK 1,531 registrations.

have some of the puppies booked in advance.

While you are waiting for your puppy, learn everything you can about dogs in general and whippets in particular. Read everything you can find, listen to friends and talk to experienced whippet people, but take everything with a grain of salt and above all try to see for yourself. Decide what you want your whippet for—purely as a pet, for showing, racing, coursing, obedience, or all of it. Few breeds are as versatile as the whippet, and there need not be any real difference between the dogs in the show ring and those in the field. In fact, the best-known bloodlines in whippets regularly produce multi-purpose dogs to a degree unknown in most other breeds, although it appears that in both England and the United States the discrepancy between "race" and "show" whippets has widened considerably during the 1980s and 1990s.

If you simply want a pet, just pick the most appealing puppy from any litter you like, make sure that it is healthy and has a happy, outgoing temperament, pay the price and take your puppy home with you. Ideally it should be around 8-12 weeks, not younger, although it does

Whippets love to run and to play

not matter if it is a bit older. Get detailed written information from the breeder about feeding, supplements, necessary inoculations and worming. Sometimes older dogs are available from breeders who have run out of space; this may be an easy way to get a sensible, affectionate, adult dog without having to go through all the extra work involved with puppies, but it is also possible that the dog has already developed habits and personality traits which you won´t like.

If you want to use your whippet for a specific competitive purpose, you should find out who´s doing well in that particular area. Visit shows and look at the judging if you want to start exhibiting; go to race tracks or coursing meetings if you are interested in the working aspects. One of the charms of the whippet is that there is a long list of activities it enjoys—add obedience, flyball, and agility to the above. Although you can´t really expect one dog to excel in more than one area, there are many bloodlines which regularly produce "multi-purpose" whippets, as opposed to breeds where the division between show and "working" types is completely watertight. Visit any kennel that will let you through the door, read books and magazines—several publications in America, Britain and some other countries are primarily or exclusively devoted to whippets. Ask questions, but be careful whom you ask and when: find someone with sufficient experience and enough success in his or her particular field to make the answers meaningful. The moment before an exhibitor goes into the ring at a show is the worst time to ask questions, but in a more relaxed mood most whippet enthusiasts would be only too glad to find a novice who is willing to listen.

When purchasing your puppy you should of course go to a breeder who is consistently producing the kind of whippet you like. You will find that person only when you have been involved in the breed for a while, watched dogs from ringside and in kennels, read pedigrees, studied books and magazines. Even so, finding a future "star" isn´t easy. In some breeds, an experienced person may be able to pick one out at a very early age—even two or three months. Not in whippets. It will never be known how many potentially great champions have been sold simply as pets because they were not especially outstanding as puppies, but every whippet breeder who has been around for a few years has experienced the reverse: a puppy which looks so perfect at two months that you can´t see what can go wrong—to find only one year later that it developed every conformation fault in the book. It says a lot for the breed (and for the kind of people it attracts) that most owners, however keen they were to show their whippet, decide to keep their "pet-quality" dog as just that—a pet—and hope for better luck with the next choice.

Nevertheless, if you are looking for a show-quality puppy, it makes sense to look at the parents, the pedigree and the puppies themselves, in that order. Both parents of course should be of as good quality as possible and have happy, outgoing temperaments, but at least you have a better statistical chance of getting a good show dog if both parents are well-known winners. A famous sire isn´t enough—the dam may have just as much influence, perhaps even more, since her behavior influences the puppy from its first day. Find out what the parents have pro-

It´s not always as easy as in this case to see that a whippet bitch is in whelp — some bitches manage to hide their condition extremely well. "Beebe" whelped eight healthy puppies twelve days after the photograph was taken.

7

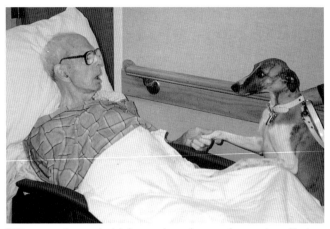

Whippets make wonderful therapy dogs: they are clean, quiet, affectionate and gentle enough for old and sick alike. "Halley" wears her Therapy Dog leash during a hospital visit.

find the same name cropping up several times in the pedigree. Very close inbreeding—half or even full brother to sister, parent to offspring, etc—is not often practiced with whippets and should be left to the experienced breeders, but linebreeding (with the same dog appearing several times in the second, third and perhaps fourth generation) is very common. It simply increases the chance (or risk) that the puppies will inherit many of that dog's characteristics. Obviously the dog which is being used for line-breeding has to be of exceptional quality, and since these key dogs are usually well-known within the breed it should not be difficult to find out something about them.

duced in previous litters—a gorgeous show winner isn't much good unless it can also reproduce its quality, and conversely a lack of quality in either of the parents can be compensated by a correspondingly more impressive stud record. Try to find out what the dogs in the parents' immediate pedigree were like—this can be a time-consuming but fascinating occupation.

It is interesting that many of the best whippet sires have been a little on the fine side, not the super-macho studs you might expect, while many of the best brood bitches have been on the heavy, perhaps matronly, side. According to some of the old breeders a small refined dog bred to a big, rather coarse bitch was usually the best combination; perhaps like some of the other old wives' tales this may have a grain of truth in it, but don't take it too seriously if you are otherwise satisfied with what you find out about your puppy's background. It is usually a sign that the breeder knows what he or she is doing if you

The chances of your puppy looking like a famous ancestor do not depend entirely on how frequently or even how closely the ancestor appears in the pedigree. Some dogs are more dominant than others and will put their stamp on offspring several generations away, while others which figure much more prominently on paper may leave only faint traces of themselves. And that undistinguished grandparent which you tend to forget about has just as much chance of influencing your puppy as one of the more illustrious names in the same generation.

When you finally have to choose from the litter, go by your instincts and pick the puppy that appeals to you most. This may not be a very scientific way of choosing a future champion, but it really is impossible to give any safe guidelines as to which puppy is going to be of star quality and which is not. In any case, it is essential that the puppy you choose is the puppy you like; with that foundation you are at least off to a good start.

Whippets more than most breeds are what you make them, and if you train, condition and raise your puppy right the chances are that it will make it to the showring in time.

Almost the only conformation detail

Whippets get along great with other animals…

which I have found that does not change too much—and which often serves as some kind of rough guide for the general quality of the dog—is a really long neck. I have yet to see a stuffy, short little puppy neck develop into a long elegant arch as time goes by. (But be sure that you can actually determine length of neck—a skinny puppy always looks as if it has a longer neck than a plump one.) The long necks usually come with generous lines elsewhere in the adult dog, too. Obviously a puppy which is always standing very cow-hocked or whose front feet are always pointing outwards, or which has some other obvious defect, should not be considered, but in the main you have to pick the one you just like and then hope for the best.

I am not alone in feeling that it is vir-

tually impossible to predict a whippet puppy's future. No less a breeder than Mrs. Doris Wear, whose Stoney Meadows Kennel for many years bred more American whippet champions than anyone else, confesses that the more she learns the harder it gets—and that she wishes she were as certain as some of the novice breeders seem to be about how her puppies are going to turn out.

Once you have made your choice, stick with it and try not to look for hidden faults or virtues in your puppy while it grows up. Between the ages of six weeks and a year, whippet puppies go through drastic changes, and the sensible owner just keeps his or her eyes shut. There isn't much you can do anyway, so remember that practically all great champions have gone through stages when they looked so

… but a little apprehension before you get to know each other is natural. None of these dogs had met before the photograph was taken: whippets are still fairly rare, but accidental encounters do occur.

bad that you might be excused for doubting their illustrious parentage. Ears go straight up in the air (particularly at the teething stage), the neck disappears into rolls of fat, that perfectly parallel little puppy front develops into an X-shape, those beautifully angulated hindquarters become as straight as a broomstick, etc. Most of these things change again, completely or partially, and, by the time the puppy is an adult, chances are that you will be so fond of your whippet that you wouldn´t want to exchange it anyway, regardless of any physical shortcomings.

Whippet puppies, as you will find out very soon, are about the most agile, lively and destructive of any puppies you can find; they are more like squirrels than dogs, the very opposite of the quiet, refined adult whippet—not nearly as fragile as they look. They can be both amusing and exasperating in their seemingly boundless energy. Leave a normal, happy whippet puppy alone in your living room for five minutes and the room will look as if a bomb has detonated in there; let the puppy into a roomful of people and it will jump over one person while trying to lick the face of a second, at the same time pulling down the tablecloth with anything that happens to be on it ...

All this activity has to be checked, for your own sake and for the puppy´s. Exercise is important, but so is sleeping and eating, and some whippet puppies tend to forget about that last part. Before you get the puppy, invest in a dog crate; this will spare you innumerable pieces of chewed-up furniture and provide the puppy with a safe, peaceful place to eat and sleep. Put the puppy in the crate for an hour or so when it is sleepy and has been fed, close the door and don´t listen to any complaints. If you put soft bedding and something to chew on inside, soon enough the puppy will learn to love its crate and go back to it for a nap on its own. When you have to leave the puppy alone for a couple of hours it is invaluable to know that it won´t be able to do any damage to itself or anything else. Locking a little puppy in a cage may seem like putting it in prison, but it´s really the best thing you can do for your puppy. The lightweight collapsible crates are ideal to take with you while travelling; they make it a lot safer to bring your dog along when visiting friends, staying in hotels or going to shows.

Crates help with the house-training too. Most whippet puppies are taught by their dams to keep themselves clean and they would much rather relieve themselves outside. If you are really consistent, a couple of days is usually all that is necessary to make the puppy understand what´s required; watch the puppy every moment it is up and about, and remember to put it outside immediately after play, sleeping and feeding. (Needless to say, you should give it profuse praise after successful trips outside and some mild scolding directly after any "mistake.")

Unlike males of many other small breeds, whippet males are normally extremely clean in their own house even while being used at stud. At one time I had three males living in the house together (in the greatest harmony, by the way), and although all of them were fairly frequently used at stud, none ever lifted a leg in the house.

Feeding and Exercise

Feeding and exercise are both extremely simple and do not differ much from the general care of other breeds. A whippet puppy will thrive on almost any good brand of well-balanced commercial dog food in combination with vitamin supplements, as long as it isn't spoiled with scraps from the kitchen. Start out with the feeding rules which the breeder gave you, and gradually cut down on the number of meals as the puppy grows up: one main meal in the afternoon, plus perhaps a small breakfast and a hard biscuit or milkbone at night is enough for any adult whippet. If the puppy doesn't finish the food, take it away immediately and let it go hungry until the next meal. It is extremely important not to spoil the puppy or try to overfeed it; the end result will be a picky, badly conditioned adult dog. Nothing is less attractive than a too-thin whippet with all the bones sticking out—unless it's a grossly overweight one rolling in fat. Perfect condition is when the body is well covered with muscles and just enough flesh to present a smooth outline— the top two or three spine bones should be just visible, but not stick up, over the top line.

The puppy itself will take care of exercise at first, especially if you give it a few good toys: a big heavy knuckle-bone which is almost too heavy to lift, a ball which is so large that it's impossible to chew on but fun to chase, etc. Lead training, after a few wild rodeo sessions and a lot

Feeding time is the best time of the day!

of praise on your part, will be no problem, but walks should be kept at a minimum until the puppy is at least 4-6 months.

Grooming

The only other things you have to teach your puppy are to stay still while being groomed and while having its nails cut. The former is fairly easy—place the puppy on a low bench or grooming table with good footing, praise profusely when it stands still and give it an easy once-over with a rubber brush, which pulls out the dead hair. The puppy will start jumping around and play-biting after a while— say "No!" firmly, hold the puppy still, and praise it as soon as it obeys. Keep telling it what a good puppy it is and it will soon start to enjoy the grooming sessions, jumping up on the bench as soon as you bring out the brush. You don´t really need anything except the rubber brush for grooming. A soft brush or a "hound glove" can be used for the final touches, but use your palms for a final rub-down and massage. The dogs love it and it gives the coat a good shine.

Whippets are easy to bathe, especially if you are lucky enough to have a raised tub. Since they love to sleep in bed and on the furniture, mine are bathed at least once every two weeks—it takes all of ten minutes per dog, including shampoo, warm rinse and towelling off. The dogs love

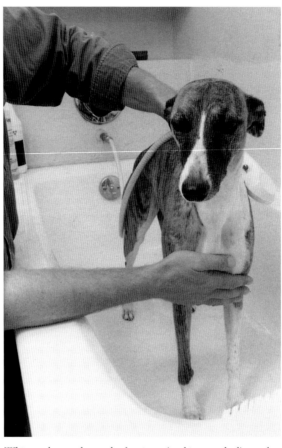

Whippets love to be on the furniture (and in your bed), so they need frequent baths and actually learn to enjoy them—although this is not always readily apparent from their expression. A raised tub does wonders for your back!

it and actually stand in line to jump into the tub!

Cutting nails is more of a problem, but regular attention to this is essential in whippets, which tend to grow extremely long nails even if exercised on hard surfaces. Long nails look unattractive and can even damage the paw, so all puppies have to learn at a very early age (starting when they are still with their

dam) to be held and subjected to this procedure. A strong-willed puppy will naturally throw a tantrum over being held so firmly that it can´t even control what´s being done to its feet: it is not the nail-cutting it objects to as much as being held absolutely still—as it must be, if you are to avoid hurting it.

Put the puppy in your lap, in a sitting position with its back towards you. Hold it with one arm as firmly as possible, take the paw in one hand and use the clippers—any of the brands available in most pet stores—with your other hand. Cut off only little snippets of the nails at first, but when you have done this a few times and the puppy realizes that it doesn´t hurt, you should try to cut as closely to the quick as safely possible: first one cut at right angles to the nail, then little pieces from the side along the nail (rather like paring cheese). Of course you have to be extremely careful—especially with a dark nail where you can´t see the quick. In case you should cut a little too close in spite of all precautions, keep some styptic powder or kalium permanganate handy to dab on and stop the bleeding. It doesn´t seem to hurt the dog as much as you feel it does, if that´s any comfort!

More time-consuming, but perhaps more restful for your own (and the dog´s) nerves, is to file the nails, which offers less risk of bleeding. But the best way is to combine the two methods: first, cut off as much as you can, then file down for a smooth, rounded appearance. The nails should be trimmed once a week on puppies, at least once every fortnight on adult dogs—more often if you are exhibiting. Professional handlers, groomers and kennels often use electric nail grinders, but don´t even think of trying to use one unless you have had it properly demonstrated by someone who knows how to use them.

After a few successful efforts, the dogs usually become resigned to the nail cutting routine; they come unwillingly but endure the procedure without complaints and go away happily—on a good day they may even fall asleep in the middle of it, which is the best you can hope for. It would be far worse for a dog to be left too long without nail cutting.

Compared to most other breeds, whippets are incredibly easy-going and without much formal training soon learn to adapt to your lifestyle. There should never be any need for shouting or physical force—most whippets are naturally civilized and seem more sophisticated than other dogs. It´s your business how much you spoil them: personally I don´t like having dogs all over the furniture, but they do need a really comfortable, soft, warm bed, a little above floor level to avoid drafts and so they can better supervise what´s going on. A comfortable old armchair with a dog blanket in it will be so much ap-preciated that they will keep off your other chairs. And if you allow your whippet to sleep on—or in—the beds, who is to stop you? The dogs will love it; they are among the cleanest of dogs and will keep your feet warm on winter nights. But since you probably won´t remain satisfied with just one dog, you may end up sleeping on the floor if you let in first one, then two, then three whippets ...

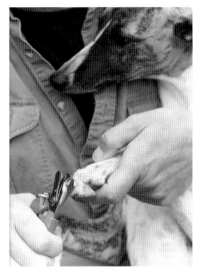

Nail cutting at least once every two weeks is important. Put the whippet under one arm in your lap, hold each foot securely and clip as close to the quick as you dare. Jewel´s expression sums up the experience: she doesn´t enjoy it but is suffering quietly and patiently...

Daily care of a whippet is so easy that you have to have kept other breeds to realize how lucky you are. You have to cut the nails every two weeks at least, and groom the coat regularly (every day when the dog is shedding if you want to keep clothes and furniture free of hair), but otherwise the routine care is very little work. If the dog gets a few walks each day, the chance to romp around loose in a safe place for a few minutes, a comfortable bed, a good square meal each day with maybe a snack in the mornings and at bedtime, the only other thing it needs is your company. It will repay the affection you show it a

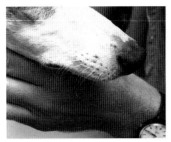

Before . . .

During . . .

After . . .

hundred times over.

The adult whippet is usually a low-keyed dog that does not need to be constantly busy, barking or digging or chasing about; it saves its energy for tremendous bursts of activity which seldom last long and is then happy to revert to a relaxed and dignified calm.

At seven years of age a whippet is officially classified as a veteran, but that fact is seldom apparent to the casual visitor; the white faces which invariably come with age only lend added beauty to the eyes and facial expression. (White faces are not necessarily linked to age, by the way: I have one bitch whose face had gone from black brindle to grey to almost white by the time she was three years old!) At ten most whippets have slowed down, physically if not mentally: it is rather touching to see a toothless and stiff little bitch boss around much

stronger and bigger youngsters, but it is necessary to make sure that the old ones are not accidentally bumped or hurt by thoughtless younger dogs. Any years I get from my whippets after ten I tend to look at as a gift; most stay healthy and active until twelve, thirteen and even longer, but it is cruel and selfish to keep a dog alive which can no longer enjoy life. The best gauge is usually appetite; when a whippet does not want to eat even its favorite food it´s time for that impossibly difficult last goodbye.

For people who like to be constantly active with their dogs there are many more high-powered breeds to choose from. For those of us who like to enjoy our dogs in peace and quiet, yet have access to an endless range of activities when we feel like it, the whippet is hard to match.

Swedish whippets up through the 1950s were mostly fawn, and there was a strong line of blues. The fawn Ch. Tundrans Bimbi (left) sired Ch. High Speeds Blue Sheik, who in turn sired Ch. High Speeds Bluebell — all were Best in Show winners in the 1950s and early 1960s.

The only whippet ever to win Best in Show at Westminster, Eng. & Am. Ch. Courtenay Fleetfoot of Pennyworth, was an English import, sired by Ch. Bellavista Barry and owned by Peggy Newcombe. "Ricky" was America´s top dog of all breeds in 1964 and went on to sire 45 champions. He was handled by Robert Forsyth—now a judge—to Best in Show at Harbor Cities Kennel Club in 1964 under judge Major Godsol (left). The trophy was donated by Mrs. Newcombe to the American Whippet Club and is now awarded at the club´s Eastern specialty every year.

Showing and Judging

It is hard to explain to an innocent bystander exactly what makes the sport of showing dogs so fascinating. Except for some brief moments of extremely superficial glory, a few ribbons and maybe a trophy or two, the dog-show exhibitor does not have much evidence of reward for an expensive, time-consuming occupation. It involves hard work, mental strain, early mornings and late nights, as well as plain boredom for anyone who does not become utterly absorbed by the strange concoction of people and dogs which makes up a show. You either like it right away or it leaves you cold forever, but the fact is that for hundreds of thousands of people around the world dog shows provide a major source of enjoyment.

The basic principle is simple. The exhibitor is asking for an expert opinion on how his or her dog compares with the ideal (set down in the standard of points) and with the other exhibits present. The problem, but also part of the charm of the whole thing, is that, regardless of how detailed and specific the standard is (see next chapter), no two judges ever think ex-actly alike—and even if they did, the dogs themselves vary sufficiently from day to day to provide the uncertainty and suspense on which much of the dog show´s attraction rest. Ideally there should be agreement among experts on what constitutes a good dog, but not necessarily on which is the better of two good ones that happen to be in the ring at the same time; and if two *great* dogs compete it is something which a crowded ringside will watch with bated breath and can discuss endlessly during post-show mortems.

Much of the fascination at dog shows lies in the constant search for perfection. The thrill when you almost find that—as an onlooker, judge, winner or even loser—makes the rest of the sport worthwhile. To the breeder, the search takes a different form than for the casual one-dog exhibitor. A true breeder is one who works towards a long-time goal; breeders have a vision in the back of their minds of what the ideal dog should be and use the shows as a yardstick to compare their dogs with those of other breeders—and also to see if someone else has produced anything which could be useful in their own breeding programs.

Skokloster Castle serves as a backdrop for the Swedish Whippet Club winners each year. In 1987, BOB (left) was the English import Ch. Houghtonhill Orbit (Ch. Novacroft Madrigal - Ch. Crysbel Skylight of Nevedith), shown by Sam Parmbäck. Best bitch was Ch. Gårdsjöns Magdalena (Ch. Colt´s Aladdin - Ch. Gårdsjöns Josefina), shown by Catharina Östring, one of the most consistently successful breeders over the past two decades. The judges Anne Knight of the Dondelayos (left) and Dagmar Kenis Pordham (Solstrand) both came from England.

The whippet is popular as a show dog in a rather different sense from many other show breeds. Larger, long-coated dogs demand an incredible amount of work if the owner is to have any chance to gain the higher awards: hours of grooming, trimming, bathing, clipping and/or conditioning before every show. But the whippet is one of the easiest of breeds to prepare and could be taken into the ring at only a few moments´ notice. This perhaps explains the unusually friendly and relaxed atmosphere around the whippet ring. But the disadvantage of the whippet´s smooth coat is that it is impossible to hide anything under it; every ounce over or under the ideal weight works against the dog´s chances in the ring. Perfect condition may vary slightly from one dog to another—one which is a little coarse might look better when quite lean, and vice-versa. The dog must also be well-muscled, although too many judges who are not especially familiar with the breed ignore this. Much of a whippet´s highly functional beauty derives from the contrast between elegance and power: the loins should bulge out just a little bit when seen from above and have a hard, resilient feel to them; the thighs should look powerful both from the side and from above, and the shoulders should be muscular without being "loaded" (excessively bulgy when viewed from the front). Some dogs can race or course regularly and still look elegant in the ring; others have to concentrate on their show career before limbering up to become working whippets.

The coat requires little attention, except a few minutes´ hand grooming and massage per day—the latter in particular aids both muscle tone and gloss. A bath before the show is essential, with a soft shampoo and special attention to clean feet, all the way down between the toes.

For show dogs, nails should be cut and filed as close as possible every week, and even the shortest of coats may benefit from thinning out the hair under the tail and tidying up around the hindquarters to accentuate the bend of the stifle. Most exhibitors in the U.S. clip the whiskers and the hair on the insides of the ears of their dogs, and trimming (euphemistically called "cleaning up") the neck can go to almost ridiculous lengths. One of the nice things about show whippets is their comparative lack of artificiality, and as far as possible we should try to leave them in their natural state.

Handling

Getting your whippet to perform well in the ring is not always easy. These are traditionally not enthusiastic show dogs; it is unusual in Britain to see whippets which actually seem to enjoy being in the ring, and when they do, few handlers or judges seem to appreciate or encourage it. In America things used to be much the same but have changed considerably over the past couple of decades; especially the all-rounder judges now place such importance on

showmanship that, through selective breeding and rigorous training, the whippet rings are full of exuberant and extroverted show dogs. It is in fact almost impossible to win at American shows unless your whippet displays at least a modicum of animation.

If you are lucky enough to have a dog with the right kind of temperament, do not ruin it by overtraining or overcorrecting. The puppy which makes a fool of you by jumping all over the ring can mature with age into a perfect show dog; it may lose its enthusiasm completely if you control it too much.

The less-extroverted puppy may need to be bribed with a piece of dried liver to show some animation; try to make the show-training sessions as much fun as possible, with lots of praise and a little playing mixed in at

The influx of English imports in American show rings reached a peak in the mid-1960s. Ch. Greenbrae Barn Dance, imported by Mrs. Margaret Hodge's Highlight Kennels, sired 63 champions — at that time a record for the breed. Barn Dance is shown in the photo on the left with his most famous son, Ch. Morshor's Whirlaway, owned and bred by Dianne Bleecker, himself the sire of 57 champions. In the ring (right photo) Barn Dance is moving with his handler Dorothy Hardy.

first, and never train for more than a few minutes at a time.

Begin with basic lead training, the dog trotting happily and willingly on a loose lead with you in a circle, in a triangle, straight back

In 1961, the American Whippet Club's West Coast specialty was held in Santa Barbara for the first time. Judge Margaret Newcombe awarded Best of Breed to Ch. Strathoak Starsheen, shown by Christine Cormany (left), with Best of Opposite Sex to Ch. Great Circle Skibbereen, handled by owner Norman Ellis of the Madcap whippets. Skibbereen was again BOS at this show the next year and won BOB in 1963.

and forth, etc. Don't use a narrow show lead at first, as the puppy will hurt itself and soon get completely turned off walking on a lead. Normally dogs walk on their handler's left side, but it is a good idea to train them to walk on your right side also from time to time—so you are not completely thrown off balance if the judge should request your dog to walk straight across the ring next to another exhibit in order to assess movement fore and aft.

Every show dog should also be used to being "set up" on a table with firm footing and also on the ground. Ideally the dog plants itself with all legs four-square (hindlegs a little stretched out so that hocks are perpendicular), arches its neck and cocks well-folded ears at attention for at least a few seconds; but in any case teach the dog to stand exactly as you place it, and to stay that way even when you stand back. If it knows that a reward, in the form of a piece of bait, is nearby this usually isn't too difficult.

"Baiting" with dried liver or whatever else the dog likes, is employed far more often in the U.S. than in other countries. It is frowned upon by some people, but the breed standard (both the English and the American version) does call for an alert expression—and if a whippet is not interested in anything else it is usually at least interested in food! Baiting is a good way to show ear carriage, but it should not be overdone so that the ring is full of flying pieces of liver, and no whippet should be expected to stay at attention all the way through a big class. Of course, the greater frequency of light ears in Britain during the 1950s may have been responsible for the strange hands-over-head style of handling which was then quite popular, ensuring that the dog would neither see nor hear anything which might make its ears "fly"; but happily this fashion now seems to have been discarded.

When you are in the ring, let your dog rest a little while waiting for your turn if the class is big, or it will be tired and have lost interest at the crucial moments. But don't assume that the judge can't see your dog when seemingly concentrating on another; many judges have a habit of throwing a glance in unguarded

Loose leash handling takes a lot of training and cooperation between handler and dog. Mary Dukes shows Ch. Starline´s Claim to Fame (Ch. Hamrya´s Lucky Charm - Ch. Ringmaster´s Gold Fever), one of the top winners in the U.S. of the early 1990s.

moments down the line of dogs they have already examined.

Study the experienced handlers, accept your losses with grace and take any victory with equanimity; there is always another show, another judge—and another dog which might or might not be able to defeat yours.

The Judge

Every exhibitor who has showed regularly for a few years should be given the chance to judge an official match, club meeting or puppy show, simply to learn that the middle of the ring is a lonely place and that it´s not always as easy as it looks to be a judge. Some exhibitors find the

experience so interesting that they decide to become real dog-show judges some day.

Ideally, all judges should be experts. They should possess a detailed knowledge of every breed they judge, not just have studied the breed´s history, development and original purpose in life. They should have watched that breed over many years before starting to judge it, picked the brains of experienced breeders, read everything available, visited major shows in areas where the breed is

(1) Good balance and angulation but stance is a little cramped and topline drops too sharply—often due to cold weather or when the dog is otherwise uncomfortable. In motion, the same dog often exhibits a correct slight rise over the loin.

particularly strong. From all this a judge can form a clear idea of what the breed should look like, which faults are important and which are minor.

This is just part of it. Judges must also be sure enough of themselves to know that they could never be swayed by outside factors and that they would honestly put up a novice´s unknown dog over the breed´s top winning champion if they really felt that this was the correct placing—and they must also be mature enough not to put up a new dog just to create a sensation. (Sometimes a much greater temptation than one would think!) Judges must be capable of making their decisions clearly, in such a manner that spectators and exhibitors can follow what is going on, and feel that the judge has given everyone a fair chance and is at least pleasing him- or herself, if no one else.

The judge must also be able to shed any personal preferences which lie outside the range of the breed standard. The type of dogs one "likes"

(2) Not the best of types—overrefined, lacking in bone and not covering enough ground. There is a strong tendency to ewe neck and instead of the desired slight rise over the loin the topline simply falls away towards the tail, causing the dog to pull its hindquarters underneath the body. Contrary to (1) this dog probably would not look better moving.

or keeps in one´s kennel must necessarily be influenced by individual taste, but as far as possible should not affect decisions in the ring. (For instance, I find light-colored eyes in a whippet very unattractive; when judging in the U.S. this presents no conflict, since the American Kennel Club standard penalizes light eyes. However, when judging in a country where the British standard prevails it would not be correct to fault a light-eyed dog, since eye color is not specified in that standard.) The same goes for judges who prefer certain markings or colors, who like dogs smaller or bigger than the ideal, etc.

One of the dangers for a judge, especially with large entries, is to slide into what is incorrectly called "type judging": by this people usually mean that the top-placed dogs look similar, as if they were related. This usually pleases the ringside audience, who feel that they know what the judge likes (and therefore know whether to spend their money on entry fees next time that judge comes around); but it is not necessarily good judging. The judge´s only duty is to put up the dogs which are closest to his or her interpretation of the standard. If the best dog is a little heavier than the ideal and the next-best a little on the light side, that can´t be helped, even if they look less pleasing from outside the ring than two near-identical but less good dogs standing side by side.

Of course in a big entry the best dogs should all possess the most important features of the breed so clearly that the lineup—at least to a knowledgeable spectator—shows some consistency. If it does not, it might be the result of bad

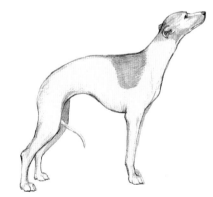

(3) Sharp contrast between the almost perfect front part with long neck, excellent shoulder, front and depth—and the hindquarters which are simply under-developed and hardly reach to the ground, which accounts for the straightness of knee and hock.

(4) Give this one a little more neck and the whole picture would be enormously improved. In fact, the neck may well be there but pulled back into the body out of boredom (one good reason for using a piece of liver as 'bait'!). The body proportions are close to perfection with a beautiful topline, great depth and angulation. Feet are a little flat and the skull a little round.

judging or of bad dogs: no judge can do more than the dogs presented to him or her permit. "Type judging" really means putting up the dogs closest to the ideal—not necessarily the dogs that most resemble each other.

Whippets should not be difficult to judge, as the breed standards used in Britain, North America and elsewhere very clearly define the main considerations. Yet from the comments of many all-rounder judges, it appears that they are regarded as one of the hardest to tackle—perhaps simply because they are such a "moderate" breed without any of the easily recognizable flashiness and extremes of many others.

The important word is balance: maximum muscular power and strength balanced by maximum elegance. A little too much of one

and you get a cart horse, too much of the other and you get a wafer-thin cartoon caricature. The impression should be of long sweeping lines in a comparatively small package—anything abrupt, hard or broken-up is wrong. The hall-mark of a top-class whippet is the long, unbroken and gently curving line which starts behind the ears, sweeps into the shoulders without any break, continues in a perceptible but slight rise over the loin, then falls very gently away over the rather long croup and ends in a dramatic curve through the stifles down to the hocks—which are sharply defined and provide about the only definite angle you should find in a whippet. The underline is similarly S-curved, with a chest which almost reaches down to the elbows, a slim waist and powerful flanks.

To acquire the perfect silhouette the dog obviously must have sufficient length of loin to avoid the cramped, wheel-back stance which has periodically been quite common in the breed. (This extra bit of loin is what allows the dog to cover a lot of ground and was what Mrs. McKay at the Laguna Kennels always impressed on me as making

(5) Not much right about this poor thing—the head is clumsy and the ribcage and loin are far too short, causing the topline to fall away sharply. Shoulder and forechest look quite good, and there is sufficient bone.

all the difference between an ordinary whippet and a top-class one.) It makes the dog look slightly rectangular—as if it were longer than tall—although the actual distance from breast-bone to buttock is not much greater than the height at shoulder.

The opposite—a short dog—can often be a striking-looking animal, particularly when it also has a long neck and upright shoulders, but it is entirely untypical. So far as running ability reflects true type, it confirms this, for while almost every conceivable conformation fault can be found from time to time in the top working hounds, I have hardly ever seen a good coursing whippet which has been too short in loin for its size.

Movement is clearly outlined in both British and American standards, but only a small percentage of whippets even approach that ideal. It seems to be more diffi-cult to produce the kind of powerful, driving, long-and-low move-ment desired in a small breed than in a big one, such as the greyhound. Sound but generally lackluster movement is

Ch. Sheridan Marial´s Nikita (Ch. Sheridan Jamoca - Ch. Sheridan Bianca), one of the most outstanding examples of "old American" bloodlines in the 1980s. He was bred by Dr. John Shelton and shown by owner Mary Beth Arthur to a breed win during the Midwest whippet weekend in 1979. Judge Eugene Jacobs owned the Whipoo whippets which were a major force dur-ing the 1950s and 1960s.

in any case preferable to the flashy but horribly inefficient "eggbeater" type of front action still seen even in some top winners. The judge should decide how much of the movement—faulty or otherwise—is due to the dog´s temperament: a happy, exuberant dog will naturally go a little higher in front, especially if kept on a tight lead, than the dog which is so bored that it´s almost falling asleep in the ring. If a dog does have the rare long, low and powerful stride, it should be easy to forgive any slight imperfections in movement coming straight towards or going away from you.

The legs should have strong hard bone all the way down to the feet. The bone should not be bladed like a bor-zoi´s but slightly flat and definitely not round. Front legs should be set under the body so as to create a slight forechest; shoulder blades and upper arms are long and lean-looking, sloping at a fairly sharp angle from one another (usually given as 45 degrees but in reality often more open). Hindquarters should be long from hip to knee and from knee to the low-set hocks. Front legs and

24

hocks should be parallel, almost perpendicular, with only a slight springy "give" at the pastern. The feet should be tight and small with nicely bunched-up toes—not quite a round catfoot but not a long oval either. The tail should be long and only slightly curved, set on and carried low, at least in adults. Again, excuses can be made for particularly happy temperaments, as long as the tail does not curl over the back.

The neck should be as long and strong as possible without detracting from overall balance, nicely molded with a definite arch over the nape and no tendency towards protruding throat ("ewe neck").

The head, although now considered quite important, especially in the U.S., has traditionally been regarded as a secondary matter in whippets; "They don't run on their heads," as the old breeders used to say. An attractive head is

Every British exhibitor's dream: Best in Show at Crufts, the biggest dog show in the world with up to 20,000 dogs in competition. For Morag Bolton from Scotland the fantasy became a reality in 1992 when her Ch. Pencloe Dutch Gold won. The top whippet of 1991, Dutch Gold (Hillsdown Fergal - Moonbeam of Pencloe and Kienford) won fourteen CCs but was retired after winning Crufts at the age of two.

simply the finishing touch to an otherwise sound, correctly made and well-proportioned dog with good running gear, and judges should never allow it to take precedence over basic construction. There is now a tendency towards over-fine skulls which is almost as disturbing as the constant problem of too-thin muzzles and

weak underjaws. Since a narrow skull often means that the eyes are set too close, giving the dog a sharp, unpleasant expression, I would rather have a slightly too wide skull with a correspondingly more powerful muzzle. The jaw should be long and strong enough to prevent the head from getting a "snipey" expression, but a

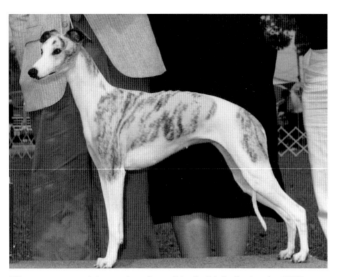

The most successful new show kennel in the U.S. during the 1980s was Bo-Bett in Florida, and its most successful representative was Ch. Bo-Bett's Snow Bunny (Ch. Bo-Bett's Wild Tobiano - Ch. Bo-Bett's Divine Dessert). Her sixteen Best in Show wins make her the top winning bitch in the breed since the 1940s. Bred and owned by Carol Harris, Snow Bunny was handled by Davin McAteer.

really good underjaw on an otherwise attractive, elegant head is extremely difficult to find.

The "scarcely perceptible" stop mentioned in the American standard must not be interpreted as requiring a borzoi-like head; the whippet has more width between the eyes and therefore appears to have more stop when the head is seen at three-quarters angle than it has at full profile. Eyes are ideally large, almost round and, at least in the U.S., dark.

Both in Britain and America light, "flying" or pricked ears are a fault, but British judges are usually not as particular about ear carriage as the Americans and often do not check them at all. Few dogs have naturally perfect ear carriage

all the time, both in the ring and outside it, and conversely few ears are so bad that they cannot be persuaded to stay something like semi-pricked for a short while. Anything from saddle-soap to hoof-grease can be tried to keep the ear soft, but my conscience (or energy?) stops short of taping, although this is done regularly and openly in many quarters. In extreme cases it has even happened that exhibitors had their dogs' ears surgically altered, which (apart from being possibly hurtful to the dog) is unethical, and if found out would disqualify the dog and make the owner liable to punitive action. (Anyone so desperate to win as to resort to this practice should revise his or her priorities anyway.)

Judges must be aware that they may not get a correct impression of ear carriage in the ring. Some experience in feeling the ear may help; it should be fine and thin, with a definite fold about halfway out, so that the outer flap is heavy enough to drop down instead of flying heavenwards. If the judge tests ear carriage by throwing a key-chain or a squeaky toy, this should not be dropped immediately under the dog's nose but far enough away for the head to be kept almost parallel to the ground. Far too many judges do this incorrectly and then criticize the dog when it looks vertically down its nose, which of course forces even the best ears to fall forwards.

Coat color is of no importance—all colors and markings should rank the same. It is easy to be impressed with an evenly and strongly marked parti-colored whippet, and it may help the judge if he or she mentally "undresses" each dog and tries to imagine what it would look like in, say, a solid fawn color. There is no such thing as a badly marked whippet, and it is sad to hear judges admit that uneven head markings, for instance, can influence their placings. Even strong pigmentation is not considered essential in Britain, and although this is required in America it has nothing to do with the dilute coat colors which periodically create a controversy here. It is quite possible for a whippet to have dark pigmentation and dark eyes together with pale coat color, and this in fact can look very attractive.

Size remains a controversial subject. It is difficult to see why, as both the British and American standards in different ways state clearly what they want. American whippets traditionally are permitted to be one or two inches taller than their counterparts in the rest of the world, but on the other hand the American Kennel Club standard includes a disqualifying size clause: more than half an inch over or under the stated limit means that the dog should be disqualified from competition, regardless of other qualities. In other countries the size requirement is less strict; excessive size is seen as a fault to be assessed against the dog´s other virtues, so a dog somewhat taller than the standard´s requirement can compensate by exceptional virtues in other areas and still defeat a less outstanding dog of ideal size. In reality, I would guess that most of the English top winners are close to the top of the size limit and quite a few considerably over it.

Few judges in Britain measure the dogs, but when they do, it should be done only as a guideline—not in order to automatically discard those over (or under) a certain level. On the other hand, some judges disregard size entirely, especially if the whole class is well above ideal height, as sometimes happens. Nobody forces a judge to measure whippets in the United States either, unless an exhibitor makes an official protest against a specific dog; then that dog has to be measured and if found to "measure out" will be disqualified. In practice, dogs of disqualifying size sometimes do win, but the risk of having your dog publicly disqualified and eventually (after three such occasions) disbarred from future showing has resulted in most oversize dogs being left at home or sold as pets.

Lewis Renwick, whose Watford Kennel was founded at the turn of the century, wrote in 1957: "I think from what I have been told, and from what I remember, Whippets of those early days were often larger than they are today, and the question then (as so often it is now), `Is the breed getting too big?´ was frequently asked. The early breeders had the same views on the matter of size as the senior breeders of today"—that the judge should not unduly penalize an otherwise good specimen for being over the ideal size.

The sentiment is still valid today. Obviously there is nothing new in the feeling that the breed is getting too big. Many of the best whippets over the years have been on the big side; and would anyone wish to sacrifice all the qualities they have given the breed—as would have happened had they been disqualified?

Black is considered a difficult color in whippets worldwide and few breeders have consistent success in breeding them. Ch. Locar Datani Total Eclipse (Timbar's Starless Night - Ch. Locar's Holiday Rambler) represents some of the most influential bloodlines for this color in the U.S.

Brindle-and-white parti-color is the most popular color in American show whippets. Ch. Alerek's Ripshin Snowy Egret (Ch. Alerek's Celebrity - Ch. Ripshin's Snow Bird) is shown at 12 months of age.

A well balanced outline, a composite from photographs of a number of top winning show whippets.

Chapter 4

The Whippet Standards

If there is to be any point in showing dogs, there must be generally accepted rules about the characteristics desirable in each breed. The official description of the ideal specimen is called the breed standard, and should be treated with deference by novices, experienced breeders and—most of all—by judges. Serious breeding of dogs is a long-term project, so standards cannot be changed every few years to follow current fashions. Establishing even a few characteristics takes decades, as it means changing the appearance of a living species from one generation to another; unless the breed standard remains fixed, the whole idea of planned breeding becomes a farce.

Most of the first breed standards were written when the sport of purebred dogs was getting organized around the turn of the twentieth century, though most have been changed since then. The first whippet club in Britain was formed in 1898, but records of its first few years are missing (the secretary left the minute-books in the luggage rack of a train at King's Cross station!). But it is known that one of the first objects was to draw up a standard to make judging easier and more uniform, and the people who wrote that standard would have included the most important early breeders within the club. Fred Bottomley of the Manorleys was chairman as early as 1907, Lewis Renwick of the Watfords was secretary from 1910 and closely involved in the club until his death in 1957; Bernard S. Fitter was treasurer from 1910 and active for several decades, becoming an honorary member in the 1950s, and Ernest Sobey was one of the founding members from the nineteenth century.

It has long been thought, and recorded in earlier breed literature, that the whippet standard existing in 1907 was the first one drawn up. Research by the late Constance O. Miller shows that the first attempts to describe the ideal whippet date back a little earlier. The following Whippet Club standard from 1903 survives (see page 34).

This is an important standard, as it is the first written description of what a whippet should look like. There is little there with which a modern fancier cannot agree almost a century later. Note the reference to a "greyhound in

Solid brindles are fairly rare in the U.S.: Fire-X Cinder (Ch. Starburst's Fast Break - Fire-X Rocking Roxanne)

Blue whippet champions are rare worldwide: Ch.Shamasan Queen For A Day (Ch. Marial's Padneyhill Illusion, CD, ARM - Ch. Stoney Meadows Modiste) gained her title at the American Whippet Club specialty in Santa Barbara 1987.

Solid fawns are far more common in England than in the U.S. and take a much larger share of the top wins. Ch. Nimrodel Eagle Wings (Ch. Nimrodel Wanderer - Nimrodel Giaconda), Best in Show at both the Northern Counties and the East Anglian Whippet Club shows in 1990.

The whippet can come in any color or combination of colors. Fashion varies, depending on location and time, but there are no "bad" colors or markings in whippets!

Black and white particolor is a striking but rare combination. Timbar´s Starlet of Morshor (Timbar´s Starless Night - Timbar´s Tempest Storm).

General Appearance Fine and graceful; a Greyhound in miniature.

Head Long and lean, rather wide between the eyes, and flat at the top.

Eyes Bright and fiery.

Nose Pointed.

Jaws Powerful and clearly cut.

Teeth Level and white.

Ears Small, fine in texture, and rose-shaped.

Neck Long and muscular, elegantly arched and free from throatiness.

Shoulders Oblique and muscular.

Chest Deep and capacious.

Back Broad and square, rather long and slightly arched over the loin.

Loins Strong and powerful.

Fore-legs Rather long, well set under the dog, possessing a fair amount of bone.

Hind-legs Strong and very muscular; stifles well bent; thighs broad and muscular; hocks well let down.

Feet Round, well split up; with strong soles.

Tail Long, tapering and nicely carried.

Coat Fine and close.

Colour Black, red, white, brindle, fawn, blue, and the various mixtures of each; it is a matter of indifference.

Height at Shoulder From 16 to 20 inches.

Weight Ideal weight 20 lb.

Scale of points

Head and eyes	10
Hind-quarters	20
Neck	15
Feet	15
Chest and fore-quarters	20
Tail	5
Loins and back ribs	15
Colour	0
Total	100

miniature", the emphasis on sound and powerful running gear and the wide divergence in size limits, as well as the comparatively slight attention paid to head, eyes and ears.

Only about a year later this standard was altered in some respects. As published in Compton´s The Twentieth Century Dog (1904), the same description reappears, except that the words "General Appearance" disappeared, the scale of points was deleted and, interestingly, the height stipulation dropped.

The "greyhound in miniature" ideal has remained controversial over the years; most breeders feel that the whippet should be almost but not quite a scaled-down version of its taller cousin—just a little shorter-coupled and less rangy. (Of course this also depends on how you interpret the greyhound standard!) The lack of any mention of size here is harder to explain.

A height clause was reintroduced in 1907: ideal height for dogs 18 in., bitches 17 in.; ideal weight for dogs 21 lb, bitches 20 lb, with

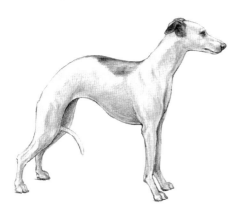

Nice angulation in second thigh and hock, but too steep in croup and very straight in upper arm!

This of course made consistent judging impossible, and it speaks well for the cooperation between the Whippet Club and the younger National Whippet Association (formed in 1936) that the latter supported an almost identical version of the former´s standard.

A clipping from the dog press shows that the situation was still not quite under control in 1945; Lewis Renwick then suggests that "members of both clubs should discuss the matter, and then perhaps a joint meeting of delegates could thrash it out and make what is at present a loosely framed standard one which will be a definite guide to breeders."

the important addition that "a slight deviation either way is to be left to the discretion of the judge". This sentence has probably caused more discussion over the years than any other part of the standard, but it should be noted first that the 1907 standard required a considerably smaller size than the first standards, second that the "discretion of the judge" clause stood for almost eighty years.

Except for the very minor addition of "creams" to the colors listed and some rearranging of the phraseology, the 1907 standard remained untouched until after World War II—an unusually long time for any standard, and probably part of the reason why the breed improved so quickly in quality.

Breed standards in those days were the sole concern of the clubs which wrote them. The Kennel Club in Britain had no say in the matter, and sometimes a new breed club would write a standard which differed considerably from that of an older club in the same breed.

Ch. Mithrandir Spider Orchid (Ch. Hardknott Mystery - Mithrandir Gavotte), bred and owned by Mrs. Pip Campbell, won ten CCs in England during the late 1980s and early 1990s.

Good movement in the show ring: Ch. Dublin's Dancing Lights demonstrates perfect form with drive and style when winning the 1982 American Whippet Club specialty in the Midwest under the author, handled by Neil Schurman. Sired by Ch. Humble Acre Williemakit out of Ch. Dublin's Emerald Isle, Dancing Lights was bred from classical "old American" bloodlines. In the background is the veteran winner Ch. Plumcreek Cinnamon Teal, one of the last few in contention for Best of Breed from 221 whippets entered.

That is exactly what happened. The Kennel Club made its approval of the breed standard a prerequisite for allocating any of the all-important Challenge Certificates needed to gain the official title of champion. When dog activities were resumed after the war years, breed clubs got together to revise and if necessary suggest changes in the existing standards. Mr. Renwick was asked by the Kennel Club to chair a meeting with representatives from the three whippet clubs then in existence. (The short-lived Whippet Club of the British Empire had apparently become defunct during the war but the Midland Whippet Club was founded only a few years later.)

The National Whippet Association was represented by Mrs. M.B. Garrish of the Fleeting Kennel and by Mr. and Mrs. Ben Evans of the Sapperly prefix, while Mr. Renwick represented the Whippet Club and an unidentified fifth person came from the Midland Whippet Club. Mrs. Garrish, who retired from active participation in the sport after judging Best in Show at Crufts in 1984, remembers that the meeting was very informal. No records of it exist, but she recalls that no major alterations of the old standard were considered necessary; it was chiefly a matter of rewording and of amplifying some points. In particular, should a definite size limit be laid down for whippets? It was decided, in Mrs. Garrish's view correctly, that this should be left to the discretion of the judge, as it had been for almost forty years before and still is today.

This whippet standard, approved by the Kennel Club in 1945, lasted for over forty years, and although it was substantially revised in 1986 it deserves to be printed in full. Its general excellence and longevity was in no small measure responsible for the great era of English whippet breeding which followed.

Ch. Nutshell of Nevedith (Eng. Am. Can. Ch. Nevedith Uptown Guy - Chilka Dairy Maid), England's top winning whippet ever. With 44 CCs and seven times Best in Show at major all-breeds show, she has a record few dogs of any breed can equal. "Shelly" was top dog of all breeds in 1989 and Reserve BIS at Crufts in 1990. Bred by Mr. and Mrs. Barker, Nutshell was usually shown by Nev Newton but is owned by his daughter Editha.

BRITISH WHIPPET STANDARD, APPROVED BY THE KENNEL CLUB 1945 (OBSOLETE)

General Appearance Should convey an impression of beautifully balanced muscular power and strength, combined with great elegance and grace of outline. Symmetry of outline, muscular development and powerful gait are the main considerations; the dog being built for speed and work all forms of exaggeration should be avoided. The dog should possess great freedom of action, forelegs should be thrown forward and low over the ground like a thoroughbred horse, not in a Hackney-like action. Hind legs should come well under the body giving great propelling power. General movement not to look stilted, high stepping or in a short or mincing manner.

Head and Skull Long and lean, flat on top tapering to the muzzle, rather wide between the eyes, the jaws powerful and clean cut, nose black, in blues a bluish colour is permitted and in livers a nose of the same colour and in whites or parti-coloured a butterfly nose is permissible.

Eyes Bright, expression very alert.

Ears Rose-shaped, small and fine in texture.

Mouth Level. The teeth in the top jaw fitting closely over the teeth in the lower jaw.

Neck Long and muscular, elegantly arched.

Forequarters Shoulders oblique and muscular, the blades carried up to the spine, closely set together at the top. Forelegs straight and upright, front not too wide, pasterns strong with slight spring, elbows well set under the body.

Body Chest very deep with plenty of heart-room, brisket deep and well defined, back firm, somewhat long and showing definite arch over the loin but not humped, loin giving the impression of strength and power, ribs well sprung; well muscled on back.

Hindquarters Strong and broad across thighs, stifles well bent, hocks well let down, second thighs strong, the dog then being able to stand over a lot of ground and show great driving power.

Feet Very neat, well split up between the toes, knuckles highly arched, pads thick and strong.

Tail No feathering. Long, tapering, when in action carried in a delicate curve upwards but not over the back.

Coat Fine, short, as close as possible in texture.

Colour Any colour or mixture of colours.

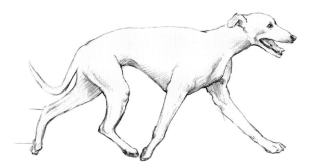

This dog shows excellent drive and reach. Note the head carriage—forward and only slightly higher than topline—and the excellent topline.

Weight and Size The ideal height for dogs is 47 cm (18 in) and for bitches 44 cm (17 in). Judges should use their discretion and not unduly penalise an otherwise good specimen.

Faults Front and shoulders: Weak, sloping or too straight pasterns, pigeon toes, tied elbows, loaded or bossy shoulders wide on top or straight shoulderblades, flat sides. An exaggerated narrow front not to be encouraged. Head and skull: Apple-skull, short foreface or downface. Ears: Pricked or tulip. Mouth: Over or undershot. Neck: Throatiness at the joint of neck and jaw, and at base of neck. Body and hindquarters: Short-coupled or cramped stance, also an exaggerated arch, a camel or humped back (the arch starting behind the shoulderblades), a too short or overlong loin. Straight stifles, poor muscular development of thighs and second thighs. Feet: Splayed, flat or open. Tail: Gay, ringed or twisted, short or docked. Coat: Wire or broken coated; a coarse or woolly coat; coarse thick skin.

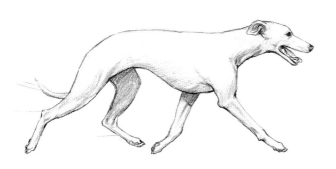

Note Male animals should have two apparently normal testicles fully descended into the scrotum.

The most important addition in this standard was that of "General Impression", an admirable summary of what the breed should look like at its best. No whippet fancier can do better than to pin up over his or her desk and learn by heart the following words:

Should convey an impression of beautifully balanced muscular power and strength, combined with great elegance and grace in outline. Symmetry in outline, muscular development and powerful gait are the main considerations …

If all breeders and judges took these words to heart there would be fewer bad whippets bred and far fewer bad whippets winning in the show ring—dogs which may not have anything particularly wrong with them point by point but which do not convey this general appearance.

Although the real differences between pre- and postwar standards are few, some of the requirements are more detailed. Expression went from the rather terrier-like "fiery" to the less aggressive "alert"; the loin changed from "slightly arched" to having a "definite arch" but not humped, and the passage specifying a "fair amount of bone" was deleted (in my opinion an unfortunate omission, as weedy bone has always been a problem in many parts of the whippet world). Feet were not required to be round any more, as this shape would hardly be functional

One of the first successful results of artificial insemination with frozen semen was Ch. Memoars Cineraria (Ch. Hardknott Maestro of Bohem - Ch. Memoars Zinnia), born in a 1987 litter sired by an English-born dog living in the U.S. out of a Swedish-bred, Norwegian-owned bitch. Cineraria has won a half dozen specialty shows in Sweden and produced several champions.

requested help from the breed clubs in an attempt to revise all standards to fit the same format. The results were controversial; in some instances, breed clubs howled in protest and refused to accept their governing body´s directives. The whippet clubs were more low-keyed but few experienced breed fanciers seem to feel that the revision which was officially accepted in 1986 offered any improvement on the traditional standard; linguistically it is certainly less elegant than its predecessor, but most of the contents were saved.

The major changes are a few deletions: of the "discretionary" admonition to judges regarding size, of the list of faults, and—most importantly—of the General Appearance paragraph, which has been chopped down from exactly a hundred words to twenty-five. (Ironically, and perhaps symbolically, this mainstay of the British breed standard has been preserved and included in the revised American breed standard, which was approved only a short time after its English counterpart.) The only addition of note in the revision was a brief and rather enigmatic sentence listed as "Characteristics": The breed is described as "An ideal companion. Highly adaptable in domestic and sporting surroundings." How a judge is supposed to be able to assess any of this in the show ring is not explained.

Obviously the 1945 description served the breed well and was accepted as the official

in a good running hound, and finally numerous additions were listed as faults—none of which contradict the old standard.

There were attempts to introduce a maximum size limit in 1932 and again in 1978, but the majority of the experienced breeders felt that it would be unwise to place overmuch importance on height.

In the mid-1980s, the Kennel Club in Britain, in a move slightly shocking to those who believed that this august organization would show respect for history and tradition, breed standard also in Australia, South Africa and (in a more or less literal translation) in the Scandinavian countries, in continental Europe and at least nominally in all other countries which are members of the FCI (Fédération Cynologique Internationale), the union of kennel clubs that governs international shows in most of the non-English-speaking parts of the world. In spite of a few protests, it has now been all but superseded by the 1986 revision. This standard is printed in Appendix I.

The Standard in North America

During the early years in America, whippets were presumably judged by whatever anyone knew of the prevailing standard in England. The American Whippet Club was not formed until 1930, but it had a somewhat mysterious forerunner in the short-lived Whippet Club of America, at its most active during the early to mid-1920s. Little is known of this organization, but some material submitted to the author by Canadian judge and bibliophile Nigel Aubrey-Jones in 1988 makes it obvious that the club sponsored racing, published a couple of interesting year books and held at least one specialty show before being dissolved—apparently following a disagreement with the American Kennel Club over the publishing of a separate racing register.

The Whippet Club of America also published what must be the first standard for the breed in the United States:

1920's WHIPPET CLUB OF AMERICA STANDARD (OBSOLETE)

Head Long and narrow, fairly wide between the ears, moderate stop; good length of muzzle, which should be powerful without coarseness. Teeth very strong, white and even in front.

Ears Rose shaped, small and fine in texture, thrown back and folded, except when excited.

Eyes Bright, intelligent , indicating spirit and fairly large.

Neck Long, muscular without throatiness, and widening gradually into the shoulder.

Shoulders Placed as obliquely as possible, muscular without being loaded.

Fore-legs Perfectly straight, set well into the shoulder, neither turned in nor out, pasterns strong with bone consistent with weight.

Ribs Fairly well sprung.

Chest Very deep and as wide as consistent with a flat shoulder.

Brisket Very deep, well cut up in loin.

Back Muscular and broad, well arched but not "wheel-backed."

Hindquarters Long, very muscular and powerful, stifles very long, wide and well bent. Hocks well bent and close to ground, wide but straight.

Feet Hard and close, rather more hare than cat feet, well knuckled up with good strong claws.

Tail Long, fine and tapering with a slight upward curve, reaching when extended well below hock joint.

Coat Short, smooth and firm in texture. In the rough variety about two inches in length and as harsh as possible to the touch, eyebrows shaggy and moustache somewhat long.

Color Immaterial.

Weight Racing weights, between ten and twenty-eight pounds.

The absence of any mention of size (as opposed to weight) and the reference to rough coat are particularly interesting; although the wire-coated variety never found favor in England and had very little success in the show rings elsewhere, it is known that some were shown both in the United States and in central Europe during the first two or three decades of the century.

When the present American Whippet Club was born, on 11 January 1930, one of its first objectives was to write a new breed standard. It was obviously inspired by the standard mentioned above:

1930 AMERICAN WHIPPET STANDARD (OBSOLETE)

Head Long and lean, fairly wide between the ears, scarcely perceptible stop, good length of muzzle, which should be powerful without being coarse.

Ears Small, fine in texture, thrown back and folded. Semi-pricked when at attention. Gay ears incorrect.
Eyes Bright, intelligent and dark.

Teeth White, strong and even. Upper jaw should fit nicely over lower.

Neck Long and muscular, well arched with no suggestion of throatiness, widening gradually into the shoulders.

Shoulders Oblique and muscular, without being loaded.

Chest Deep and capacious, as wide as consistent with speed. Ribs fairly well sprung.

Forelegs Straight and rather long, held in line with shoulders. Elbows neither in nor out, moving freely with point of shoulder. Pasterns strong. Fair amount of bone.

Feet Either cat or hare foot is permissible, must be well formed, with strong pads and claws well knuckled up.

Hindquarters Long and powerful, stifles well

bent, thighs broad and muscular, hocks well let down.

Back Broad and square, rather long and well arched over the loin, which should be strong and powerful.

Tail Long and tapering.

Coat Close, smooth and firm in texture.

Color Immaterial.

Height Dogs from 18 to 20 inches. Bitches from 17 to 19 inches.

The American standard of 1930 was as brief as the British version then current, but already differed from it in some important respects. Eyes had to be dark; the back was not "slightly" but "well" arched; and the feet were to be "either cat or hare foot", thereby anticipating to some degree the change in the British standard. The stop was "scarcely perceptible", which encouraged a more "snaky" type of head than commonly seen in Britain, and finally—most important—the size was given as more than an inch over the British ideal. These discrepancies were the beginning of a widening gap between British and American ideals.

By 1944, shortly before the British standard was revised (but basically unchanged), the American standard was radically altered: ideal height was raised a further couple of inches, to 19-22 in. for dogs, 18-21 in. for bitches—with the addition that these were not intended as definite limits, only approximations. The nose was to be entirely black—while the British standard specified several acceptable nose colors. Incorrect ear carriage should be 'strictly penalized' and eyes should be not only dark but also round, indicating once again the greater American preoccupation with head and expression. There were some other changes in the wording, and the first outright ground for disqualification: an undershot mouth.

After eleven years, in 1955 a completely rewritten and much more verbose standard was approved. General appearance was included for the first time, requiring the whippet to be a dog of "moderate size, very alert, that can cover a maximum of distance with a minimum of lost motion." The stipulation on eye color was temporarily loosened a little; "oblique eyes" were to be severely penalized and there was a rather peculiar sentence concerning forelegs, requiring them to be "held in line with the shoulders and not set under the body", actually making it sound as if a straight upper arm was desirable—hardly conducive to the angulation needed in a working running breed. Straight upper arms have long been a problem in some lines; fortunately this clause was abandoned in later versions of the American standard.

The 1955 standard held until 1971, when the "General Appearance" paragraph was rephrased. Even more detailed requirements were introduced concerning lack of pigmentation, disqualifying eye color and now also a disqualifying size—one half-inch or more above or below the specified measurements.

The trend towards amplification was continued in 1976, when a new whippet standard was approved by the American Kennel Club. It contained no drastic changes from the previous version but included a lot more detail, especially concerning legs and feet, topline, tail and movement, as well as the

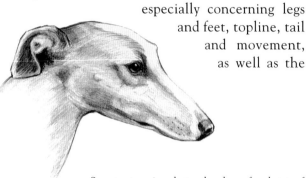

Sweet expression, but rather down faced: top of skull and top of muzzle not parallel.

proviso that old scars and injuries should not necessarily spoil a dog's chances in the showring.

AMERICAN WHIPPET STANDARD APPROVED BY THE AMERICAN KENNEL CLUB ON 9 MARCH 1976 (OBSOLETE)

General Appearance A moderate size sight hound giving the appearance of elegance and fitness, denoting great speed, power, and balance without coarseness. A true sporting hound that covers a maximum of distance with a minimum of lost motion.

Head Long and lean, fairly wide between the ears, scarcely perceptible stop, good length of muzzle which should be powerful without being coarse. Nose entirely black.

Ears Small, fine in texture, thrown back and folded. Semipricked when at attention. Gay ears are incorrect and should be severely penalized.

Eyes Large, dark, with keen intelligent alert expression. Lack of pigmentation around eyelids is undesirable. Yellow or dilute-colored eyes should be strictly penalized. Blue or china-colored eyes shall disqualify. Both eyes must be of the same color.
Muzzle Muzzle should be long and powerful denoting great strength of "bite" without coarseness. Teeth should be white and strong. Teeth of upper jaw should fit closely over teeth of lower jaw creating a strong scissors bite. Extremely short muzzle or lack of underjaw should be strictly penalized. An even bite is extremely undesirable. Undershot shall disqualify. Overshot one-quarter inch or more shall disqualify.

Neck Long, clean and muscular, well arched with no suggestion of throatiness, widening gracefully into the top of the shoulder. A short thin neck, or concave curvature of the top neckline sometimes called ewe (opposite of arched), should be penalized.

Shoulders Long, well laid back, with flat muscles, allowing for moderate space between shoulder blades at the peak of withers. The length of the shoulder blade equals the length of the upper arm. A straight shoulder blade, short upper arm, a heavily muscled or loaded shoulder, or a very narrow shoulder, all restricting low free movement, should be strictly penalized.

Brisket Very deep and strong, reaching as nearly as possible to the point of the elbow. Ribs well sprung but with no suggestion of barrel shape. Should fill in the space between the forelegs so that there is no appearance of a hollow between them.

Back and Loin The back broad, firm and well muscled, having length and a strong natural arch over the loin, creating a definite tuck-up of the underline. A short loin creating a cramped stance should be penalized.

Topline and Croup The topline runs smoothly from the withers with a graceful and not too accentuated arch beginning over the loin and carrying through over the croup, with the arch being continuous without flatness. A wheel-back, flat back, dip behind shoulder blades, or a back that falls away sharply creating a cut-away appearance should be penalized. A steep or flat croup should be penalized.

Forelegs Straight, giving appearance of strength and substance of bone. The points of the elbows should point neither in nor out, but straight back. When the dog moves, the joints allow free movement from the point of the shoulder to give a long low reach. Pasterns strong, slightly bent and flexible. Bowed legs, tied-in elbows, legs lacking substance, legs set far under the body so as to create a fore-chest, weak or straight pasterns should be strictly penalized.

Feet Feet must be well formed with hard, thick pads and strong nails. Nails naturally short or of moderate length. Toes should be long, close and well arched. Feet more hare than cat, but both are acceptable. Flat, open, or soft feet without thick hard pads should be strictly penalized.

Hindquarters Long and powerful, stifles well bent, hocks well let down and close to the ground. Thighs broad and muscular. The muscles are long and flat and carry well down toward the hock. Sickle or cowhocks should be strictly penalized.

Tail The tail long and tapering, reaching to the hipbone when drawn through between the hind legs. When the dog is in motion, the tail is carried low with a gentle upward curve; tail should not be carried higher than top of back. A curled tail should be penalized.

Coat and Color Close, smooth and firm in texture. A coarse or wooly coat should be penalized. Color immaterial.

Gait Low, free moving and smooth, with reach in the forequarters and strong drive in the hindquarters. The dog has great freedom of action when viewed from the side; the forelegs reach forward close to the ground; the hindlegs have strong propelling power. Lack of front reach or rear drive, a short, mincing gait with high knee action should be strictly penalized. When moving and viewed from front or rear, legs should turn neither in nor out, nor should feet cross or interfere with each other. Crossing in front or moving too close should be strictly penalized.

N.B. Old scars and injuries, the result of work or accident should not be allowed to prejudice the dog´s chance in the show ring, unless they interfere with its movement or ability to perform.

Size Ideal height for dogs, 19 to 22 inches; for bitches 18 to 21 inches, measured across the shoulders at the highest point. One-half inch above or below the above stated measurements will disqualify.

DISQUALIFICATIONS
Blue or china-colored eyes.
Undershot.
Overshot one-quarter inch or more.
A dog one-half inch above or below the measurements specified under "Size."

One small but important change was suggested by the American Whippet Club and approved by AKC in late 1983. Following the publicity given to certain breeding experiments carried out by one individual who claimed to have produced long-coated whippets from pure-bred smooth stock, any type of coat other than the traditional smooth was listed in the standard as disqualifying.

Following the same route as the Kennel Club in England, the American Kennel Club towards the end of the 1980s requested the breed clubs to change their standards to fit into a set format. Many refused, feeling that it was putting the cart before the horse if breed standards which had been used as a guiding light by breeders for decades were to be refashioned simply to suit the tastes of kennel club staff and aspiring judges. In whippets, where the standard has been revised regularly every few years, it would be impossible to maintain this kind of lofty stance, and the American Whippet Club after months of diligent work agreed on a standard which is published in Appendix II.

One further revision was allowed in 1993, changing the wording of disqualifying size from "half an inch" over or under the stated limit to "more than half an inch." A small but embarrassing mistake concerning the unpigmented "eyelid" still remains (it should of course be "eyerim").

Obviously, what is considered a good whippet in America is not necessarily a good whippet in Britain or in many other countries. A dog of quite acceptable size according to one standard might be considered far too big or too small according to another; pigmentation and eye color which are considered unimportant in one country can actually disqualify an otherwise top-class whippet according to another set of rules. In spite of this, the best dogs around the world differ far less in appearance than one might think—in fact many of the top winning American dogs fit as well into the British standard as any of the British dogs do, and vice versa, and an increasing number of whippet fanciers around the world find that they can benefit by importing or breeding to dogs from many different countries.

Ch. Robmaywin Stargazer of Allways (Ch. Evening Star of Allways - Ch. Mistral's Mrs. Miniver), the top winning male in England up to the 1960s. In 1958 he became the first whippet to win the Hound Group at Crufts. One of his champion daughters helped found Shalfleet in England, another the Highlight Kennels in the United States.

Ch. Elysian A-Few Perrier (Ch. Plumcreek Walk On Water - Ch. A-Few Marthasville) won three American Whippet Club specialties in the early 1990s. Judge Anthony Gutilla (Lazebrook) gave him Best of Breed at the AWC Southern specialty, handled by Jan Swayze Pence.

A group of whippets with wellrounded talents — at least 37 titles for show, lure coursing and obedience titles between them! From left to right, in the back: Dual Ch. Shamasan Bitterblue Columbia, Dual Ch. Bitterblue's Loco Weed and Dual Ch. Bitterblue's Raybar Peyote. In front, from left: Ch. Aymes N Raybar's Tumbleweed, Ch. Sithean's Lolita Bitterblue, Ch. Bitterblue's Prairie Fire, Bitterblue's Gun Runner, Bitterblue's Ffire and Ice, and Ch. Bitterblue Shamasan Magenta.

All have at least a Senior Courser or Field Champion title in lure coursing (Peyote, Tumbleweed and Prairie Fire are Lure Coursers of Merit), and all except Magenta have the CD degree in obedience. Dual Champions have AKC titles in both conformation and lure coursing. Loco Weed, Peyote and Tumbleweed have passed the Canine Good Citizen test and Prairie Fire is a Register of Merit sire. Paul and Linda Garwacki in Massachusetts are the proud owners.

Chapter 5

The Multi-purpose Whippet

Hardly any breed of dog is used for a greater variety of purposes than the whippet. It may be family pet, show dog or breeding animal, in some cases an obedience performer, but the whippet´s original purpose in life was to be a hunting dog coursing live game. Thousands of people around the world still pursue the sport of organized open-field coursing with sighthounds after live game or derivative sports, lure coursing or racing on different types of track. An interesting aspect of this is that the bloodlines which have played the most important part in development of the show whippet have also frequently had great influence on the working whippet. When a breed is used both for show and for utilitarian pursuit, there is eventually a division of types; but this has not yet happened in whippets to nearly the same degree as in most others.

Coursing

In coursing, the hounds run down and kill the quarry by sight, strength and superior speed. Many thousands of years ago humans began to use half-wild camp dogs to help with the hunting, and coursing as it developed over the centuries was often a necessary means of survival. With the arrival of an agricultural society, and much later of guns, coursing lost much of its basic importance and developed into a sport, a sort of competitive test for the fastest and most efficient hounds run according to a detailed set of rules.

Coursing has existed wherever sighthounds were known. Salukis have coursed hare and gazelle in Arabia and the Middle East for thousands of years, the borzoi was used in imperial Russia for the aristocratic sport of wolf hunting, and in Britain the large wire-coated sighthounds—deerhounds and wolfhounds—have pursued their quarry since medieval times. The most popular coursing breed has always been the greyhound, particularly in England where the first greyhound coursing club, started in 1776, is still in existence. Greyhound coursing in England has been governed by the National Coursing Club since 1857.

Organized whippet coursing is a relatively new sport. Obviously whippet-type dogs

Whippets love warmth, but they also love to run and can even come along on a ski trip, as shown by Peter Wounder and his whippets enjoying a Scandinavian winter.

have been used for private, unofficial coursing wherever hares were available for hundreds of years, but although some private meetings were held by members of the Whippet Club in England during the 1950s, the Whippet Coursing Club was not founded until the summer of 1962. It is not affiliated with any other club but has strong connections to the Whippet Club through some of its members—notably Mrs. Dorrit McKay of the Laguna Kennels, for many years secretary of the Whippet Club and chairman of the Whippet Coursing Club.

The first meeting was held at Fawler on 1 December 1962 with sixteen dogs running. With the help of friendly landowners and farmers the club was soon running up to a dozen meetings per season in the south of England. Its

two most important trophies—the Nicholl cup for dogs and the Laguna cup for bitches—were presented during the first season and have remained the most coveted coursing trophies for whippets in England. (The Nicholl cup was won outright by Miss Gay Robertson's Madishan Moonlake after three successive victories in 1974, 1975 and 1976, and was replaced by the Moonlake cup.)

By 1971 whippet coursing had become so popular that two more clubs were started— the East of England Whippet Coursing Club by Mr. and the Hon. Mrs. Richardson in Essex, and the East Anglian Whippet Coursing Club by Mrs. Daphne Gilpin (of the well-known Wenonah whippets and greyhounds) in the Peterborough area. At least one more club has been formed since, the Woolley Whippet Coursing Club, and as a central body for the four clubs the National Whippet Coursing Club was formed in 1972, consisting of a chairman, a secretary and two representatives from each club.

The man behind much of the organized whippet coursing in England is Col. E.G. Walsh, whose articles and coursing stud-book compilations have been invaluable to the sport; and also his dogs—not carrying a kennel prefix but registered with names having the initials EW—have been very successful. Several of the well-known show kennels regularly participate in coursing-club activities. Lady Selway of the Ballagans was an early member, as were the late Mrs. Cleeve of the Dragonhills, Lady Anderson with her Tweseldowns, Mary Lowe of the Nimrodels, Joanna Russell and Caroline Brown with the Martinsells, and Hilda Meek of the Chancericks.

Obviously not many exhibitors are willing to risk a damaged toe or a scratch from barbed wire on their show dogs, but those which have coursed have given a good account of themselves. Mrs. Lowe´s great show winner in the 1970s Ch. Nimrodel Ruff finished his show title, then coursed for three seasons, then went back into the ring and won several more Challenge Certificates. In the 1980s, Susan Baird´s Ch. Sound Barrier was the leading dual winner, with three challenge certificates and the Moonlake cup for 1982 and 1983 to his credit. He carries well-known show blood from his sire Ch. Waycross Wishing Star and his dam Sunday Best was sired by Tweseldown Lariat out of a litter sister to Ch. Tweseldown Whinchat, the bitch line which is behind so many bench winners, including the redoubtable Ch. Nimrodel Wanderer, as well as some good coursing stock.

The influence of Mrs. McKay´s kennel has been particularly strong, at first mainly through the orange brindle-and-white stud dog Ch. Laguna Light Lagoon. He himself did not race or course but proved to be an outstanding sire, particularly of coursing whippets. Although carrying the Laguna prefix, "Freckles" was actually bred by Miss Clay of the Tantivvey Kennels out of a sister to the internationally famous Diver. The sire was a gorgeous young show dog called Laguna Lightstep who won his Junior Warrant many times over in 1963 and who might have become a champion in Britain if he had not been exported. As Freckles´ four grandparents were Laguna champions Limelight, Leading Lady and Ligonier and Fleeting Fancy Free, the breed's first leading coursing sire was indeed bred from the best show stock imaginable. His most successful son was probably the previously mentioned Madishan Moonlake.

The rules for whippet coursing in Britain are based on those of the National Coursing Club for greyhounds. Only whippets registerable with the Kennel Club, over 12 months of age, and not exceeding 20 inches at the shoulder, may take part. The size rule has been attacked many times but stands firm: "The whippet is a `little´ dog and if bred oversize it loses type," to quote Col. Walsh.

The meetings take place between November and February on grounds where plenty of hares can be expected. Knowing where to find the hares is an art in itself: for instance they do not like sheep but can often be found in a field of bullocks; on flat land it is worthwhile to walk every field, but on hilly land hares prefer the middle level in the lee of the wind. Two dogs are run at a time by the slipper, from special fast-release leads; he needs to be an expert in order to make split-second decisions on whether a hare is suitable to be coursed. The judge is always on horseback; both slipper and judge are usually professionals licensed by the National Coursing Club.

At a "walked" meeting the field—consisting of the participants, their dogs and spectators—spreads out and walks in a line some twenty yards behind the slipper and the two dogs about to be released. The length of slip—the "law" given to the hare—must not be less than 35 yards. At a "driven" meeting the hare is driven towards the field by a line of around 25-40 "beaters." When a hare is raised and the dogs are slipped, the field is expected to stop and hold on to the non-runners: no easy task, since even a small whippet suddenly is stronger than a giant when seized by the desire to course—and there is a heavy fine for loose dogs. The judge follows the coursing pair of dogs and awards points for each dog´s speed up to the hare, for turning the hare less or more than a right angle from its course, for a go-by (passing the other dog on the straight run by at least a length), for a trip (when the hare is struck but not held), and for the kill.

Each dog wears a knitted collar: the top dog of each pair wears red and goes into slips on the left-hand side, while the bottom dog wears a white collar and goes on the right-hand side.

For a winner to be declared it is not necessary for the course to end in a kill. In fact only about one in four do, for the hare can weigh half as much as a whippet and is often its equal in speed and agility. If the hare goes to ground or finds a thicket the dogs will usually give up the chase, as they hunt by sight only—not by scent.

When there is a kill it is usually surprisingly fast. The dog grips the neck of the hare and kills it instantly. There are exceptions to this, but a "hard mouth" is much desired. Participants must see that any hare caught is dead before the dogs are attended to. The dogs do not usually suffer any hardships other than those caused by sharp stones, barbed wire, etc.

The winners of each course are run against each other until the final winner of the meeting can be determined. If there is a shortage of hares, a draw sometimes has to be declared.

Coursing remains a controversial sport in Great Britain, outlawed in many other countries. Bills to ban it have several times been read in Parliament, but have so far not gone through. In early 1983 the Waterloo Cup for greyhounds, which has been run annually since 1836, was disrupted by protestors who ran over the plowed fields, scaring away the hares by shouting and setting off firecrackers. If coursing is eventually outlawed the enthusiasts—according to Col. Walsh—will go back to private coursing, with fewer dogs at a time, no card, no slipper, no judge on horseback: "In this country certainly man has pursued hares with dogs ever since they first joined up together a great many thousand years ago, and many of us will go on doing so until the last bit of open land is covered in concrete and the last hare is shut up in a wild animal park."

For those who keep whippets entirely as pets around the house it is a fascinating, almost frightening, experience to see how deeply the coursing instinct is embedded in the whippet´s psyche. Many whippets can go straight from sleeping on the couch to perform the activity for which they were bred without any training whatsoever. Although open-field coursing is outlawed in many European countries it is impossible to prevent a whippet from chasing after a hare wherever the opportunity offers itself. While living in a densely forested area of Sweden, which did not provide ideal coursing grounds, my own dogs regularly—unasked but often successfully—coursed hares. The bitches were invariably more efficient than the males, and the most enthusiastic of all was a superbly show-bred, rather over-refined and shy little

The coursing instinct is born early in whippet puppies. A glove or a plastic bag tied to a string at the end of a long pole can cause endless excitement.

Participants and gallery on the way to a Whippet Coursing Club meet in England.

bitch which most observers would see as a "typically exaggerated" bench specimen rather than as the frighteningly utilitarian hunting machine she was.

In the period 1983-1993 whippet coursing in the UK has continued to flourish despite the pressure from the anti-fieldsport lobby which increasingly besets all forms of hunting with dogs, both scent- and sighthounds.

Major Anthony Loch publishes annual statistics of the top winners with all four whippet coursing clubs, which are of great interest to those who study coursing form. He has devised a Hall of Fame which, while an indication of excellence, is based on the number of times a dog runs in relation to its wins, so inevitably some important winners and sires of winners will slip through the net as not having chalked up enough evidence.

One such dog is Mrs. Rawlings´ Ch. Chyton Copy Press, twice the winner of the Whippet Coursing Club´s Moonlake Cup, the only champion besides the previously mentioned Ch. Sound Barrier to achieve this. Copy Press has an excellent coursing pedigree as well as carrying classic show bloodlines. His sire was Moonlake Master Copy of Chyton, a CC winning son of Ch. Deepridge Mintmaster out of Moonlake Miss Chiff, granddaughter of Ch. Nimrodel Ruff. His dam was Sweet Briar, litter sister to Ch. Sound Barrier.

In general coursing breeding continues to incorporate and make use of well-established show bloodlines. While fewer coursing winners are actually sired by or out of bench champions than used to be the case, most coursing pedigrees today stand up to critical examination. The one or two outcross matings to racing dogs—for speed—which have taken place have not been noticeably successful; as with coursing greyhounds, increased speed has tended to lead to a lack of stamina and guts. The strict 20 inch height limit adhered to by the National Coursing Club is doubtless largely responsible for the fact that most coursing dogs running under NCC rules have retained an enviable uniformity of type.

A look at the list of Hall of Fame winners proves that show breeding is still represented. Ch. Sound Barrier has proved an important sire of coursing stock, in spite of the fact that his premature death shortened his career as a stud dog. There are progeny of several other champion sires: Moonlake Mint Sauce (by Ch. Deepridge Mintmaster), Ballagan Rouge

Dragon (by Ch. Samoems Silent Knight of Shalfleet), Nimrodel Pegasus (litter brother to Ch. Nimrodel Peerless, by Ch. Poltesco High Seas ex Ch. Wipstych Grandiflora), and Moviestar Madam (by Ch. Nimrodel Wanderer).

The most effective coursing kennel, as in the past, is still without any doubt at all that of Mrs. McKay´s world-famous Lagunas. Now bred in partnership with her daughter, Lilah Bond-Gunning, the Lagunas continue to perform brilliantly on the field. Laguna Leader (not to be confused with his much older champion namesake in Sweden), a black dog of solid Laguna breeding, has consistently won at all stages of his career and is also proving a useful coursing sire. Another black, Laguna Larmite, has also swept the board. He is sired by Wyemere Black Casanova who carries lines back to the famous Bey Noir/Rosefinch mating mentioned elsewhere.

The breeding of most coursing winners in England today is still interrelated with the foundation sires and bloodlines on which the Whippet Coursing Club was founded in 1962. The great early sires were Apbrenin Piquet (by Eng Aust Ch. Playmate of Allways), Ch. Dragonhill Woodpecker, Nimrodel Bilberry of Allways, and Ch. Laguna Light Lagoon. In later years their

Two whippets are being put into slips by Roger Upton during an open field coursing meeting in England.

descendants are still producing the best results. It is good to know that the bloodlines that played such a part in the support and founding of the Whippet Coursing Club are still there to be seen, even if some of their owners are not as active as they used to be.

In the United States, open-field coursing "for the pot" was common around the turn of the twentieth century, particularly in the wide open spaces of the western states. The sport did not get organized until 1961, when through the efforts of borzoi breeder Lyle Gillette an advisory committee on sighthound coursing was set up. A few years later the title Pacific Coast Coursing Champion was recognized; when open-field coursing spread to other states this was changed to Coursing Champion (CC) added after a dog´s name. Later the higher Award of Coursing Merit (CM) was added. The main difference between the two open-field coursing titles is that while the Coursing Champion may have won 90 of the 100 points required in competition with other breeds, the Award of Coursing Merit whippet has won all its points against others of the same breed. Forty points are awarded to the winner of a meeting, 30 to the runner-up, 20 to the third, 10 to the fourth and 5 to the fifth.

The only time a whippet has ever won the Grand Course for all sighthounds, the most important open field coursing event in America, was in 1988. The winner was the bitch Windyglen's Spuds McKinsey, CC, CM, seen with owner Don Papin.

Dogs are judged on desire (enthusiasm), speed, agility and endurance, with extra points for a "touch" or "take". One unassisted or two assisted kills are compulsory before either coursing title is granted.

Meetings for more than one or possibly two sighthound breeds are unusual in Britain, but most of those held by the sport's governing body in the U.S., the National Open Field Coursing Association, are open to all sighthound breeds. In the first fifteen years a total of 32 American whippets became Coursing Champions (counting also the early Pacific Coast champions), and seventeen won the Award of Coursing Merit (all except three of those also held the CC). Eight of the coursing champions have also won a track-racing title and several have excelled elsewhere too: four were show champions. The brindle dog Ch. Whirlaway's Apache holds the triple show, racing and coursing titles; Epinard Shelby of Wyndsor has track-racing, lure-course and obedience degrees in addition to his coursing championship, and Amberwood's Maximilian has the track-racing, lure-course and award of open-field coursing merit titles.

Prior to the 1980s old American blood was heavily represented in the coursing field, but during the 1980s and 1990s English racing blood was introduced that crossed well with the American lines. In the 1970s Emberson of Course sired most of the successful coursing winners. The top kennel names during that time were Regalstock, Canyon Creek, Epinard, Darbe and Sheridan. During the 1980s and 1990s the top kennels have been Windy Glen, Windward, Kentfield and Flyaway. During the 1970s the most points by a coursing whippet were accumulated by Darbe's Liberty Bell Windward, who had 510 coursing points, as well as her Award of Racing Merit, Field Champion and coursing titles. During the late 1980s more whippets amassed 500 or more points. The most points ever accumulatd by a whippet were won by a male named Kentfield's Karillon, SC, CM (sired by Ringdove Quantock - Kentfield's Diana,); at just three years of age he had accumulated over 1000 points in open field coursing. This record still stands at the time of writing, and at five years of age Karillon is still active in the field and adding to that phenomenal total (at latest count, his total was 1077 points).

The highest number of points ever attained by a bitch were won by Windyglen´s Spuds McKinsey, CC, CM. Her total to date stands at almost 800 points. Several other fine whippets have point totals close to these superior athletes, proving that whippets in the field are to be taken very seriously as swift, keen hunters.

During the early coursing years, the number of whippets competing was small—barely more than ten or so at mixed and breed hunts—but then a fresh interest in testing the athletic prowess of the breed emerged and numbers rose dramatically; some breed hunts in Californa received entries from 20-30 whippets or even more at some hunts. Mixed hunts also felt the influx of more whippets, with the end result being stronger competition for the whippet´s big cousin, the greyhound, and many mixed hunt wins for the breed. Whippets soon came to be looked upon as worthy opponents and given the utmost respect and admiration.

There are about 55-60 NOFCA hunts per year, but half of these are breed hunts for the other sighthound breeds. If one is willing to travel to California, New Mexico, Minnesota, Wyoming and Utah during the winter months, it is possible to compete with whippets in approximately 30 hunts. Most coursing enthusiasts, even the most dedicated ones, usually only compete in their own area. They can be seen each weekend walking through all kinds of brush and rough terrain regardless of weather, tossing good-natured banter up and down the gallery. After many hours in the field a feeling of real comradery develops. It helps to have a good sense of humor and a flexible attitude; walking can be tiring and the elements less than ideal.

The most important hunt is the two-day Grand Course, held at the end of each coursing season. Entry to this event is by invitation only and is open to hounds which have accumulated a set number of points during the season—usually 50-60 points. Competition is fierce for the highly prized title of Grand Course winner and many finely tuned sighthounds turn out for

The whippet, in spite of its gentle appearance and sweet nature, is an effective hunting machine and killer of game. An early California courser, Rockabye Checker, CC brings back her prey.

57

this annual event. In 1988 a whippet, Windyglen's Spuds McKinsey, owned by Don Papin, won the ultimate title of Grand Course winner. Prior to Spuds' win many whippets had placed highly, some had even gotten as far as second place, but none had ever won "the big one" before.

A list of top open field coursing winners is included in Appendix III.

Lure Coursing

Some time after the advent of organized open-field coursing, a variation which did not involve the pursuit of live game started to become popular. Lure coursing in some ways is a combination of open-field coursing and track racing: the dogs follow an electric lure which consists of an artificial rabbit (usually simply a white plastic bag) attached to a line guided by pulleys along a predetermined course, which on its way across the field makes several twists and turns in imitation of a live running hare.

Although as yet practiced mostly in the United States, lure coursing has quickly gained in popularity and since 1972 has been governed by the American Sighthound Field Association; in 1991 the American Kennel Club also recognized lure coursing as a field trial event, which means that the sport now has two independent governing bodies. All the disqualifications listed in the American Kennel Club standards apply, which means—among other things—that over- or under-sized dogs cannot compete. The exceptions from show rules are that monorchids, neutered dogs and spayed bitches may enter.

The course is laid out before the trial, usually in a fenced area, and may vary in length from around 500 yards to 1,400 yards or more. It always includes some straight runs as well as a number of twists and turns and can often be run both up- and downhill. Three dogs are run at a time and points are awarded towards the title of Field Champion (F. Ch.), added after the dog's name. Once a dog has earned its field championship it competes in special stakes for the higher Lure Courser of Merit (LCM) title. There are now over 300 trials with 10,000-13,000 entries per year for all the sighthound breeds added together.

Since the beginning in 1972, well over a thousand whippets have earned their Field Champion title. The first was the male Tiger Rag of Keynote (who also had the Companion Dog degree in obedience) in December of 1972. Over 200 of the field champions also earned the higher Lure Courser of Merit title—the first one was Turfside's Joker in 1976. Well-known show dogs frequently win at the lure course trials—a show champion, Ch. Flippet's Appraxin Marshall, LCM, was in fact the top lure courser of 1978 and Ch. Buncrana's Sligo, CD, LCM won in both 1987 and 1988. Dual Ch. Paris Seaworthy Simon, LCM II set all sorts of records in 1991 by being both top sighthound in ASFA and the first whippet to become a field champion under AKC rules. (For good measure, he had also won the American Whippet Club futurity as a puppy!) ASFA titles are added after the dog's name, AKC titles before: the "Dual Ch." title thus means that Simon is both a conformation and a field champion of American Kennel Club records, and the roman numerals after the LCM title indicate that Simon has won additional points over what's necessary for that title itself: several whippets have won LCMV, LCMVI and even higher.

The first whippet to gain show, racing and lure-coursing titles was the bitch Ch. Silverado Sue of Sea Aire, who also produced several field champions and was one of only a few whippets ever to hold the Tracking Dog degree usually reserved for bassets, bloodhounds, German shepherds and the like.

The first sighthound litter where both parents were field champions was bred from two whippets; sired by Happy Trails Mister Rufen, F. Ch. out of Ch. Domino Allegra, F. Ch; both parents also had an obedience degree and two from their litter also won the LCM award. Probably the most outstanding dam of field champions ever, however, was the obedience-titled top lure courser Greyfriar's Phoenix, LCM, owned by Paul and Linda Garwacki; all her lifetime total of fourteen puppies (from two different litters, sired by Ch. Saturn's Star Duster, F. Ch. and Ch. Timbar's Shadow of the Moon) won at least one field champion title, six were LCM, five were conformation champions and several obedience titled for good measure! The best known of the puppies, the almost solid red Ch. Bitterblue's Prairie Fire, CD, LCM also proved a successful sire of lure coursing and show stock. Equally successful in both areas, and

closely related through the Saturn's line (which comes down from Hound Hill and Stoney Meadows) are the Wistwinds of Greg and Carolyn Mountan: among their many lure coursers of merit Ch. Wistwind's Eli was unusual in that he gained his coursing titles before his conformation championship and finally topped that off with an AWC specialty Best of Breed.

The most important annual lure-coursing event, the so-called International Invitational, has several times been won by whippets: in 1978 by the attractive mostly brindle bitch Timbar's Saturn Sun Maid, in 1983 a litter mate to Prairie Fire, Bitterblue's Castle Ffire, and in 1986 by Buncrana's Sligo (who did not gain his show title until after retirement from coursing).

At an informal lure coursing meet, the dogs are not even necessarily muzzled. Blankets of different colors make it easy for spectators and judge when the winner is announced.

Agility is a sport which could have a big future in whippets. "Zaza" clears one of the jumps in the obstacle course.

The list of all-time top lure coursing whippets by the end of the 1980s was also headed by Sligo, followed by Ch. Sundance Haut Brion and Ch. Sligo's brother Ch. Buncrana's Fullerton—an impressive record in that all top three lure coursing dogs also became conformation champions. Since fourth place was occupied by Haut Brion's half sister Jack's St. Paulie Girl, the top placements were very much a family affair: both Haut Brion and St. Paulie Girl were sired by Ch. Sundance Super Devil (son of the English import Ch. Dondelayo Shaun), while Sligo's and Fullerton's sire Ch. Whippletree's Isaac, CD and dam Polly Flinders of Kristobel, CD occupied seventh and eighth place, with Elysian Like The Night and Whippletree's Ice Magic in front and

Comet's Maxine The Charmer and Free Wynd's Lord Farley of Fife behind them. All these of course also have the Lure Courser of Merit title.

Racing

Whippet racing, in spite of a somewhat tarnished image in its early days, has come to public notice more than any other whippet activity. After flourishing during the second half of the last century in Great Britain, it lasted well into the 1920s and 1930s before interest waned. Since the war there has been a great upswing in interest again—now as a clean family sport—not only in Britain and North America but also in Australia, Scandinavia and parts of continental Europe.

When the bloody sports of dog-fighting, bull-baiting, ratting and cockfighting were outlawed in Britain, most of them during the second half of the nineteenth century, the people who had enjoyed these activities turned to a corrupted form of coursing, in which two dogs and a rabbit were turned loose in a fenced area and wagers were laid on which dog would kill the rabbit first. The dogs were of whippet type but often had been cross-bred with terriers or even bull breeds for gameness—one pair of dogs could be expected to go through as many as fifteen rabbits in one morning.

When this bloody sport was prohibited, interest, particularly in the mining areas of northern Britain, turned towards "rag racing", as the primitive form of whippet racing was called. There were neither hare nor starting traps, sometimes not even much of a track; the dogs were simply hand-slipped across a field of 100-150 yards length and—egged on by shouts of encouragement—ran for dear life towards their owners who stood waving a "rag" made of white cloth or rabbit skin at the other end of the field. As any whippet owner knows, all whippets love to run, and at the end of the race the dogs were allowed to make a spectacular leap for the rag, often grabbing it and swinging around full circle without letting go! The dogs were not muzzled and fights between them at the end of the race were common.

Over the years various refinements were introduced. The track usually was divided into five or six lanes by a length of string attached to wooden stakes in order to ensure an uninterrupted run for each dog. The starter fired a gun to mark the beginning of a race and the "slippers" who started the dogs became increasingly important: the finer points in their throwing action—hands on the dog's collar and around base of tail—when launching the dog on to the track could make all the difference between a flying start without breaking stride and a nasty fall before the race had even begun. The ragger's ability to establish and keep contact with his dog from the moment it was handed over to the slipper and while walking down the length of the track, all the while waving the rag and shouting to the dog, was almost equally important.

Handicapping by weight was introduced quite early, as the dogs could vary in weight from under 15 lb to around 35 lb. The most important development of whippet racing was no doubt the introduction of betting. The prize money itself was sizeable, particularly to miners who did not earn in a month what their whippets could win in a week. The unlicensed bookmakers who swarmed around the whippet tracks first helped racing to flourish and then eventually brought about its downfall.

Whippet racing in those days was often a disreputable sport, with no governing body to control the proceedings and no official rules. Dogs were entered under false names in order to get better odds, slippers could be persuaded to help or break certain charges a little, the favorite could be fed just a little too much the day before an important race, and an also-ran could be encouraged to give the performance of a lifetime by one of the old and tried pick-me-up drugs. There were attempts to improve the image. In 1895 the Prince of Wales (afterwards King Edward VII) was treated to a display of whippet racing at the Ranelagh Club in London, but the procedure was so much cleaned up—no firing of pistols, no shouting, the owners uncomfortably dressed up to the nines and told to behave, not even authentic racing dogs used—that Freeman Lloyd in his usual outspoken way called it "the tamest and least exciting whippet handicap ever witnessed." It was not repeated.

The great showman P.T. Barnum experienced a brief moment of success in the sport when he brought round-track whippet racing with his circus to London in the 1890s, but generally whippet racing did not catch on outside

Northern Britain and had virtually died out by the time of World War II. There was a brief but spectacular revival of rag racing in the mid-1950s when several clubs were formed in Northeast England and brought the sport to its highest level of sophistication, with permanent race tracks equipped with electrically operated traps, floodlighting, covered stands and even photo finish. The peak was reached in the early 1960s when four clubs were operating in a relatively small area, with tracks at Furness/Barrow, Dalton, Millom and Whitehaven. There were nine meets with well over 100 races each week during the summer and over 300 dogs participating. Betting was still the main attraction, but with the introduction of betting duty in 1966, interest fell away until most of the tracks were closed by the mid-1970s.

By the time rag racing was revived, modern whippet racing, with the dogs running after a mechanical lure instead of to the rag, had already been born. Several clubs were formed in the North during the 1940s, often with their own tracks, and when the British Whippet Racing Association was formed in Yorkshire during the summer of 1967 it was already possible to attend whippet racing every weekday in that part of England. Although the BWRA does not require the dogs entered to be purebred (some are indeed publicly recognized to be the result of a greyhound/whippet cross), it maintains records of all dogs registered and issues identification cards with the dogs' names permanently recorded.

The introduction of a mechanically driven "hare" meant that races no longer had to be run on the straight. Longer "bend" races with one or two turns of up to 350 yards proved popular. The most important of the association's annual events are the bend and straight National Championships run every year. Each region holds its own qualifying races, from which the first and second in nine different weight classes go to the National finals. The winner in each weight division there attains the title Racing Champion. Dogs and bitches run separately, the bitches usually being faster. Weight divisions start with dogs weighing up to 16 lb, and go up to 32 lb by 2 lb stages. The association has even made an effort to keep the old sport of rag racing alive, awarding the title Rag Racing Champion to the winner of the yearly contest.

The leading bloodlines in this part of the racing population usually have little in common with most purebred show or coursing stock. It is no secret that there is a good portion of greyhound blood close up in the pedigrees of many of the top BWRA racers, and even collie and terrier crosses in some cases. According to the racing publication Whippet News, some of the racing strains were kept alive during the war through an infusion of Staffordshire Bull Terrier blood. I remember this being rumored about some of the unregistered stock present at a race meeting in southern England in the early 1960s; certainly those dogs not only looked much heavier and coarser than pure-bred whippets but also had temperaments far removed from the gentle friendliness of the true whippet.

The leading post-war sire of BWRA stock has probably been the fawn heavyweight

Bilko, sire of such great winners as the black R. Ch. Little Lucy—winner of around a hundred races on both bend and straight tracks—and the parti-colored R. Ch. Snowflake. Bilko was grandsire of the amazing R. Ch. Good As Gold, who won the BWRA Supreme Dog Champion award for four years in a row. The other great stud was Blue Peter, the only whippet to have a race track named after him, the sire of numerous racing champions.

Purebred whippet racing started in 1968 when Mrs. Ian Lowe—whose Nimrodel whippets have been equally successful showing, coursing and racing—proposed that the Whippet Club should set up a subcommittee to maintain the official whippet standard for racing and to avoid a division in types such as had long been evident in show and racing greyhounds.

The Whippet Club Racing Association was born a few months later and acts as a national governing body for purebred whippet racing with at least eighteen affiliated regional clubs and around two thousand dogs registered under its rules. To be eligible for a WCRA passport the dog has to be registered with the Kennel Club, have a five-generation pedigree of acceptable breeding and must not measure more than 21 inches in height or weigh less than 14 lb.

Dogs are run in weight classes ranging from 16 lb to 30 lb and race over a distance of 150 yards straight or 240 yards with two bends. The first championship meeting was held in May 1970 in conjunction with the Camberley all-breed open dog show; the following year a title was established to be awarded to dogs which had won at least two championship finals. The Kennel Club gave the Whippet Club permission to grant those dogs the title Whippet Club Racing Champion (WCRCh.); during the club's first fifteen years this was awarded to over a hundred dogs. Four or five championship meetings a year have usually been held in various parts of the country, each with 150-200 whippets competing.

The leading sire of pure-bred racing whippets during the first years was Russetwood Pageant, a parti-colored show winner, litter brother to the lovely Ch. Russetwood Portia and sired by Ch. Laguna Ligonier (himself quite a keen racer when given the chance) out of a daughter of Ch. Laguna Limelight. Pageant sired Mystic Pepe, one of the few "double" racing champions—both BWRA and WCRA—who himself has proved to be an excellent sire. The great coursing sire Ch. Laguna Light Lagoon is also behind many racing champions, particularly through his sons Laguna Larkin (sire of five WRChs), Clipper of Hardknott (sire of WCRCh. Jack's Boy, one of the top sires with five racing champions to his credit) and Tarbuck of Heatherpard.

Show-bred stock from other leading kennels also won well on the track in those years. The well-bred black Ebzan Noudini Bey Noir (Ch Ladiesfield Bedazzled ex Fleeting Fashion Plate) when mated to a Nimrodel-bred bitch by Ch. Poltesco Peewit produced an historical litter which has broken all previous records for consistency: three became racing champions, with WCRCh. Chancerick Kondor equalling Pageant's record by siring six racing champions and his brother WCRCh. Chancerick Koh-i-noor siring four. A third brother, Chancerick Kaspar, won a challenge certificate in the show ring and sired one of the most outstanding coursing dogs of the early 1980s, Maximilian of Chyton.

The greatest racing winner under WCRA rules has probably been the pretty white-and-black bitch Karyon Sootican Princess, better known in racing circles as WCRCh. Pickety Witch. (All racing dogs have two names—one registered Kennel Club name and one racing name.) Born in 1973, she won an amazing ten of the association's racing championships in one of the most competitive weight divisions, nine of them in a row. Her pedigree shows an almost unbroken line of well-known show names within a couple of generations, her sire being of Allways breeding and her dam sired by Shalfleet Saga. The last-named was a well-known show dog in the early 1960s, owned by the Martinsell Kennel and the sire of well-known dual-purpose winners. Although almost none of the dogs owned by Shalfleet have been either raced or coursed, the ability is obviously there; in addition to Saga, several of Mrs. Wilton-Clark's own stud dogs have sired racing and coursing winners for other kennels.

More proof of the show whippet's ability to produce racing winners was offered by the WCRA's "superstar" point scores in the early 1980s. In 1982 the top dog was WCRCh. Binfield Rocket (also known as Firehawk Silver Sea), sired by the aforementioned Tarbuck of Heatherpard out of a bitch of Wingedfoot breeding. Top bitch the same year was WCRCh. Blue Frost Lady who is sired by Chancerick Kondor. The leading kennels where numbers of WCRChs are concerned at that time were Laguna, Casaloma and Kemerton; the two latter almost never appear in the show ring but breed from the same bloodlines as most of the show kennels.

The Whippet Club Racing Association is still responsible for pedigree whippet racing in the UK in the 1990s. Despite a number of attempts to infiltrate the pedigree scene with cross-breds, the purity of British whippet blood is safeguarded by the WCRA. In terms of breeding and bloodlines, however, the racing whippet has moved away from the common heritage of bloodlines shared by the show and coursing whippets. Two things have played a part in the difference in overall type and construction of the racing whippet to his show and coursing cousin. First, breedings planned with only speed in mind and with total disregard for other factors have produced some very untypical stock. Second, the running of weight groups favors the breeding of tall, light-boned specimens to a degree that would not find favor in the ring or on the coursing field. The American system of graded races seems to produce a much more uniform type of whippet.

In the United States whippet racing was popular during the early days in California, with dogs from the Arroyo, Lazeland and Strathoak kennels competing. For a few brief years in the 1920s and 1930s whippet racing was in fact quite a fashionable sport in Los Angeles, with Hollywood stars participating. There was even a popular MGM short film, of the type then used to introduce the evening's full-length movie, which brought whippets to the attention of thousands of viewers in cinemas across America—Whippet Racing, produced and narrated by multiple Academy Award winner Pete Smith. (The film was found intact in the Turner Entertainment archives in 1993, has been transferred to video and is currently in the American Whippet Club archives.)

The sport reached a peak in the East with the arrival of the Maryland Whippet Club in 1930 and lasting until after the war. The driving force there appears to have been Felix Leser of the Freemanor Kennels who—just as some British fanciers at the same time—experimented with cross-breeding. His pure-bred show bitch Ch. Broadway Admiration was bred to a bull terrier; according to Freeman Lloyd the final result of this cross a few generations later was the black bitch Try Me, seven-eighths whippet and "unquestionably one of the very fastest of her kind— including the straight-bred whippet—ever seen in the United States." Whippet

During a brief period in the 1920s and 1930s, whippet racing was a fashionable sport in Hollywood, attracting many fans from the movie industry. Lew Cody, a star of Hollywood silents and early talkies, is training his dog to the rag at the MGM racing championships.

racing was even featured at the great Morris & Essex dog show several times, through the benevolent interest shown in the sport by the show's patroness Mrs. Geraldine Hartley Dodge. (Her kennel manager Mr. McClure Halley was in fact one of the most successful early whippet exhibitors.)

Mr. Leser's best-known dog was the blue male Freemanor Racing Ravanell, who, although quite ugly judging by his pictures, appears to be pure-bred. Several of Mr. Leser's Freemanor dogs did well in the show ring too and the line from some of his best winners has been carried down to the present day.

The Maryland club even tried obstacle races as a novelty. These were popular with the audience but not apparently with the dogs; in the first meeting only one entry completed the race—the other five fell and failed to finish.

Modern whippet racing in America owes much to the enthusiasm of Mrs. Wendy Howell of the Great Circle Kennels—then in California, later in Ireland. (One bitch which she brought with her from the United States later became one of the most outstanding coursing dogs for Mrs. McKay's Laguna Kennels in England.) In 1958 Mrs. Howell persuaded the organizers of the Chicago International Kennel Club to put on whippet racing as a spectator event at their all-breed dog show. A team of Great Circle dogs was brought in from California and younger enthusiasts such as Mr. and Mrs. Eugene Jacobs of the Whipoo Kennels were encouraged to participate. Both Great Circle and Whipoo were great forces in the evolution of the American show whippet as well.

Since then whippet racing in America has continued to grow. Louis Pegram, who had been active in whippet racing in Maryland during the 1930s and 1940s, was instrumental in convincing the American Whippet Club to sponsor whippet racing as an amateur sport and breed improvement program. In the 1960s he authored the official rules and regulations for National Point Racing and in 1967 introduced the title Award of Racing Merit (ARM) to honor the top racing whippets. Up to the end of 1992, only 273 whippets have earned the ARM certificate, 27 of which are also conformation champions. There were no provisions for cross-breed racing in the same way as had been done in England, which created a controversy which has dogged AWC racing since the 1980s; some dogs were imported from England which had been refused admittance into the English WCRA stud-book registry because of dubious ancestry. Because they were in fact registered by the Kennel Club in England they were accepted by AKC, and consequently also by AWC, but their tremendous success in racing has if anything assisted in making an even more clear distinction between "show" and "racing" lines in

recent years. The most recent show champion to be top racing whippet in the U.S. was Ch. Marial´s Whitewater, ARM, ORC in 1988; and the most recent whippet to gain both AKC champion and ARM titles in the same year was Ch. Marial´s Monte Carlo, ARM (Ch. Marial´s Gazon Illusionist ex Ch. Marial´s Memphis), in 1987.

Today the AWC sponsors a program of whippet racing across North America (including Canada) open to whippets which are eligible for registration with the American Kennel Club, and which do not have any of the disqualifications specified in the official breed standard. Initially that included dogs which were spayed, in season or monorchid; in late 1987, after lively debate pro and con within the American Whippet Club, spayed and neutered whippets were permitted to race in a separate category, and in September 1992 they were allowed to compete on equal terms. So far, no spayed or neutered racers have earned the ARM title, however.

Adult racing is done in six-dog races, 200 yd. straight. Puppies between 8 and 13 months race 150 yd. in four-dog races. As in England, the dogs are muzzled and wear colored and numbered racing coats. About 35 official meets are held annually in many different parts of the country with anything from 700 to over 1000 entries per year; each meet has an average of 20-50 adult whippets competing. In recent years the biggest individual meet has been hosted by the Jersey Rag Racers, often with 50 whippets competing.

The dogs are graded by the racing secretary according to past performance, as either

A, B, C, or D racers: A for consistently excellent racers, D for average or first-time runners. A good time is considered 12.0 seconds for 200 yd., an outstanding time 11.5 seconds.

Meets sponsored by the AWC and having at least twenty adult starters employ a point system which eventually can earn an outstanding dog the Award of Racing Merit certificate (abbreviated ARM, used after the dog's name). The point system is fairly complex but usually gives 15-25 points to the winner of a meet. Since this certificate was introduced in 1967, only about 200 whippets have earned it. The most outstanding winner was the famous Van Oorschot's Toro, whose record will be difficult for any other dog to beat. Out of the 140 heats he ran in, Toro won 132 and was High in Score at 33 out of a possible 35 meets. Toro retired at the Santa Barbara races in 1979 after having won there for six consecutive years. Sired by an imported French dog, Midst du Pilier Rouge, out of the show bitch Ch. Van Oorschot's Val O'Legendary, who gained her title at, among other shows, the AWC specialty in Santa Barbara. Toro was also the leading sire of ARM winners in the 1970s and 1980s with over twenty of these to his credit.

Up to the 1980s, the leading sires in addition to Toro were the great multi-purpose dog Epinard Shelby of Wyndsor, CD, and Ch. Pinetop's Opening Knight, ARM. The former was titled in obedience, track racing, open-field coursing and lure coursing, and owned by Jean Balint's dual-purpose Wyndsor Kennel in California; the latter was bred from two of Norman Ellis's Madcap champions back to the old Meander line, and owned by Dr. John Shelton's well-known show kennel Sheridan. The leading brood bitch was the great producer Topper's Wistful of Regalstock, with a record 12 ARM

Racing exhibition, Santa Barbara Kennel Club, 1972.

offspring. The most successful racing kennel names have been Regalstock (owned by David Rosenstock) and Wyndsor, followed by the Arthurs' Marial Kennel, which has been at least as successful in the show ring.

In the 1980s and early 1990s, the Lyth dogs of Tony Lewis—who arrived from England in 1979 with 10 whippets and at least one "lurcher"—have dominated racing wherever they have been able to compete; the top spot in AWC racing has gone to either a Lyth dog or a Lyth descendant every year for the past decade except one. The great racing sires Lyth Djon, Lyth Jasper, Lyth Satus and Regalstock Lyth Router have sired the most ARM winners

One of the top performing working whippets of the late 1980s, Kentfield's Kalypso — top sighthound in open field coursing in 1989, oval track racing national champion 1989, and a lure coursing Best in Field winner.

Although most racing in America is on straight tracks, oval-track racing has recently been introduced on the West Coast. The National Oval Track Racing Association was formed in California in 1975 and for many years it organized what is called the California Whippet Derby over 383 yd. (350 meters) at Santa Barbara during the same weekend as the American Whippet Club races and the specialty show. Some of the best ARM racers not surprisingly have dominated the first "bend" races. The North American Whippet Racing Association

was founded on the West Coast in 1988, partly as a result of AWC's acceptance of the questionable English imports; in May 1990 NAWRA banned Tony Lewis and his dogs for life. The formation of NAWRA is no doubt part of the reason that AWC racing activities have dropped off somewhat in the late 1980s. The most recent separate racing organization is the dual-purpose Continental Whippet Alliance, which was founded by Douglas and Mary Beth Arthur and has averaged more than a dozen combined race and conformation meets per year between 1991 and 1993.

Obedience

A sighthound is hardly the most natural choice for anyone wanting to start in obedience, as the very nature of these dogs' original purpose in life—coursing—predisposes them to be more independent and less eager to please than most other breeds. There are exceptions, and some whippets in fact have the kind of extroverted, razzle-dazzle temperament which in combination with a close relationship to the handler helps to achieve success in this field.

Obedience work with whippets seems to be particularly popular in the United States. There have been examples of successful obedience whippets in Britain—Ballagan William Wallace in the 1960s was one—but no whippet is known to have become an Obedience Trial champion in Britain so far. Some of the other European countries do not even offer an obedience title. The Swedish Kennel Club does, and at least two whippets have become obedience champions there since the late 1960s. The first was the elegant little fawn bitch Fedha-Mwezi (by Int. Ch. Laguna Leader), and the second the fawn dog Owelyns Dream (by the Tarragon son Bocachica Orpheus).

In the U.S., hardly a month goes by without a whippet being awarded the official Companion Dog title by the American Kennel Club. The CD is the lowest of the obedience titles, but whippets also regularly graduate on to the Companion Dog Excellent level and at least twelve whippets have earned the Utility Dog title. The first was Picardia Priscilla, owned by Dorothea Hastings who became better known as a professional handler and breeder of many show champions carrying the Hollypark prefix. The obedience titles are added after the dog's name, and the higher title always takes the place of a lower: thus Picardia Priscilla, CDX later became Picardia Priscilla, UD.

Most of the Utility whippets carry kennel names known from the show ring: Great Circle, Crestfield, White Acre, Sheridan, Pathen, etc. Sheridan Seabiscuit, owned by Betz Leone, even won the Lure Coursing of Merit title in addition to her obedience degree! At least two of the Utility dogs were also show champions: Ch. Mojo's Bold Benares of Remleaf, UD and a bitch which must be one of the most titled whippets anywhere—Amigo's Cosa Caliente, bred by Nubby and Walt Errickson's well-known kennel in New Mexico and owned by Pam Sehmer. "Cali" is a show champion in America, Canada and Mexico, a lure-coursing Field Champion, a Utility Dog in obedience and one of the only four whippets known to have been awarded the Tracking Dog (TD) title. Her official name therefore should read Am. Can. Mex. Ch. Amigo's Cosa Caliente, F. Ch., UD, TD.

The first Obedience Trial champion whippet in the United States was crowned in 1981 and has an interesting background. Sporting Fields Mad Hatter, alias "Jo," was bred in Mr. and Mrs. James E. Butt's famous show kennel but developed such bad rickets as a puppy that he was going to be put to sleep. However, Jo had an engaging personality and instead he was given to Jodie Martin as a pet. The rickets were treated and eventually disappeared, and Jo remained a charming pet for several years. When his owner started to compete with her German Shepherd dog in obedience, Jo was miserable about being left out and was put into training—at five years of age—just so he could come along to the shows. Jo quickly earned his CD degree, ending up with a first-place win among all breeds and a near-perfect score of 197 points. When he took seven consecutive first places in the Open A classes to complete his CDX title, obedience people were beginning to sit up and notice the whippet which was beating the golden retrievers and border collies. Getting through to the UD took a whole year, but Jo again won several first placings at large shows, and at ten years old he finally collected the 100th point necessary for the Obedience Trial Championship. Along the way, Jo had twice scored the highest points in trial award, each time with 198 points—no mean feat for a low-keyed whippet in competition with fast, flashy working poodles and retrievers.

Miss Martin believes that whippets can be very competitive in obedience if trained properly. They do require careful handling, and the better you know your dog and can read its reactions the better success you will have. She says: "The biggest mistake people can make when training whippets is not to correct them. A whippet will easily "con" you if allowed to get away with it, and needs to know he will be corrected if he doesn´t obey." The corrections need to be diplomatic, however, as whippets are very soft dogs, get depressed easily—and then quit. Utility training can be especially confusing and the dog needs a lot of reassuring along the way.

Miss Martin´s younger dog, Ch. Sporting Fields Santana, proved to be a true

Sighthounds are usually not enthusiastic obedience dogs, but whippets frequently do well.
Cantagree´s Remarque (Molly) does the broad jump and retrieves a dumbell.

dual-purpose dog, winning his show title and CD at the same time, sometimes winning the High in Trial award the same day as Best of Breed. He completed his CDX degree quickly and competed successfully in the AWC obedience trials as a veteran.

The obedience classes at the American Whippet Club´s annual national specialty have been a popular feature since this event was first instigated, rather humbly, with seventeen entries in 1987. Interest has increased considerably since then; there have been as many as 70 entries in the 1990s. Some of the winners have done well in both conformation and obedience judging, such as Yorktown True Colors, who managed to take home both Reserve Winners Bitch and Highest Scoring in the regular obedience classes at the 1993 show.

The two top winning whippets in all-breeds competition at American shows are Ch. Sporting Fields Clansman ("Buoy") and his great-grandson Ch. Sporting Fields Kinsman ("Luke"). Between them they won over a hundred Best in Shows during the 1970s, 1980s and 1990s. Luke poses in front of a painting of his ancestor.

A Breed is Born

Few things can be more amusing—or ridiculous, depending on your point of view—than a breed historian´s attempt to prove the noble and ancient ancestry of whatever kind of dog he or she happens to specialize in. Literary and artistic evidence of the most nebulous kind is dragged forward as proof that the breed existed in its purest form thousands of years ago, conveniently disregarding the fact that breeds as we know them are an invention of the nineteenth century. Pedigrees, stud books and the rules which govern the sport of pure-bred dogs did not come into being until quite late: the first dog show was held in England in 1859 and the Kennel Club there was founded in 1873.

Of course some types of dogs are indeed very old. In little pockets in time and geography over the centuries there have always been people possessed by a passion for breeding animals in a controlled manner with the clear object of improving—or preserving—specific features from previous generations. Dogs have been bred this way far less frequently than horses, cattle and most other livestock, however. Certain characteristics of favorite dogs —hunting ability, guarding instinct, attractive appearance—may have been considered so desirable that a family, a village or even a larger group of people may have attempted to breed dogs which kept those qualities as true as possible over a comparatively long time, avoiding contamination by outside influence. But early attempts at pure breeding in dogs did not usually last long, and in the end only the most functional and generally desirable traits lived on through the centuries.

When dogs and humans first got together some 10,000 or 15,000 years ago it was for mutual advantage. Dogs´ tendency to raise an alarm whenever strangers, hostile or otherwise, approached was useful, and the dogs would be fed and encouraged to stay around the camps. Some mutual bond of understanding must have been necessary for the next step in the dog/human relationship: a dog by its nose or speed would be a far more efficient hunter than a human being, and together they proved an unbeatable combination. In open terrain where the prey could spot hunters from afar, a good nose or a strong bark would not be much help to

Modern artists, like those of past centuries, have often used whippets as models. Lucian Freud (b. 1922) is one of the world's foremost contemporary representative artists towards the end of the twentieth century. His Double Portrait, oil on canvas, is from 1985/86. Private collection.

long-legged hunting hounds were regularly portrayed throughout the Middle East. Some of the dogs bear a close resemblance to today's greyhounds, smooth-coated salukis and pharaoh hounds, but they all appear to be fairly large—and it is in any event far too early to think in terms of specific pure breeds.

Hunting with sighthounds remained popular long after society had become agricultural and no longer needed hunting dogs to provide meat for the table. The thrills of the chase and the beauty of the hounds made coursing a sport much favored by the ruling classes wherever suitable land was available. In the second century AD, the Greek historian and philosopher Arrian even wrote a textbook on coursing with greyhounds. The bedouins in Arabia hunted on horseback with their salukis, the boyars in imperial Russia made a grand and dangerous spectacle out of wolf

Whippet stamp from Bermuda, 1993.

hunting with borzois, the Romans brought greyhounds to the British Isles which gave rise to deer and wolf coursing with wire-haired sighthounds among the Celts.

The sighthound group today forms an independent, officially classified group of breeds in many European countries; in the English-speaking countries it is a sub-group of the

the dog, so gradually a type of dog specifically suited for open-field hunting—coursing—was developed, with longer limbs, lighter body, keen eyes and above all tremendous speed—ready at a moment's notice to take off after any prey available, overtake it and kill it. This was the ancestor of the dozen or so modern breeds now loosely grouped as sighthounds—on the basis of ancestry and what may be termed general greyhound characteristics.

The first known pictures of definite sighthound types date from around 6000 BC. During the following centuries various elegant,

Hounds and consists of the Afghan hound, borzoi, greyhound, Irish wolfhound, Ibizan hound, pharaoh hound, saluki, Scottish deerhound and whippet; often the Italian greyhound is included as well—some even claim that the African basenji

and Rhodesian ridgeback are sighthounds. There are several other, much rarer sighthound breeds, such as the Italian cirneco dell´Etna, the Spanish galgo, the Moroccan sloughi, and the azawakh from Africa.

There had been small, smooth-coated sighthounds in ancient Egypt and Rome—Cleopatra is reputed to have owned several—and these were the ancestors of both the whippet and its smaller cousin, the Italian greyhound. No one bothered to differentiate between the varieties; there were big sighthounds, small ones and medium-sized ones, but they did not have separate names, nor were they necessarily kept from breeding together until many centuries later. Complete outcrosses with heavier types of dogs no doubt occurred as well; but these would have been less useful for hunting, and less attractive to look at (an important factor in ancient Greece), so they would hardly have been encouraged.

The smaller whippet-like type proved to be an extremely efficient rabbit courser, able to twist and turn and catch its

The Italian Jesuit priest Giuseppe Castiglione lived in China for fifty years. At his death in 1765 he had became the Imperial Court´s most celebrated painter. This is only one of his many elegant dog paintings, printed as a modern Chinese stamp.

prey in much smaller areas than the faster but more cumbersome greyhound. These dogs lived on throughout the decline of the Roman Empire and prospered during the Middle Ages and the Renaissance, judging by frequent appearances of small or middle-sized smooth-coated sighthounds in the art of that period—invariably in scenes with elevated themes. The quality of the dogs portrayed is distinctly superior to anything that appeared in several later centuries, so these whippets, as we might now begin to call them, must have

The magnificent set of fifteenth century French tapestries called The Lady and the Unicorn, now in the Cluny Museum in Paris, includes representations of several small, exquisite sighthounds of unmistakable whippet type. This detail from one of the tapestries is often called The Whippet.

Ch. Fleeting Flyaway, one of the few brindle champions of her era and daughter of Sapperly Tiptree Pilot, with her owner Mrs. Molly Garrish in the early 1950s.

been held in high regard in their own time. The size varies from small Italian greyhound through middle height up to full-grown greyhound size; even in our own time there is no universal agreement on the size limits which chiefly distinguish these three breeds. (The height in whippets alone can vary as much as 5 inches from what is considered correct in some parts of Europe to what is ideal according to the American breed standard. It would not be impossible

to pick out an extremely large or small animal of either breed and pass it off—size- if not type-wise—as a different breed in another country.)

The common notion that the whippet is a relatively new breed of slightly disreputable origin is due to later circumstances. In Britain, during the eighteenth and nineteenth centuries, the small whippet-like dogs came into the hands of people who could not afford to keep a greyhound; indeed, most people were prevented by law from doing so until the mid-fifteenth century, as the great lords wished to keep the exclusive sport of greyhound coursing to themselves. The whippet became known as "the poor man´s greyhound" and was frequently used for poaching and rabbit coursing to fill the pot. It was also appreciated for various sporting purposes, providing entertainment and an opportunity for a wager when pitted against others of its kind in chasing a poor bewildered rabbit within a fenced-in area. Later the whippet´s instinct to follow a fluttering rabbit-skin was used as the basis for flat-out "rag racing," the humble forerunner of today´s highly mechanized track racing (see Chapter 5).

Early whippets were sometimes crossed with other dogs, most often terriers, which were supposed to give the breed more heart and also provided the rough coats sometimes seen well into the twentieth century. Wire-haired whippets have always been regarded as cross-breeds in Britain, but they were occasionally shown in America as late as the 1920s; several wire-coated British dogs of unregistered background were exported to the European continent and shown there. There are records of wire-haired champion whippets in Germany during the 1920s and 1930s, with attempts at a revival through Bedlington terrier crosses after the war. The Fédération Cynologique Internationale which governs canine affairs on the continent officially listed wire-haired whippets as a separate breed until the late 1960s, when an inquiry from the author brought about a hasty end to official recognition of the already-extinct variety.

One breeder in the U.S. has repeatedly attempted to produce whippets with a long, silky borzoi-type coat, with protestations that these dogs have been bred entirely from pure whippet stock. Even if this is correct there is no evidence that an earlier long-haired variety ever existed; the shiny, short smooth coat has been regarded as the most desirable variety for well over a hundred years. In the 1980s the breeder involved in producing the "long-hairs" was investigated by the American Kennel Club, and such doubts were raised about the record keeping and pedigrees of his dogs that a whole series of the dogs were expelled from the AKC Stud Book. The fact that the same kennel also housed Shetland sheepdogs does not appear to be completely incidental.

Ch. Saxon Shore Amber Waves (Ch. Rolling's Viktor - Ch. Rafina Rhianda of Kamara) has sired more than 60 champions in the 1980s and early 1990s. Owner and breeder Dan Lockhart.

Crosses between whippets and other breeds—even bull terriers and collies—have been recorded as late as the 1930s and 1940s, both in Britain and the U.S., and one of the two big national organizations for whippet racing in Britain does not limit its registrations to purebred stock. Some of their racers have documented greyhound blood quite close up in their pedigrees, but of course none of these can be used for producing pure-bred Kennel Club-registered stock. In 1979 the Whippet Club Racing Association, which allows only purebred whippets to compete, banned a number of dogs belonging to an owner who had allegedly misrepresented their breeding. Although all evidence was submitted to the Kennel Club, no further action was taken and the dogs are still registered with that body—and therefore also eligible for registration in other countries. This caused problems in North America to which several of the dogs were exported, resulting in new legislation for participants in American Whippet Club racing.

Lady with a Whippet, nineteenth century. Oil on canvas, 28 x 22. F.R. de Leub

Although the word whippet (or corruptions of it) appeared as early as in the sixteenth century, it did not necessarily mean then what it does today. The Oxford Dictionary of English defines a whippet in 1550 as "a lively young woman; a light wench"; later the word came to be used for a "nimble, diminutive or puny person" and by 1610 for "a small breed of dog." From the descriptions it doesn´t sound like a very attractive little dog at all, nor like a typical whippet: a "whappet" was "a prick-eared curre" addicted to "wapping or yelping"—even Milton refers to it in a derogatory fashion, equating the "bauling whippets" with "shinbarkers" and other "infestations" of this world.

As late as 1841 the whippet is described as "a dog bred betwixt a greyhound and a spaniel." Around the same time, on the European continent a school of artists known as Les Animaliers were sculpting exquisite bronzes of whippets and Italian greyhounds, clearly defining the differences between the breeds which are so much more subtle than mere size. Some of the nineteenth-century bronzes resemble the best dogs of today more closely than their live contemporaries in the UK seem to have done, although it is true that one particular Mêne bronze has been labelled alternately as a whippet and as an Italian greyhound in the art-sales catalogues!

Shortly before the outbreak of World War II, Mardormere Kennels imported Ch. Flornell Glamorous, who became the top whippet bitch ever shown in America, winning Best in Show 21 times — a record which still stands a half century later. Bred by Stanley Wilkin in England, Glamorous was sired by Tiptree Monk and inbred on Tiptree Golddust.

All this changed with the appearance around the turn of the twentieth century of the great British breeders. During the next few decades they lifted the whippet from relative obscurity to its present position as one of the most universally respected and admired breeds of the dog world.

The two whippet bitches are probably the sisters Ch. Lady Bibi and Ch. Madame Superb (English imports by Tiptree Golddust), shown with a greyhound companion at the Salmagundi Kennel in the 1930s prior to their purchase by Mrs. Anderson´s Mardormere establishment.

Chapter 7

The Early Whippets

Any student of a breed needs to know something about the ancestors named in the pedigrees of the dogs that dominate the breed today. Most of the important whippets we have now are intensely linebred to certain key dogs of the past, and these in turn were closely bred to still earlier dogs, which in turn descend over and over again from a few dogs of the early twentieth century.

Many of these dogs appear hundreds of times far back in modern pedigrees. But to trace today's dogs back to their roots one must go through innumerable of pages of old stud books—and the line inevitably vanishes as soon as the note "unregistered" or "parents unknown" appears after an ancestor's name—sometimes as soon as within fifty years, always within a hundred. It is a fascinating exercise to draw up extended pedigrees for the old champions; patterns emerge, and it becomes clear just how much influence certain individuals and families have had—and not always those that seemed to be the most successful in their own time.

The whippet has had an unusually large supply of new blood added to its gene pool until fairly recent times by unregistered dogs picked up from the race tracks. Even if some of these outsiders were more closely related to the show stock than their lack of official pedigree might suggest, they are probably responsible for two important factors in the breed's genetic make-up. First, the whippet is a remarkably healthy breed, free from almost all known serious hereditary defects that plague other breeds. Second, there is a wide divergence in type, size and quality even in the best-known and most successful lines. Compared to other dogs, the whippet is one of the most difficult to breed with any degree of consistency throughout the litters.

Stud books, extended pedigrees and the like do not tell us much about what the key dogs were actually like. Old photographs are often difficult to find, seldom technically good and sometimes incorrectly labelled. Few of the old breeders bothered to write down pertinent details about their dogs, and when they did, it was colored by a very human desire to paint them as brightly as possible. Breeders of tomorrow will benefit from modern technology: taped interviews, video recordings of important dogs, hundreds of photographs will be available. I would give much for a few filmed moments of Champions Shirley Wanderer, Willesbeaux, Watford Brilliant, Towyside Tatters, Mica of Meander and the early Tiptree dogs—even some of relatively recent dogs such as Ch. Bellavista Barry and Ch. Laguna Lucky Lad. Unlike a movie camera, human memory does not retain all details about a dog seen more than thirty years ago.

Old issues of dog magazines, clippings and breed columns, odd photographs and the few whippet books available offered some help. Most important, in my quest through largely unchartered territories I had to turn to breeders who were there themselves. They offered fascinating insights in a bygone era; some of them generously sent whole boxes of fascinating photographs and clippings along with their memories for this book, and I only wish it could all be published. There is a tremendous amount of research (if that lofty term may be applied to such a humble occupation) to be done.

I have attempted to concentrate on the dogs, kennels and bloodlines which have had most influence in shaping the breed as we know it today. An occasional outstanding show winner can change the future of a breed by making judges and breeders aware of certain new or different qualities, but the great producers have been the main focus of my attention.

The first organized dog show in Britain was held in 1859, but this was for setters and pointers only. The first mention I have found of whippets as show dogs dates from 28 July 1876: according to C.H. Lane's now exceedingly rare Dog Shows and Doggy People, the annual exhibition of "Sporting and Other Dogs" in Woodside Park, Darlington, that year featured "classes including Whippets, Non-Sporting Puppies, etc" apart from the usual gundog classes. The judge was a Mr. J. Fisher; there is no record of the dogs exhibited. This may not have been the only—or even the first—show where whippets were classified. The same year the famous dog writer Stonehenge (pseudonym for C.H. Walsh) mentions when writing about Italian greyhounds that some of these weighed as much as 10 or 12 lb and would "these days be classed as whippets," implying that the latter breed must already have been fairly well established on the show scene by then.

It took twelve more years for the whippet to become recognized by the Kennel Club in Britain. At its meeting on 16 April 1890, a letter from Herbert Vickers requesting official recognition for the whippet breed was read. The club decided henceforth to accept whippets into its stud book and to offer classes for them at the shows. Judging by the stud book entries for that year, the first three shows with officially recognized classes for whippets were held in Leeds, Tunbridge Wells and the Crystal Palace in London.

Of the first five whippets listed in the Kennel Club Stud Book of 1891, one was black and white, one fawn and white, two "brown and white," and one was not described as to color. This is fairly typical of the color range over the next few years—the solid fawn dominance was to come much later. Two of these first dogs were to live on in the pedigrees of all modern whippets. Mr. Vickers, of Clumber Park, Nottinghamshire, owned the fawn-and-white bitch Herndell, born in 1886 and sired "by Charlie out of Lizzie," and also owned her son Zuber, later the breed's first champion. The brown-and-white Zuber, born in 1889, was sired by a dog named White Eye, described as a 'world famous' 21.5 lb racer, black with one white eye. In 1888 he clocked at an even 12 seconds over 200 yards. His owner subsequently challenged any dog of the same weight, offering £100 with White Eye given a yard start; but he found no takers, and White Eye was never beaten in his prime. Zuber's litter-brother Paleface was also brown and white, so the parti-colored pattern was strong within this family.

Zuber won at his first show, beating his dam at Tunbridge Wells, but only placed third at Crystal Palace. His record improved over the years until he finally became a champion—probably in 1896, although he was not listed as such until the 1898 stud book, when he was already nine years old. The requirements for the title were then more complicated than today, and for a long time Challenge Certificates were not necessarily offered separately to both sexes.

In 1897 Zuber's brown-and-white son Enterprise also became a champion. Judging by his photographs he had very light ears which he carried almost erect; since he was frequently pictured with ears pointing skywards this was probably not then regarded as such a serious fault as it is today. He was also owned and bred by Mr. Vickers, who that same year won a CC with a brindle-and-white daughter of Enterprise. In the next few years Herbert Vickers fades out as new and more ambitious kennels emerge, but a hundred years later, his two champions are at the back of every whippet pedigree in the world.

Two events before the turn of the century proved that whippet interest had grown, not by leaps and bounds but at least steadily. In 1894 Freeman S. Lloyd published his book The Whippet and Race Dog, now a collector's item, dealing mainly with the racing aspects of the breed and written "to make money for rent" as Mr. Lloyd confessed forty years later, when he was still drawing royalties from it! He later moved across the Atlantic, became known as the dean of American dog journalists and was active both as a judge and a writer well into the 1930s. He did not show or breed whippets but owned a little black 16 lb. bitch called Alice Tatham.

The second big step occurred in 1899. A group headed by the Duchess of Newcastle asked the Kennel Club to acknowledge the newly formed Whippet Club as the official breed organization. The Duchess is mostly remembered for the many borzoi and fox terrier champions carrying her "of Notts" banner, but she was an occasional whippet exhibitor as well and a great supporter of the newly sanctioned breed. The application was granted on 5 October 1899, with the Duchess as president. The emergence of a breed club had a stimulating effect. The number of whippets listed in the stud book doubled within a year, and from then on between 20 and 30 whippets were placed at championship shows each year until World War I; then in 1915 only nine whippets were listed, in 1917 and 1918 none.

Several of the kennels which had great influence on the breed's later development were started before the century turned. Although short-lived, none was more important than Albert Lamotte's Shirley Kennel. After showing several bitches of usually unregistered parentage for a few years, Mr. Lamotte crowned his first and most influential champion in 1902. Ch. Shirley Wanderer's show record was not more impressive than that of many others, but as a stud dog he made history. Himself sired by old Ch. Enterprise out of a bitch with unregistered parents, Wanderer was fawn in color, and so were most of his winning offspring; we know that all his sire's known family were parti-colored, so the solid fawn gene probably came from his dam. That would explain the large proportion of fawns in later generations, when Wanderer's most famous son Ch. Manorley Maori was bred to a sister of Wanderer's dam and thereby produced W.L. Renwick's first champion, Ch. Watford Glory. Mr. Lamotte drowned when the Berlin went down in the English Channel during World War I, but the influence of his dogs was enormous.

A much longer career was in store for the Manorley Kennels of the brothers F. and J. Bottomley, of Manorley Hall in Bradford, Yorkshire. Their names first appear quite inconspicuously in the stud book for 1895, but three years later the brothers had their first champion; they then totally dominated the scene until dog shows ceased for a few years in 1917. Most of the ten champions carrying the Manorley prefix were owned by Fred Bottomley, but only one or two of these were homebred. Obviously the brothers had a knack for picking up unknown stock at the race tracks and turning them into show dogs after they had been re-registered to carry the Manorley prefix. Complete changes of names were quite common in Britain until well into the 1930s (as they still are in some parts of the horse industry); it was possible for a dog to have a different name from one year to another, which of course complicates things enormously for anyone researching pedigrees.

The first big winner for the Bottomleys was the red-and-white Manorley Model, the breed's first champion bitch in 1898. She was of undistinguished background but proved a lasting winner—she was almost nine years old when she won the last of her ten CCs (three of them at Crufts). For the future, the most important of the Manorley dogs was Ch. Manorley Maori. He is described in the stud book as "blue"; color denominations then may easily have differed from current ones, and Mr. Renwick, who bred to him, described Maori as fawn, but in any case this is the only British whippet champion registered with this color until the 1980s. Maori was originally shown and used at stud under the name of Shirley Tramp and must have belonged first to one and then to the other of the two leading kennels of this time, although shown or bred by neither. He was born in 1902 and exhibited to most of his ten CCs by J.W. Proctor; during his final years he was owned by J.W. Marples of the famous Our Dogs publishing family. Maori was the best son of Ch. Shirley Wanderer; his dam is listed as a blue with unregistered parents. He sired only two champions but must have been popular as a stud dog, since he appears over and over in various combinations in most of the later pedigrees.

Maori's niece Ch. Manorley Moireen had an even more spectacular career. She won her first CC at Crufts as a puppy and repeated that win for the next four years, was defeated in 1911 (by a non-champion which never won another CC!) and then came back for her fifth and final Crufts CC in 1912—a record which has never been equalled at that show. Moireen was an unevenly marked red and white, her face at least half white (shades of her distant ancestor White Eye?). She ended up with a total of eighteen challenge certificates—a breed record which it took sixty years and modern bitches like Ch. Harque The Lark and Ch. Dondelayo Roulette to surpass in the 1960s and 1970s.

The judge who awarded Moireen her final CC at Crufts was Gertrude, Lady Decies, herself owner of the first two brindle whippet champions—the litter brothers Manorley Maxim and Marco. The first black-and-white champion, Manorley Magpie (incidentally the only one of that color until 1950), was owned by Sir Edmund Chaytor, Bt., who with Lady Chaytor remained a regular exhibitor for several years and helped reorganize the Whippet Club after the war.

These dogs disprove some commonly held notions (besides of course proving the Bottomley brothers' talent for buying and selling winners for other exhibitors): first that whippets were not owned or shown by the upper classes, second that all whippet exhibitors were men, and third that whippets in those days were predominantly fawn. In fact some of the most active early breeders and exhibitors were obviously pillars of society; women appear regularly on the lists of exhibitors (Lady Decies even handled her own dogs in the ring, in full late-Victorian regalia with voluminous skirts and cartwheel hat), and of the 26 champions whose colors are listed in the stud book up to 1923 only eleven were fawns, the rest parti-colored and/or brindle.

The fashion in color changed during the next decade, no doubt due to the dominance of solid fawn blood from Ch. Shirley Wanderer. Fawns continued to outnumber all other colors in Britain until the early 1960s, when the glamorous pieds and parti-coloreds began to catch on again—not so much a "new" color fad as a return to the colors which had originally been predominant.

Fred Bottomley remained active in the breed for a long time, showing and judging regularly through the 1920s and 1930s and even attending some shows after World War II, but the Manorley success story basically belongs to the pre-1920 era. There is one exception: the famous Ch. Manorley Manala, who won his title more than forty years after the first dogs carrying the same prefix. But Manala was bred by a niece of the brothers and did not have any Manorley breeding until the seventh and eighth generations of his pedigree.

Around 1920, the torch was handed to two newer breeders, Captain W. Lewis Renwick of the Watfords and W.L. Beara with his Willes dogs. Both had been in the breed since the turn of the century, but neither reached their peak until after 1920. These two strong personalities dominated the next two decades, until the outbreak of World War II. It is impossible to deal with one without mentioning the other, so intertwined were their dogs' bloodlines.

Captain Renwick lived in London but came from a north of England sporting family, famous for racehorses and cattle as well as dogs. His niece Dorothy Whitwell, née Renwick, had the successful Seagift Kennels of the 1950s; her sister Mrs. V. Williams started the still-famous Toydom pekingese; their cousin Lionel H. Renwick introduced the pharaoh hound to Britain and is an international judge. Lewis Renwick

Zuber's son Ch. Enterprise. Note the pricked ears, which were obviously not considered a fault worth hiding at the time.

started in whippets as a fourteen-year-old, with a bitch named Shirley Pride, bred from unregistered parents and "on the big side" but nevertheless a prizewinner in the first years of the century. When she was due to be bred, her young master was away at school; he advised his father to breed her to "the most expensive stud dog advertised." This turned out to be Ch. Manorley Maori, at the fee of 2 guineas, and the result of this union was Watford Glory, a champion in 1911 and at the back of almost all modern pedigrees.

A further connection between Watford and the Manorleys was made through Capt. Renwick's acquisition of the great brood bitch Ch. Manorley Mimosa, also by unregistered parents but dam of four champions. One of these, Ch. Falside Frivolity, owned by Lady Decies, won eleven CCs—including one at Crufts under B.S. Fitter in 1913; the following day she won the trophy for best bitch in show (all breeds), which "was a wonderful performance for a

The first whippet champion — Zuber, born in England in 1889 and ancestor of all modern whippets.

Enterprise´s son Ch. Shirley Wanderer, the first sire of major importance in the breed.

Whippet at Cruft´s, and the only time that this has happened," according to Mr. Fitter´s breed column in 1955.

But it was not until 1920 that the most important of Watford´s bitches was acquired. Judging at Crufts that year, Capt. Renwick awarded the CC to an almost six-year-old, almost all-white bitch named Kemmel, which until that date had an undistinguished show record. She was going to exert much influence on the breed.

Renwick purchased Kemmel after the show and promptly won four of the seven bitch CCs available that year with her. Kemmel´s breeding record is even more impressive: bred to three different dogs, one of them her son and another her near-blood brother, she produced offspring which dot the pedigrees of later years with amazing regularity. The most important of these was probably Watford Bon, a small red-and-white dog who did not win high show awards himself but sired several champions, including the all-conquering Ch. Watford Brilliant.

Pedigree 1. Ch. KEMMEL, white bitch with fawn head markings, born 1914

Sire: Heritor (fawn)	Student	Manorley Merman, by Ch. Manorley Maori (ped 5)
		Ch. Watford Glory, by Ch. Manorley Maori (ped 5)
	Hyacinth	St Clement´s Spring (unregistered)
		Wallingford Warning
Dam: Ch. Delphine (white)	Ch. Shirley Sunstar (fawn)	Prince George, full brother to Ch. Manorley Maori (ped 5)
		Shirley Poppy
	Falside Fascination (black/white)	Hip Hurray
		Topsy

Ch. Manorley Maori, a popular stud dog in the years prior to World War I, was sired by Shirley Wanderer. He was registered as blue but is said to have been fawn.

87

Ch. Watford Brilliant, whose achievements as a sire were not equalled for several decades. Brilliant´s breeding went back at least a half dozen times to Zuber, Enterprise et al.

However, as early as 1921 the fawn bitch Watford Maisie won eight mixed-variety classes, as well as a "Grand Challenge Cup and Best in Show" at the Bridgend show, under the great all-rounder judges Messrs. Houlker and Marples. According to the dog press, Maisie thereby proved "that whippets can beat terriers," obviously something which could not be taken for granted then. Maisie, described by Lewis Renwick as being "of the Greyhound type," became a champion the next year.

Pedigree 2. Ch. WATFORD BRILLIANT, fawn dog, born 1922

```
                                          Fortune's Wheel, by Manorley Merman (ped 1)
                           Better Luck (fawn)
                                          Senorita, by Ch. Shirley Wanderer son
Sire: Watford Bon (red/white)
                           Ch. Kemmel (ped 1)

                           Student (ped 1)
Dam: Regan Maid (unregistered)
                                          Sundial, sister to Better Luck (above)
                           Sequence
                                          Falside Fairy, by Manorley Merman
```

Brilliant, earlier registered as The Sheik and according to Renwick´s advertisements unbeaten for four whole years, set a new record by siring six champions—a figure not exceeded in Great Britain until the late 1950s. His dam was unregistered, but her pedigree is known and shows that Brilliant was line-bred many times over to the old great names.

There were many other Watford champions, including one of the first Best in Show winners recorded. The modern method of judging this competition—with each breed winner entering a group competition and a final run-off between the undefeated group winners—was not imported from the United States until 1939.

All told there were eight Watford champions in Britain, but only three of these were homebred. Much of Lewis Renwick´s influence came through his activities as a respected judge, regular contributor to the dog press and president of the Whippet Club over a long period. After the war he chaired the committee which revised the breed standard and finally wrote the excellent little Whippet Handbook, published shortly before his death in 1957.

W.L. "Willie" Beara, of Appledore in Devon, never wrote a book and refused to judge, even when invited to officiate at Crufts. But he was the greatest whippet-breeder of the prewar era. Charles Douglas Todd described him as "a big man in every way, in outlook as well as physique ... he made everyone who met him feel on good terms with themselves and the world in general." Until his time, breeding plans seem to have followed the simple maxim "breed a nice dog to a nice bitch and hope for the best." Beara inbred and linebred consistently, and was the first to establish anything like a true line of dogs, in the sense that they did not merely carry the same prefix to their names but were closely related. He did not even use a kennel name as such; most of his dogs were simply registered with the prefix Willes, though several champions he bred were shown by other kennels under their own prefixes. This may be one reason why the full impact of his breeding program is seldom recognized; the fact remains that he bred ten champions in Britain, twice as many as anyone else until well into the 1970s.

Mr. Beara won his first Challenge Certificate in 1903, but not until 1912 did he acquire the black-and-white bitch Falside Fascination which was to put him on the map. Her pedigree represented lines totally different from those then winning, with little to indicate that she would be of particular importance as a brood bitch; nor did she reach the top in the show ring. However, when bred to Ch. Shirley Sunstar, she produced the first ever predominantly white champion, Delphine, mentioned above as Ch. Kemmel's dam, which of course means that Willie Beara had a hand in the Watford winners too. In fact, when later breeding the famous dog that became known as Ch. Willesbeaux, Beara might have been trying to copy Kemmel's pedigree, so closely are the two related.

Pedigree 3. Ch. WILLESBEAUX, brindle dog, born 1920

		Treffynnon Sunstar, probably Shirley/Manorley bred
	Search light	
		Treffynnon Frivolity, by Ch. Shirley Sunstar (below)
Sire: Willesbea (fawn)		
		Student (ped 1)
	Spray	
		Hyacinth (ped 1)
	Ch. Shirley Sunstar (ped 1)	
Dam: Winstar (brindle) (sister to Ch. Delphine, ped 1)		
	Falside Fascination (ped 1)	

Kemmel's and Willesbeaux's dams were full sisters and their sires too were closely related. So the two most important kennels of prewar days, the Watfords and the Willes, were building on practically identical bloodlines—and they became even more closely related when Kemmel and Willesbeaux were bred together. It was through linebreeding to their sons and daughters, as well as to other Willesbeaux offspring, that Willie Beara was able to achieve his record of home-bred champions.

Willesbeaux, in spite of a brief career at stud in England, sired five champions and has been, if anything, more important in later pedigrees than his great rival Watford Brilliant. The later Beara dog which had the biggest influence was not a champion himself; Willesberg was too big to do much winning, but he sired five champions up to World War II, when show activities were interrupted. His pedigree demonstrates the kind of well-planned linebreeding that was Beara's forte, with nine lines to the near brother-sister team of Willesbeaux/Kemmel and a few more to Willesbeaux's dam, Winstar. Hardly any photographs or descriptions of Beara's most important whippets have survived.

Pedigree 4. **WILLESBERG**, fawn dog, born 1930

Sire: Ch. Silver King (fawn)	Scissors of St. Clair (fawn)	Telepathy
		Rhyl Boy, ex a Watford Bon daughter (ped 2)
		Country Girl, by Ch. Willesbeaux (ped 3)
	Splash	Watford Bon (ped 2)
		Ch. Kemmel (ped 1)
	Ch. Watford Playful (fawn/white)	Ch. Taffy's Pride, by Watford Bon (ped 2)
		Watford Worry, by Ch. Willesbeaux - Ch. Kemmel
	Poppy (fawn/white)	St David (unregistered parents)
		Willeslil, full sister to Willesberyl below
Dam: Willesberyl (fawn)	Ch. Willesbeaux (ped 3)	Willesbea (fawn)
		Winstar (brindle)
	Watford Watch	Watford Mystic
		Watford Whisper
	Willesbelle	Winstar (ped 3)

Popette
Willesbelle

Other exhibitors who had success before World War II included the great all-rounder judge J.J. Holgate, of the Southboro´ Kennels, who showed his daughter´s early Ch. Signorina to eleven CCs. Ernest Sobey, whose father had shown whippets in the late nineteenth century, was a mainstay, both as a breeder and as an officer in the Whippet Club. Bernard S. Fitter was less a breeder than a showman par excellence; his Willesberg son Ch. Boy Scrounger collected eleven CCs in the mid-1930s—more than any whippet male before him.

Both Ernest Sobey and Bernard Fitter remained popular judges well into the 1950s, but not even they had as long a career in the breed as Mrs. "Poppy" Martin. She owned her first whippet in 1910 and remained involved in the breed until her death in 1984. She bred her first champion in 1926 and a few years later showed the cream Ch. Poppysilver, bred by Willie Beara with whom she worked closely for many years. There was also the beautiful Ch. White Poppy, and after the war Mrs. Martin´s greatest winner was Ch. Poppytarquin, who in 1956 became the only black whippet known to win Best of Breed at Crufts.

Another kennel which spans more than half a century is Barmaud, founded by James E. Barker. He showed his first champion (again bred by Beara) in the early 1920s and a few years later bred the influential fawn sire Ch. Lashaway. Mr. Barker´s son continued the kennel and his granddaughter Mrs. Jennifer North-Row still shows and breeds under the same prefix.

Others who had great success in their own day did not make such a lasting impression. Halford Adcock owned the great Ch. Willesbeaux during part of the dog's adult life and made good use of him in his kennel "of Oxon," noted for a whole line of champions in America. Eventually, even Willesbeaux himself was shipped off overseas: the Whippet Club of America yearbook noted in 1925 that "The famous sire of the Oxon Kennels Ch. Willisbeaux [sic] was imported in 1924 by Mr. Ray Dunham; so far he has been little in competition in this country but has sired several litters from which great results are expected. Another son of Willisbeaux[,] Restless got winners at the first Whippet Specialty Show and later won his championship."

The Primley dogs of H. Whitley enjoyed a run of success based on an unregistered brood bitch, but Mr. Whitley remains best known as owner of the greyhound which in 1928 won the first Best in Show award offered at Crufts. Mrs. Barry Adams exhibited several champions of Willes breeding under her "of Ynys" suffix immediately before the war, and Mrs. Minne Howden bred the lovely Ch. Zanza Zanita, who is behind most of the Tiptree dogs through a breeding to her own litter brother.

Capt. H. Price Jones only bred two champions in Britain and one in America, but as one of these was Ch. Towyside Tatters and another Am. Ch. Towyside Teasle he deserves a mention. Tatters won a CC from the puppy class at Crufts in 1922 in a "record entry" of 62 (which does not necessarily mean that this was the number of dogs present; multiple entries for each dog were more common then than now, and at Crufts in those days the figures usually refer to the combined entries in special classes added by the Whippet Club and the short-lived British Empire Whippet Club. The biggest entry recorded before the war, 117 entries at Crufts in 1929, consisted of about 40 exhibits). Lewis

Renwick, who put Tatters to the top in 1922, said that he "excelled in front, neck and body"; he thought that he was a "future great." He did indeed win five CCs that season but does not appear to have been given much opportunity as stud dog and sired only two champions—one of these born when Tatters was ten years of age. His full importance was not realized until many years after his death, when Stanley Wilkin´s strongly Tatters-influenced breeding program started to bear fruit in the Tiptree dogs. No photographs of Tatters seem to have survived.

Pedigree 5. Ch. TOWYSIDE TATTERS, slate-fawn dog, born 1921

                                          Ch. Shirley Wanderer
                      Ch. Manorley Maori (blue)
                                          Princess Alice
Sire: Towyside Smoke
                                          Boy Sprinter, by Ch. Shirley Wanderer grandson
                      Ch. Girl Scout (fawn)
                                          Manorley Maggie, inbred to Ch. Shirley Wanderer

                                          Ch. Watford Myth, by Ch. Shirley Sunstar
                      Watford Mystic
                                          Montana Maid, by Ch. Manorley Maori son
Dam: Watford Myrth
                                          Manorley Merman, by Ch. Manorley Maori
                      Ch. Scilla (fawn)
                                          Senorita, by Ch. Shirley Wanderer son

The other influential Towyside champion, Teasle, was closely related to Tatters and is forever inscribed in the history of American whippets as the dam of the famous foundation bitch, Ch. Syndicate of Meander.

England´s most successful whippet sire ever was Ch. Laguna Ligonier. Born in 1960, he sired eleven champions in England and many more in other countries. He had over a hundred champion grandchildren in the United States alone.

Chapter

The Modern
Whippet in Britain

Dog activities in Britain came almost to a standstill during World War II. Many kennels were disbanded for lack of food or adequate help, and only the most dedicated breeders kept going with a small nucleus of their most valuable bloodlines, hoping for better times. With the renewed enthusiasm of the first postwar years, annual whippet registrations increased from just over 100 in 1942 to more than 700 five years later. They then remained fairly stable during the next decade, with a slow increase up towards the 1,000 mark. In 1960 the second big jump occurred, with over 1,500 registrations, and over 2,000 in 1965—putting the whippet perilously near the Top Twenty popularity charts. The danger of overpopulation which has threatened so many breeds was never realized for the whippet—in later years registrations have remained fairly constant around the 1,500 mark. It is difficult to compare current figures with those from the 1970s, since the registration system employed by the Kennel Club was changed several times, but it is safe to say that the whippet is more popular in Great Britain than anywhere else. (The registration total has been exceeded by those in the U.S. in recent years, but there are still at least three or four times as many whippets per person in England as in America.)

Entries at the first postwar shows also bear witness to the upswing in interest, much of it due to the breed clubs' activities; apart from the Whippet Club there was now also the National Whippet Association, founded in 1936 at the instigation of Mrs. Conway-Evans of the Conevan Kennels. In the autumn of 1945 each club organized its first independent "open" whippet show—meaning that no challenge certificates were available. The National was first off the mark and on 13 October received a world record of 263 entries in the sixteen classes—more than twice that of any earlier figures. The number of exhibits was 74, so each dog must have been entered in an average of three or four classes.

Only a month later the Whippet Club had 180 entries in thirteen classes at its show, held on the same site as the National show—the Scottish Drill Hall in London, which remained the battleground for many of the big

93

whippet events in more recent years. The two experienced judges, J. Emlyn Owen at NWA and James E. Barker at the Whippet Club, each selected a bitch for his Best in Show winner; Seagift Sonata and See for Charming respectively. Neither became a champion; Sonata died shortly afterwards. She was owned by Mrs. M.B. Garrish, whose Fleeting prefix has a prominent place in the breed´s history. See for Charming belonged to Mrs. Kay Chapman, who later bred a long line of glamorous English champions.

The next year both clubs held their first championship shows. At the National´s show in May, Charles Douglas Todd judged 238 entries in sixteen classes. The Whippet Club event in June was held in conjunction with the Afghan Hound show, with the whippets outnumbering the then relatively rare Afghans by far, with 167 entries in fourteen classes judged by W. Lewis Renwick.

The Challenge Certificate in dogs at both shows went to the light brindle Mighty Atom, subsequently the breed´s first postwar champion; his owner, George Silk, is still showing his Wyemere dogs almost a half century later. Mr. Todd gave Mighty Atom the BIS award as well, while Lewis Renwick preferred his bitch winner, White Statue of Conevan—an all-white who also became a champion, but above all was a brood bitch of the utmost importance. From her come all the top-producing Brekin bitches, and through them also most of the champions of the 1960s and 1970s. Mr. Renwick described Statue as being of correct size, with lovely outline, good substance and quality, indeed hard to fault; Mr. Todd felt that

she failed in feet and was too fat. (Incidentally, the disposition to put on weight easily seems to have been inherited by many of her latter-day descendants.)

One of the unluckiest dogs at these shows was the eight-year-old fawn Sporting Chance. Owned by Miss Bottomley, he was sired by one of the last Watford dogs out of a sister to Ch. Manorley Manala, and so brought some of the oldest names into the postwar period. In spite of his age, Sporting Chance was reserve best dog at both shows; Lewis Renwick even called him "the best type of all the dogs." Although he never became a champion, through a breeding to White Statue of Conevan he figures prominently in almost all modern pedigrees.

The experts disagreed strongly about the general state of the breed after the war. Lewis Renwick believed that the bitches were far better than the dogs, found many faulty mouths and felt that true movement was conspicuous by its absence. Mrs. Minne Howden (Zanza) wrote that the dogs seemed to be getting too big, but Charles Todd found not only a vast improvement in most respects since before the war, but even felt that some of the exhibits could have been bigger to advantage, as the larger dogs were "invariably better balanced" all round! The whippets shown immediately after the war did indeed seem to be smaller than many of those of the 1930s, judging by a number of candid snapshots showing whole classes in the ring with their handlers. Those early dogs almost certainly averaged around 20 in. at the shoulder, so when size increased again in the 1960s it was more a reversion to earlier times than a new development.

Many of the old breeders remained active for years after the war, usually as judges. The most important influence, however, came from a group of new people, and it is necessary to backtrack a little to see the foundation on which most of them built. Of Stanley S. Wilkin, Tiptree Kennels, it was written that "Nobody ever showed so many dogs and won so little for so long and yet still stuck to his guns and his ideas." Mr. Wilkin had started his kennel in 1930 and died in 1946, so does not strictly speaking belong to the postwar period. However, during most of his own time it would have been impossible to guess the impact the Tiptree dogs would have on a later generation; he never owed a single champion and by prewar contemporaries was given credit for little more than breeding a lot of dogs ("hundreds of litters" according to one writer) and being an aggressive and flamboyant salesman. Stanley Wilkin advertised freely and apparently had his own printing press from which flowed an unending line of "blotters, calendars, pictures, poems" publicizing his Tiptree

Tiptree Jink had tremendous importance as a sire — almost every whippet in the world now carries his blood many times over. This head study is unusual in that English whippets even today are seldom pictured with alert ear carriage. Jink also demonstrates excellent neck carriage, an intelligent expression and the undeniable style which endeared Tiptree dogs to breeders worldwide.

whippets. It probably did not help his reputation that he actively (but unsuccessfully) campaigned for a change in the British standard that would allow for the bigger dogs wanted in the U.S. This would have been of much more interest to him—as American fanciers were clamoring for his large and glamorous dogs—than to other breeders whose dogs were not in such demand overseas. Apart from numerous exports to America, Tiptree dogs went to Africa, India, Holland, Norway, Portugal and even the West Indies.

Stanley Wilkin bought his first three whippets in 1930, one dog and two bitches, none of them from a well-known breeder. The male was registered as Tiptree Jink, a fawn who never made it into the Kennel Club stud book and whose sire is sometimes listed as unregistered, sometimes as a brindle-and-white brother to Ch. Watford Brilliant. (This is not necessarily contradictory, as he could have been registered late in life.) The dam was extremely well-bred, with Ch. Towyside Tatters as sire and a daughter of Ch. Willesbeaux as dam—so Jink possessed the very best prewar blood. The two bitches also had Tatters close up in their pedigrees. With these three

The Tiptree Kennels of Show Whippets, Goldhanger, Essex, England

Tiptree Golddust

Tiptrees Jink, Jane & Monk

THE FOUNDATION SIRES OF THE TIPTREE KENNELS

Tiptree Mee Mee
Beat two champions whilst still a puppy
C.C. and Best in Breed, L.K.A. London, 1939

Ch. Tiptree Evon
Unshown in England

Ch. Tiptree Iris
C.C. Richmond and £27 in London, etc.

Ch. Tiptree Veronica
Unshown in England

The above four are now all in America

After World War II, most kennels worldwide based their breeding on English Tiptree stock. This advertisement from the early 1940s features the three most important Tiptree stud dogs — Jink, Golddust, and Monk — as well as four youngsters, all exported to the United States. Evon, Iris and Veronica all became American champions.

Mr. Wilkin founded his kennel in Goldhanger, Essex. (The famous Tiptree preserves and marmalades were produced by his family there, and apparently the offices still bear pictorial evidence of Stanley Wilkin´s interest in whippets. One wonders if the present directors are aware that the Tiptree name is in certain small circles as well known for whippets as for orange marmalade.)

When bred to his own full sister, Jink sired the only two English champions bred by Mr. Wilkin— Tiptree Silver Dream and Tiptree Golden Dream, both owned by other exhibitors. A brother to Jink´s dam was bred to Jink´s full sister, and this tight linebreeding resulted in another fawn, Tiptree Golddust. He never got into the stud book either, but sired the white-and-fawn Tiptree Monk, who had moderate success at the shows and has been the dog most used for linebreeding of all the Tiptrees.

Monk´s dam was a complete outcross—her pedigree even to the fifth and sixth generation contains hardly a single familiar name, so for better or worse she may have provided some of the features which made Tiptree a distinct strain. Dogs of this line seem to have had more consistently attractive heads than any others, with alert expressions, neat ears and arched necks—perhaps one of the reasons why they were much sought after in the U.S., where head properties have traditionally been more important than in Britain. Size was often a problem, but Stanley Wilkin also "straightened up the Whippet of his day in front," according to Charles Todd, although in the early days they tended to be slab-sided.

The most important fact about the Tiptree dogs is their close proximity to that early great Ch. Towyside Tatters (introduced in the prewar chapter). Mr. Wilkin appears to have consistently collected Tatters' blood from whatever source was available, and all the later Tiptrees as a consequence were closely linebred to him. This brings the pedigrees back astonishingly soon to the oldest dogs; Tatters was a grandson of Ch. Shirley Wanderer (born in 1900), and the Tiptree dogs cover as much as four decades in just a few generations.

In spite of the conspicuous lack of show ring success for his dogs, Stanley Wilkin worked out a breeding program that proved to be of great importance for most of the major postwar kennels of the 1950s and 1960s. The Sapperly, Samema, Laguna, Allways and Wingedfoot champions were nearly always of Tiptree breeding. When the exhibitors honored Stanley Wilkin´s memory with a silent minute at the National Whippet Association show shortly after his death, it was an overdue tribute to someone whose ideals probably had more influence on the whippet of today than anyone else´s.

The linebreeding which Stanley Wilkin steadfastly believed in is best exemplified by the influential stud dog Sapperly Tiptree Pilot, sire of six of the early postwar champions in Britain and owned during most of his life by the Sapperly Kennel of Mr. and Mrs. Ben Evans.

Pedigree 6. SAPPERLY TIPTREE PILOT, fawn-&-white dog, born 1942

```
                                      Tiptree Monk, by Tiptree Golddust (below)
                     Am. Ch. Tiptree Noel (ped 23)
                                      Tiptree Christine, by Tiptree Golddust (below)
     Sire: Tiptree Progress
                                      Tiptree Jink, out of a Ch. Towyside Tatters daughter
                     Tiptree Naomi (silver-fawn)
                                      Highland Lassie, by Ch. Towyside Tatters (ped 5)

                                      Silians Tatters, by Ch. Towyside Tatters (ped 5)
                     Tiptree Golddust (fawn)
                                      Silver Phyllis, sister to Tiptree Jink, above
     Dam: Tiptree Stella
                                      Zanza Zagreb, by Ch. Towyside Tatters (ped 5)
                     Zanza Zarella
                                      Ch. Zanza Zanita, by Ch. Towyside Tatters (ped 5)
```

Tiptree Christine and Stella were full sisters, as were Zanza Zagreb and Zanita. This means that Pilot carried ten lines to Ch. Towyside Tatters through closely related stock. Pilot did not become a champion, although according to Stanley Wilkin (in a letter written to Mrs. M.B. Garrish only a few weeks before his death) he was "good enough to sweep everything before him." The reason was not his age, as earlier supposed; Pilot was only three years old in 1945 but does not seem to have been at any of the first postwar shows. Mr. Wilkin explains that Pilot "perhaps will never be a champion because he lost the tip of his tail in a door sometime ago, altho´ Evans hopes to make him one."

Mr. and Mrs. Evans later had great success with two of Pilot's sons, the white-trimmed fawn Ch. Sapperly Heralder (out of a Tiptree Jink daughter) and the solid fawn Ch. Sapperly Kinsman. The former was the most consistent sire, with as many champions as Pilot himself, but the latter assured his place in breed history through one outstanding son, the great Ch. Wingedfoot Marksman of Allways.

It appears to be nothing more than coincidence that two great whippet sires just after the war were both named Pilot. The white-and-fawn Ch. Pilot Officer Prune was a great winner, with three of his seven CCs won at the National club shows and Best in Show at the Bath all-breed championship show in 1947—the first known such win for a whippet in Britain. Prune went on to shatter all previous records by siring no less than nine champions in Britain and several more in the U.S., Sweden and Australia.

Pedigree 7. Ch. PILOT OFFICER PRUNE, fawn-&-white dog, born 1945

```
                                        Willesberg (ped 4)
                    Ch.  Conquisitor (fawn)
                                        Ch.  Tiptree Silver Dream
Sire: Happy Landings (fawn)
                                        Ch.  Manorley Manala
                    Silver Wings (white)
                                        Oxted Dainty Maid, by Tiptree George

                                        Willesberg (ped 4)
                    Silverbeige of Luss (silver)
                                        Whoopee
Dam: Silver Nymph (silver-blue)
                                        Blue Cloud of Highmead
                    Fantasia of Marvin
                                        Happy Morning
```

In 1947 Ch. Pilot Officer Prune won Best in Show at Bath, the first time a whippet had taken such a win at a championship show for all breeds in England. He also sired nine English champions, a record at the time, and is credited with adding great refinement and glamour to later generations.

According to Prune's owner and breeder Mrs. Kay Chapman, neither Silver Wings nor Happy Landings were outstanding, apart from being of ideal size, and Prune's dam is described simply as "a little blue bitch which lacked in substance but was an excellent ratter." So the champion qualities must have been inherited from the double dose of Willesberg and the Tiptrees.

In many ways Prune was a different type from those then being shown, perhaps more "modern," certainly more refined and elegant than most. Lewis Renwick describes him as being higher on leg and not having the strength of some other champions, and according to some breeders—who admired him and sent their bitches to him nevertheless—Prune could move with that high hackney-like front action which is still often a problem in the breed. But he was of ideal size and must have had tremendous class, glamour and all-over quality. His name is carried on into later pedigrees, most of all through the great Ch. Bellavista Barry, but also through Mrs. Chapman's own Ch. Flying Officer Kite (BIS at Bournemouth 1949) and other champions from the Springmere, Seagift, Ballymoy and Peppard kennels.

Mrs. Chapman remained virtually unknown outside England, never judging, seldom advertising and never using a prefix for her dogs—yet she bred more champions than most of the more famous kennels. Some of the best were Tea for Teresa, Jay for Jewel, Bouquet, Telstar Moon and the lovely little brindle-and-white dog Ch. Walhachin in the 1970s, a son of Ch. Laguna Light Lagoon with at least half a dozen lines back to Prune.

The biggest success story directly after the war was probably that of Mrs. Dorothy Whitwell's Seagift Kennel. Mrs. Whitwell was born into the famous Renwick "livestock" family and had been a successful exhibitor of pointers and setters before the war. She soon reached the top in whippets also; during the next fifteen years she showed more whippet champions than anyone had done before her in Britain—sixteen in all. The dogs were of differing backgrounds and varied in color from nearly all white to solid black. Although Seagift was more a show kennel than a breeding establishment, their exports played a major part in establishing some of the best-known American kennels, such as Pennyworth and Canyon Crest.

In Britain the Seagift blood is now difficult to find, as most of Mrs. Whitwell's champions (some carrying other kennel names—Fleeting, Hillgarth, Ravenslodge, etc) were exported before they were bred. One of the few kennels which carried on the Seagift lines was Mrs. Carmi Cleeve's Dragonhill, which together with Lady Anderson's Tweseldowns and Mrs. Mary Sheffield's Hillgarths provided the basis for the Poltescos and the later Nimrodels, forming a numerically small but high-quality family of distinct type and almost always solid fawn color.

The whippet side of the Seagift Kennels was disbanded around 1960, but Mrs. Whitwell showed her famous greyhounds under the same prefix for several more years and later became one of the most-travelled international all-rounder judges.

In 1950, when the Whippet Club held a slightly belated fiftieth anniversary show at the Royal Horticultural Hall in London, there was a new record entry of 276, made by 127 exhibits in eighteen classes. The famous all-rounder Leo C. Wilson judged dogs and Ben Evans of the Sapperlys judged bitches. Mr. Wilson brought out three dogs to choose from for his final award; each was outstanding, yet very different in type. The famous Ch. Pilot Officer Prune was the most elegant, Ch. Seagift Sherriff supremely well balanced, the young Laguna Liege less eye-catching when standing but moving "like a thoroughbred horse," which eventually won him both the Challenge Certificate and Best in Show over the fawn bitch

Ch. Shirleymoor Setfair.

This win marked the first major success for Mrs. D.U. McKay, whose Laguna Kennel achieved world fame a few years later and has remained an important factor in the breed´s development worldwide for over fifty years, first mostly in the show ring, later exclusively in the field. Dorrit McKay´s first whippet had been acquired from Stanley Wilkin almost by accident in 1939; going up to Goldhanger to look at a horse, Captain and Mrs. McKay dropped by to see the whippets on the way and came home with a new dog instead of a horse. This was Tiptree Joan (by Tiptree Monk out of a Tiptree Jink daughter), later bred to one of Mr. Wilkin´s dogs for a litter which included the homebred fawn bitch Jovial Judy, dam of Liege.

Liege was sired by Ch. Sapperly Heralder and played his own part in the development of the Laguna story. But even more important was an acquisition in 1951. The white-and-brindle bitch Brekin Ballet Shoes, then already two years old, had won well for her breeder Lady Danckwerts and soon became a champion when owned by Mrs. McKay, but above all she was an excellent brood bitch—perhaps the best example of what may be the strongest bitch line ever in the breed.

The value of this pedigree is obvious: linebreeding to the unlucky "war baby" Sporting Chance, plenty of Tiptree blood (Golden Pencil was in effect 100% Tiptree) and also several lines to the older Watford and Manorley dogs. Ch. Balaise Barrie, not to be confused

with his grandson Ch. Bellavista Barry, was the last dog shown by Miss B. Bottomley, niece of the old Manorley brothers from the turn of the twentieth century.

Pedigree 8. Ch. BREKIN BALLET SHOES, particolour bitch, born 1949

```
                                        Grey Owl, by Watford Mystery
                        Balaise Beau Geste
                                        Take Me, sister to Ch. Manorley Manala
Sire: Ch. Balaise Barrie (fawn)
                                        Sporting Chance (below)
                        Samema Silver Shoes
                                        Springmere Fascination

                                        Watford Sapper Officer, by Tiptree Jink (ped 6)
                        Sporting Chance (fawn)
                                        Take Me (above)
Dam: Ch. Brekin Spode (white/fawn)
                                        Golden Pencil, by Am. Ch. Tiptree Noel (ped 27)
                        Ch. White Statue of Conevan (white)
                                        Samema Sunray, by Ch. Manorley Manala
```

Ballet Shoes was only one of several extremely influential brood bitches carrying the Brekin prefix. The key to Lady Danckwert´s breeding success was obviously Ch. Brekin Spode, herself a Best in Show winner at Leicester in 1948 and successfully bred to three different stud dogs. The most important litter was sired by Balaise Barrie; Ballet Shoes put Laguna firmly on the world map, her sister Brekin Bright Spark was the dam of Ch. Bellavista Barry, and Brekin Brown Sugar produced Eng. Am. Ch Ravenslodge Solitaire, who is behind a long line of O´Lazeland champions in the U.S.

When Spode was bred to Mrs. Garrish´s fawn stud dog Fleeting Hillgarth Sovereign, she produced Brekin Fiesta of Fleeting (the dam of champions in both England and Australia); and when bred to Sapperly Tiptree Pilot she pro-

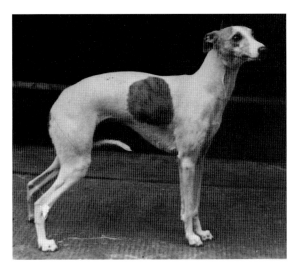

Ch. Brekin Ballet Shoes, cornerstone for the Laguna Kennels and granddam of England's all-time top sire Ch. Laguna Ligonier.

name: Wingedfoot Marksman of Allways. The success was immediate. "The Great Marksman" is remembered mostly as a sire but was also a record-breaking show dog with a total of thirteen CCs.

Pedigree 9. Ch. WINGEDFOOT MARKSMAN OF ALLWAYS, fawn dog, born 1950

```
                      Sapperly Tiptree Pilot (ped 6)
        Sire: Ch. Sapperly Kinsman (fawn)
                                  Flight Lieutenant
                      Joyous Greetings
                                  Springmere Sweet Mavis

                                  Am.Ch. Tiptree Noel (ped 27)
                      Golden Pencil
                                  Tiptree Naomi (ped 6)
        Dam: Bolney Starshine of Allways (fawn)
                                  Ch. Willesblair
                      Silver Lady of Luss (white)
                                  Heatherblade
```

duced Brekin Willow Pattern, dam of the famous trio of Fieldspring champions used in the Allways and Wingedfoot breeding programs. All these dogs are behind hundreds of champions all over the world. It is doubtful if any other bitches have had such a pervasive influence on the breed as Ch. Brekin Spode and her daughters.

If the Brekin line dominated in bitches, the leading stud dogs during most of the 1950s usually came from two kennels which worked so closely together that it is hard to say where one begins and the other ends—Wingedfoot and Allways. Charles Douglas Todd already had long experience in the breed when he decided to start a "proper kennel" in 1950. He acquired a fawn dog puppy from Mr. and Mrs. Fred Jones's kennel of Allways and added his own new prefix to its

Since Tiptree Progress and Golden Pencil were full brothers, this is again linebreeding to Mr. Wilkin's dogs, with Willes blood close up on the dam's side.

Marksman's record of siring ten British and numerous overseas champions was unchallenged for two decades. Most of the winners by him were from the Allways or Wingedfoot kennels; others were bred by Test, Brekin, Boughton, Shalfleet or Mrs. Chapman. In 1960, when I first saw Marksman he was an old dog (he died in 1963), but his qualities were still in evidence: close to ideal size, good bone structure and excellent soundness, great angulation fore and aft, overall balance and beautifully cadenced movement. He was more short-coupled than many breeders like today and tended to fall away rather sharply over the loin. His head and ears were not the most elegant, which may explain why in spite of his enormous influence in Britain and Europe he never achieved the same popularity in the U.S.

Most of Marksman's descendants bore his definite stamp, both in color and type. Ch. Wingedfoot Wild Goose was close to his father in looks, almost emulated his show record, but is best remembered as the sire of one of the most admired English whippets of all time, the gorgeous Ch. Wingedfoot Claire de Lune. She was a stunning parti-color, whose visual image I have forever tried to keep alive in my memory after seeing her both in the show ring and at Wingedfoot Kennels. Mrs. McKay in a weak moment once described her as the best whippet she had ever seen. Claire of course got her color and much of her looks from her dam, the nearly all-white Ch. Wingedfoot Hildegarde, and was an excellent representative of the successful "nick" between Marksman and the Fieldspring champions mentioned earlier. Hildegarde eventually was exported to Holland as a brood bitch for the Kafiristan Kennels there; Claire went to South Africa where she founded the famous Tula Kennels.

The most important early sires in Fred and Bobbie Jones's kennel were Ch. Fieldspring Bartsia of Allways and his nephew Ch. Evening Star of Allways, both correctly sized, sound and attractive little gentlemen, each the sire of five champions in Britain and others overseas. Evening Star, when inbred to his half-sister, sired a dog whose show record surpassed that of any other male whippet in Britain: Ch. Robmaywin Stargazer of Allways, the winner of seventeen CCs, the Hound Group at Crufts and Best in Show at the Three Counties championships show in 1958.

Pedigree 10. Ch. ROBMAYWIN STARGAZER OF ALLWAYS, fawn dog, born 1956

Ch. Wingedfoot Marksman of Allways (ped 9)
Sire: Ch. Evening Star of Allways (fawn)
        Fleeting Hillgarth Sovereign
    Ch. Fieldspring Betony (fawn)
        Brekin Willow Pattern

Ch. Wingedfoot Marksman of Allways (ped 9)
Dam: Ch. Mistrals Mrs Miniver (fawn)
        Ch. Sapperly Kinsman (ped 9)
    Fleeting Frieze
        Fleeting Filigree, by Fleeting Hillgarth Sovereign

Stargazer was a powerful, masculine dog with tremendous ring presence. In England he sired only two champions, but he plays a bigger part in many pedigrees than this might imply; he has other champion descendants in Scandinavia, central Europe, Australia and the U.S. His daughter Am. Ch. Selbrook Highlight was the dam of eight champions and founded Mrs. Hodge's Highlight Kennels in the U.S.

Around 1960 the scene changed. Mr. Todd moved to Rhodesia with some of his dogs, and although he came back to England before his death in the mid-1970s the Wingedfoot era was basically over. The Allways Kennel was disbanded after the death of Fred Jones, although his widow, now Mrs. Bobbie Cooke, has maintained an active interest as a judge and as president of the Whippet Club. The most important subsidiary to these two kennels, Mrs. Dorothy Lewis and her Test dogs, carried on for a few years, exporting numerous dogs all over the world and showing her last champion shortly before her death in 1965—

the parti-colored Ch. Dancing Girl of Test, strongly inbred to Stargazer and Marksman.

Many other changes took place in the 1960s. Registrations almost tripled in ten years, and, as the registration figures are the basis for how many Challenge Certificates are allocated to each breed, the number of CCs awarded in whippets gradually increased from 20 per year in each sex throughout the 1950s to 37 in 1993. Competition at the championship shows which offered CCs grew progressively stronger, usually with 100-200 whippets exhibited at the major shows, even more at some of the most important breed club events. Since there is no separate class for champions in Britain, the up-and-coming stock has to defeat mature champions in order to gain their titles, and it is therefore much more difficult for a dog to become a champion in Britain than anywhere else. In spite of the higher entries, far fewer champion titles are awarded than in almost any other country—usually not to more than ten or fifteen whippets each year.

Several new whippet clubs were granted championship status by the Kennel Club in the 1960s. The Midland Whippet Club was founded in 1948 but did not hold its first championship show until 1964; the Northern Counties Whippet Club started in 1955, gained championship status in 1963 and had the colorful American importer-exporter of many breeds, Anton Rost, judging over 200 entries at its first show. Scotland, East Anglia, South Yorkshire, the North East, Wales and Northern Ireland now all have their own clubs which organize annual champion-ship shows (the NIWC and the South Yorkshire Club since the early 1980s, the North Eastern Club for the first time in 1992).

The heritage from Wingedfoot and Allways was carried on into the present by several kennels. The Harques of Mrs. Ann Argyle and the Shalfleets of Barbara Wilton-Clark bred almost exclusively along these bloodlines until well into the 1970s. Ann Argyle´s first champion was bred by Mrs. Chapman but sired by Marksman, and as a result of intelligent linebreeding Harque could present five more beautiful fawn champions during the 1960s. The most successful of these was the great Ch. Harque The Lark, who surpassed the almost sixty-year-old breed record held by Ch. Manorley Moireen and had won a record nineteen CCs in the early 1970s. The Lark also soared to previously unscaled heights by twice winning Best in Show at all-breed championship shows and twice being runner-up; she was also BIS at the Hound Association show and won at least eight Hound Groups—one of the best show records for any whippet in Britain. Lark was an elegant yet powerful bitch with more showmanship than is commonly seen in the breed; this, coupled with soundness, perfect conditioning and Mrs. Argyle´s impeccable long-leash handling, made them almost invincible for several years.

During the 1970s and 1980s Mrs. Argyle introduced different blood, producing winners such as the fawn Ch. Harque To Pegasus (by Ch. Deepridge Mintmaster), the brindle Ch. Harque Yonder (by Ch. Dondelayo Buckaroo out of Lark) and the parti-colored Ch. Harque

To Equerry (by Ch. Akeferry Jimmy ex Yonder). The bottom line in the pedigrees still goes back to Wingedfoot and Allways, however. In the 1980s Mrs. Argyle became increasingly active as a judge—including at Westminster in the U.S. (although regrettably not for whippets) and Crufts, where she judged Best in Show in 1991. Her brindle dog Ch. Harque To Milo (by Hillsdown Fergal) has continued the long line of champions into the 1990s, however. Mrs. Argyle died in early 1994.

Pedigree 11. Ch. HARQUE THE LARK, fawn bitch, born 1966.
Also showing pedigree of Ch. Harque To Gamecock (fawn dog, born 1963) and Ch. Harque To Rosa (fawn bitch , born 1960)

```
                        Ch.  Allways Wingedfoot Running Fox (below)
            Ch.  Runway Controller (fawn)
                        Evening Mist
Sire: Harque To Beaumont (fawn)
                        Ch.  Wingedfoot Marksman of Allways (ped 9)
            Ch.  Wingedfoot Tu Whit Tu Whoo (fawn)
                        Eh for Adorable

                        Ch.  Wingedfoot Marksman of Allways (ped 9)
            Ch.  Allways Wingedfoot Running Fox (fawn)
                        Perpetual Motion
Dam: Rosaday of Knotnum (fawn)
                        Cornish Rhapsody
            Bringhurst Thimble
                        Fleeting Flicker
```

The Shalfleet Kennels started in 1952. The first whippet Barbara Wilton-Clark acquired was a monorchid, the second one also, but with the third purchase she hit the jackpot: Wingedfoot Bartette was classically bred by Bartsia out of a Marksman daughter and became the dam or granddam of all the homebred Shalfleet champions during the 1960s and 1970s. Almost the day that Bartette arrived, Barbara purchased her first greyhound from the world-famous Treetops

Kennels of Mrs. Judy de Casembroot; the Shalfleet success in that breed has always gone hand in hand with the whippets and helped make the kennel one of England´s top show and breeding establishments for many years.

The first Shalfleet whippet champion was the glamorous parti-colored Ch. Shalfleet Selbrook Daylight (litter sister to Ch. Selbrook Highlight in the U.S.), not homebred and rather different from the solid, no-frills fawns usually shown by Shalfleet. When mated to a son of Bartette´s she produced two champions, one of them the outstanding red-fawn Ch. Shalfleet Story. The most important whippet winner from this kennel during the 1970s was Story´s great-granddaughter, the exquisitely correct Ch. Sequence of Shalfleet, winner of 15 CCs as well as one or two Hound Groups—making her one of the top winning bitches of all time.

Pedigree 12. Ch. SEQUENCE OF SHALFLEET, fawn bitch, born 1971

```
                        Ch.  Robmaywin Stargazer of Allways (ped 10)
            Shalfleet Skyliner (fawn-white)
                        Ch.  Shalfleet Story, inbred to Ch. W. Marksman of A. (ped 9)
Sire: Ch. Shalfleet Sailing Free (fawn)
                        Ch.  Evening Star of Allways (ped 10)
            Ch.  Shalfleet Starstruck (fawn)
                        Shalfleet Sceptre, inbred to Ch. W. Marksman of A. (ped 9)

                        Ch.  Robmaywin Stargazer of Allways (ped 10)
Dam: Shadow of Andreovna (fawn-white)
                        Moonlight Cloudy Hunter
            Josie of Foxstones
                        Tintara of Foxstones (unregistered)
```

In the 1970s Shalfleet added some Ligonier blood to these intensely linebred Marksman lines. A son of Eng. Am. Ch. Laguna Leisure sired the gorgeous near-white Ch. Shalfleet Silver Knight of Skyeboat, and a brindle son of Ch.

Deepridge Mintmaster was acquired as part outcross, Selbrook Brandy of Shalfleet. Although hardly shown he proved consistently successful at stud; when bred to Sequence he sired the lovely Ch. Shalfleet Sequilla (winner of eight CCs), and he is behind all the later Shalfleet champions.

In 1979 Barbara Wilton-Clark imported a dog from Holland, the first time that a breeder brought in a foreign whippet in a deliberate attempt to upgrade British stock, which by this time was frequently the target for devastating criticism from many breeders. She had judged the young brindle dog Samoems Silent Knight in Holland and felt that he would be suitable for breeding to her own stock in England—particularly as his dam was an exported Shalfleet bitch and his sire went back to the old Wingedfoot exports of the 1950s. After completing his title on the European continent, Silent Knight went through six months in quarantine and promptly thereafter added both the Shalfleet suffix and the British championship to his name. He won nine CCs and the title of Top Whippet for 1980. Two of his sons were among the top winners for 1982—Barbara Wilton-Clark's own fawn Ch. Shalfleet Silent Wish and Roger Stock's group-winning parti-colored Ch. Shalfleet Showman of Courthill, later exported to India.

The brindle Silent Knight daughter Ch. Shalfleet Shablis was co-owned by her breeder with Canada's Max Magder, whose Lorricbrook prefix was already well known on both the American continents. A few years later a dog bred by Mr. Magder in Canada from part American Misty Moor and part English Shalfleet background, Lorricbrook Runaway, became Shalfleet's (and England's) second imported whippet champion. With Barbara's retirement from the world of dog showing and the harsh English climate to the sunny island of Tenerife in the late 1980s, Runaway went to Tim Teillers' Samoem Kennels in Holland, won the FCI World Show in 1989 under the author, and added several European titles to his U.S., Canadian and English championships.

Ch. Sequence of Shalfleet was perhaps the most successful of all Barbara Wilton-Clark's whippet champions, winning fifteen CCs during the mid-1970s. Shalfleet was equally well-known for Greyhounds prior to the kennel's closure in the late 1980s.

Although Mrs. Wilton-Clark's active involvement in recent years has been limited to judging assignments, the Shalfleet banner has kept flying in England through a couple of successful champions shown by Kathy Thomas: the brindle bitch Shalfleet Songwriter of Faracre and the fawn dog Shalfleet Still So Sharp at Faracre, both of pure old Shalfleet background. The most successful kennels currently active with similar background are now Shelagh Thompson's Walkabouts, Mrs. M.B. McConkey's Barmolls and Lady Sarah Neill-Fraser's Baxendales. The Walkabouts started with Wingedfoot breeding in the 1960s; the brindle Silent Knight son Ch. Walkabout Warrior King, the parti-colored Ch. Walkabout Whirlpool of Baxendale, and the two fawns Ch. Barmoll Blaze of Gold and Ch. Barmoll Beeswing at Walkabout have all won Best in Show at breed club championship shows over the past few years; the latter two are both out of the remarkable Ch. Barmoll Beejapers, one of the most successful brood bitches the breed has seen in many years and descending surprisingly closely from the old Wingedfoot dogs on which Shalfleet was founded several decades earlier.

Other kennels which showed the first of several champions in the late 1950s or early 1960s were the Ladiesfields, often black or blue, of Mrs. Margaret Wigg, the Springmeres of Miss J. Stevensen and the Peppards of Mr. and Mrs. D. Gollan, the Porthursts of Mrs. Diana Ticehurst and the Trevelmonds of D. Armstrong. Miss I.B. Clay's Tantivvey prefix had been famous in Dalmatians since the 1930s, long before whippets were added; and Gillian Ussher, MRCVS, apart from showing her Iniskhelltr dogs with much success, has remained editor since the first edition in 1972 of the valuable Whippet Biennial, published by all ten of the British breed clubs in conjunction. (The North-

ern Counties Whippet Club yearbook which preceded it in the 1960s is now a rare collector's item.) Lady Selway's Ballagans also go back a long time but have often been located in other countries: France (where Lady Selway showed her first champion in the 1940s), the U.S., Singapore, etc.

A separate, numerically small but very successful line has been maintained by the previously mentioned Tweseldowns and Poltescos in cooperation with Mrs. I.H. Lowe's Nimrodel Kennel. Although making up only a small percentage of the breed population they have produced such excellent specimens as the

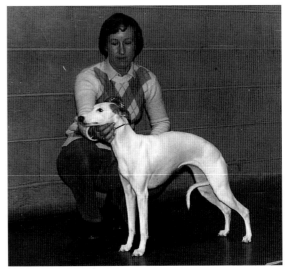

Ch. Barmoll Beelzebub (Garnstones Nearco of Shalfleet - Brandy Smash of Barmoll) with owner Mrs. B. M. McConkey, winning Best in Show at the Midland Whippet Club show in 1981. Through her daughter Ch. Barmoll Beejapers, Beelzebub is granddam of several champions in the early 1990s.

Ch. Welstar Royal Mint (Ch. Nimrodel Wiveton - Ch. Welstar Minted Model) became a champion in 1979 but had his best show season as a nine-year old veteran. In 1986 he won BIS at the Whippet Club championship show and added several of the nineteen CCs which made him England's top winning whippet male up to that time. Bred by Linda Jones, Mint was owned by Mr. & Mrs. F. Hempstock.

Ch. Nimrodel Wanderer, a grandson of Royal Mint's, overtook his record by winning 22 CCs during the latter half of the 1980s, before his death at eight years of age. He was bred by Mary Lowe, owned and shown by June Minns.

Pedigree 13. **Ch. NIMRODEL RUFF**, fawn dog, born 1970

		Tweseldown Merdeka, by Dragonhill Socklet
	Poltesco Phoenix	
		Poltesco Peri, by Seagift Sportsman
Sire: Ch. Poltesco Peewit (fawn)		
		Ch. Bellavista Barry (ped 15)
	Poltesco Clemwade Merry Maid (fawn)	
		Poltesco Fantasia, by Ch. Evening Star of Allways (ped 10)
		Ch. Ladiesfield Topaz, by Ch. Allways Wingedfoot Running Fox (ped 11)
	Ch. Dragonhill Woodpecker	
		Ch. Dragonhill Curlew, by Dragonhill Hillgarth Spring Salad
Dam: Nimrodel Wintersweet		
		Apbrenin Piquet, by Ch. Playmate of Allways
	Nimrodel Sweet Amber (fawn)	
		Langford Poppet

important sire Ch. Poltesco Peewit—sire of the Crufts winner Ch. Poltesco Periquita, Ch. Nimrodel Ruff and Ch. Nimrodel Willow Daughter. Ruff's grandson Ch. Nimrodel Wiveton is the sire of Ch. Welstar Royal Mint (whose photograph adorned the initial edition of this book), and Willow Daughter's brother sired Lady Anderson's classic Ch. Tweseldown Whinchat. All these are fawns of various shades: Ruff, Mint and Whinchat have won at least ten CCs each, and both Willow Daughter and Wiveton were runner-up to BIS at all-breed championship shows. Ruff was one of the few champion whippets which actively participated in coursing and in his later years proved a

tremendously successful sire in both the field and the show ring.

Royal Mint, like his grandsire, had a remarkably long career. His triumphant return to the show ring in 1986, at an age when most whippets have long since retired, won't be forgotten easily; at the age of nine he became the top-winning male whippet at breed level ever in England with 18 CCs. It seemed entirely fitting that Mint's own grandson, the powerful Ch. Nimrodel Wanderer, should take over Mint's mantle; by the time of his premature death at the end of the decade, Wanderer had collected an impressive 22 CCs. Bred by Mary Lowe, Wanderer was always superbly shown by his owner June Minns, one of the best whippet and greyhound handlers England has had, and in fact he fought it out for Best of Breed at some shows with his most successful daughter, Ch. Baldrey Limited Edition of Juneric, also shown by Mrs. Minns.

Pedigree 14. Ch. NIMRODEL WANDERER, fawn dog, born 1984

```
                    Ch. Nimrodel Ruff (ped. 13)
Sire: Nimrodel Dragoon
                                  Ch. Danegeld Piper's Tune, by Ch. Peppard Topflight
                    Nimrodel Dipper
                                  Ch. Dragonhill Tawny Owl, by Ch. Poltesco Peewit (ped. 13)

                                  Ch. Nimrodel Wiveton, by Bartonia of Brough (below)
                    Ch. Welstar Royal Mint
                                  Ch. Welstar Minted Model, by Ch. Shalfleet Silver Knight of
                                  Skyeboat
Dam: Nimrodel Wanton
                                  Bartonia of Brough, by Ch. Iniskhelltr Lovely Silver
                    Nimrodel Wissie
                                  Nimrodel Wissendine, by Ch. Nimrodel Ruff (above)
```

The "top dog" crown has toppled remarkably often in England; from Stargazer in the 1950s and Tarragon in the 1960s it was just a short step to Royal Mint in the 1970s and Wanderer in the 1980s. In the 1990s the new record-setter has been Ch. Tilegreen Tornado, who topped Wanderer's total by two CCs in 1993; he is of primarily different bloodlines and will be referred to again later.

Going back a few years, an outsider dog which managed to break through the Winged-foot-Allways dominance proved to be of tremendous value for whippets all over the world. The flashy red-fawn-and-white Ch. Bellavista Barry, star of Miss Dorothy Cuzner's small kennel, was the sensation of 1956 and won eight CCs in all, two of them at Crufts, under such highly respected breeders as Lewis Renwick (at what must have been the last show he judged), Charles Todd of the Wingedfoots and Mrs. Garrish of the Fleetings.

I saw Barry shown in the veterans' class when he was eight years old, and was struck by his beautiful flowing lines, so much more generous than those of most of the dogs winning in his day. He was always considered to be big and he sired some large offspring too, but he became a popular stud dog, and in the early 1960s the British rings were full of his winning children. The most successful were probably the glorious pair, the red-and-white Ch. Blik's Ringmore Bardolph (14 CCs) and the mostly white Ch. Teighways Tasmin (13 CCs), which won the double at Crufts in 1962 under Mrs. "Poppy" Martin, but Barry's most important claim to fame comes through two sons who are both among the greatest whippet sires of all time: Ch. Laguna Ligonier in England and Eng. Am. Ch. Courtenay Fleetfoot of Pennyworth in the U.S.

Fleetfoot won his first CC in 1961 and the next year tied with Ligonier for top honors in the breed (each with half a dozen CCs that year). Fleetfoot won the Hound Group at Blackpool, but then went on to even greater glory in the U.S, and it was left to Ligonier to carry on the line in England. His breeder Dorrit McKay had realized Barry's possibilities early on and took her brindle top winner Ch. Lily of Laguna to him in 1956. This resulted in the lovely blue-fawn-and-white Ch. Laguna Leading Lady, an important bitch in her own right through her descendants at Greenbrae and Dondelayo. The Barry-Lily combination was repeated in 1960 and Ligonier was born.

It seems appropriate that it was C.H. Todd—owner of the previous top sire Marksman—who awarded Ligonier his first CC and Best of Breed at Windsor in 1961, since this dog in many respects started a new era and later became the top sire of the breed himself. Ligonier built up an enthusiastic following among breeders all over the world: it is a rare pedigree—especially in England, America and Scandinavia—which does not contain his name several times a few generations back.

Pedigree 15. **Ch. LAGUNA LIGONIER**, brindle-&-white dog, born 1960

<pre>
                    Ch. Pilot Officer Prune (ped 7)
Sire: Ch. Bellavista Barry (fawn/white)
                         Ch. Balaise Barrie (ped 8)
                    Brekin Bright Spark
                         Ch. Brekin Spode (ped 8)

                         Fleeting Hillgarth Sovereign
                    Ch. Fieldspring Bartsia of Allways
                         Brekin Willow Pattern, out of Ch. Brekin Spode (ped 8)
Dam: Ch. Lily of Laguna (brindle)
                         Ch. Balaise Barrie
                    Ch. Brekin Ballet Shoes (ped 8)
                         Ch. Brekin Spode
</pre>

With a pedigree like this, it is not surprising that Ligonier proved an exceptional sire. The Kennel Club records show that he sired over eighty litters between 1961 and 1972 out of bitches of every possible denomination; at least fifty of his progeny either gained entry into the British stud book through their wins at major shows or became champions in other countries. The total tally of eleven English champions may not sound impressive when compared to later American figures, but then the British title is about ten times as difficult to gain as any other—and Ligonier also sired eight champions in the United States (some dogs winning in both countries) and several more in Scandinavia, central Europe and Canada.

Ligonier was not a big dog, close to the 18 in. mentioned in the British standard, and since his elegant dam was not large either, the tall Ligonier children (and there were a few)

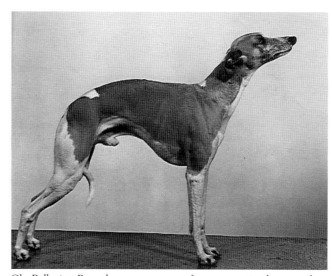

Ch. Bellavista Barry became even more famous as a sire than as a show dog. Among his most notable sons were Chs. Laguna Ligonier in England and Courtenay Fleetfoot of Pennyworth in the U.S., both remarkable stud dogs in their own right.

Ch. Walkabout Warrior King, sired by the Dutch import Ch. Samoems Silent Knight of Shalfleet, won Best in Show at the National Whippet Association show in 1987. Owned and bred by Mrs. Shelagh Thompson, his pedigree is almost pure Shalfleet, going back to the Allways and Wingedfoot kennels of the 1950s.

must have inherited their size from the Barry side of their pedigrees. Ligonier would be considered broad in skull by some judges today and could have had a stronger underjaw, but his head was long and large-eyed which made it seem extreme at that time. (I remember that the American professional handler Tom Gately, later a judge, said that the one thing which might prevent Ligonier from winning in the U.S. was not his size but his head.) The ears were excellent, the neck long and beautifully molded, the shoulders long and sloping with sufficient angulation of upper arm (although some of his progeny were fairly straight); the topline beautiful and the hindquarters powerful with ideal angulation at both knee and hock. His body was both deep and wide with a brisket that reached down to his elbows, and his feet were tight and small with nicely bunched-up toes. He was completely sound both coming and going and moved quite well from the side, very smoothly if not with the tremendous drive and long stride we sometimes see these days. He had excellent bone but some of his progeny tended to be on the fine side.

In temperament Ligonier was unlike most of the other Lagunas—usually tough, sturdy, happy-go-lucky dogs, prepared to throw their arms around any stranger and love everybody. Ligonier was much more aristocratic and withdrawn, definitely a one-woman dog with eyes for Dorrit McKay only. He seemed very aware of his special importance and in his quiet way was definitely the "leader of the pack" at Laguna. Most of his puppies seemed to revert to the more outgoing temperament.

It is above all Ligonier´s great producing sons which have provided his ticket to immortality. The colorful Ch. Tantivvey Diver (out of a Fleeting bitch) left for Pennyworth in the U.S. while still in the middle of a successful show career and before he had sired more than a handful of litters in Britain; however, his few descendants at Fleeting, Cockrow, Crysbel and Baydale are behind champions the world over, and in the U.S. Diver proved to be a big success as a sire. Two other Ligonier sons of particular American importance were the litter brothers Ch. Greenbrae Barn Dance and Ch. Coveydown Greenbrae Wayfarer, with close to a hundred champions in the U.S. and Canada between them. Their half-brother Eng. Am. Can. Ch. Laguna Leisure sired winners on both continents, but was most influential in North America through his Alpine and Plumcreek descendants, while Int. Ch. Laguna Lancelot broke new ground in central Europe and Int. Ch. Laguna Leader sired a record 25 champions in Scandinavia.

In Britain, the most important Ligonier sons have been Ch. Deepridge Mintmaster and Ch. Towercrest Flarepath Taurus—each a classical winner and sire in his own right and each Best of Breed at Crufts. In spite of similar fairly pale brindle-and-white color and an obvious likeness to their sire, they were of rather different type. Taurus was a blood brother to Laguna Leisure (same sire, the dams full sisters): an extroverted, showy dog with excellent substance and a lovely alert expression. His six champions in Britain were from the Oakbark, Garganey, Fairfoot, Faircorn and Flarepath kennels.

Mintmaster on the other hand was not a happy showman and also quite tall by British standards. He was nevertheless regarded by most judges as virtually impossible to fault—a model in flowing long lines and daisy-cutting movement. (My vote for "best ever" in England would probably fall on either Mintmaster or on Taurus´s gorgeous son Ch. Garganey Bartemus, who in spite of a brilliant show career seems to have been largely overlooked at stud.) Mintmaster was an outcross, carrying some Wingedfoot and Springmere blood on his dam´s side, but sired five champions in Britain for the Oakbark, Peppard and Harque establishments as well as for his owner Miss Hawthorne´s small and highly successful Deepridge Kennels.

Some other memorable Ligonier champions: the fawn Ch. Sticklepath Saracen, who won the last of his nine CCs at nearly ten years of age; the exquisite bridle-and-white Ch. Russetwood Portia, who won at least two Hound groups (as well as Best of Breed at this writer´s first British judging assignment in 1967) and whose brother Russetwood Pageant turned out to be one of the top racing sires of all times; the dark brindle Ch. Peppard Premium Bond; the part American-bred "smutty fawn" Ch. Badgewood Sewickley, and many, many others.

The Laguna influence, not necessarily through Ligonier, is evident in most of the important British winners and producers after 1960. One of the most outstanding whippets ever was the red-fawn-and-white Ch. Laguna Ravensdowne Astri, purchased as a puppy by Mrs. McKay but later owned by Mr. and Mrs. E. Wood of the Flarepath Kennels. (I still have a scribbled note from Mrs. McKay in 1964, offering me a parti-colored bitch puppy at the grand price of £25; the puppy was Astri, and I have never stopped kicking myself for passing up that opportunity.) She won fourteen CCs and was the first whippet to go Best in Show twice at all-breed championship shows—at Blackpool and Cardiff in 1967, making her one of Britain's top dogs of any breed that year. She also turned out to be the best brood bitch in a family of outstanding producers.

Astri was bred several different ways, usually within her own family. By her uncle Taurus she had Puddledock Kennel's Ch. Flarepath Astrinomical; by a grandson of her sire came the Crufts winner Ch. Flarepath Astrinought of Lowglen and the excellent brood bitch Flarepath Aquaria (dam of three champions at Oakbark); and by her own sire—also owned by the Woods—Astri produced the dam of Ch. Lowglen Newbold Cavalier, one of the top British sires of all time. Since one of Astri's full sisters was the dam of Laguna Leisure, and another of Towercrest Flarepath Taurus, both by Ligonier and both previously mentioned, it should be obvious that the Flarepath/Ravensdowne bitch line rivals even that of the earlier Brekins in importance.

Pedigree 16. Ch. LAGUNA RAVENSDOWNE ASTRI, fawn-&-white bitch, born 1963

```
                              Ch. Robmaywin Stargazer of Allways (ped 10)
              Trevelmond Starsign (fawn)
                              Ch. Trevelmond Masquerade, Allways/Laguna breeding
Sire: Ch. Ravensdowne Bright Star (fawn/white)
                              Samarkand's Victor of Thistlecroft
              Samarkand's Sea Nymph
                              Sparkling Cascade

                              Ch. Sapperly Kinsman (ped 9)
              Ch. Laguna Liege (fawn)
                              Jovial Judy
Dam: Little Loo of Laguna
                              Ch. Bellavista Barry (ped 15)
              Little Lucy Locket of Laguna (sister to Ch. Laguna Ligonier)
                              Ch. Lily of Laguna (ped 15)
```

The single biggest influence from this family has come through Ch. Lowglen Newbold Cavalier, a classical blue-fawn-and-white, who after a brief show career was retired to stud at the Lowglen Kennels and sired a total of nine English champions.

Pedigree 17. Ch. LOWGLEN NEWBOLD CAVALIER, fawn-&-white dog, born 1969

```
                              Ch. Laguna Ligonier (ped 15)
              Ch. Towercrest Flarepath Taurus (white)
                              Flarepath Ravensdowne Vega, sister to Ch. L. R. Astri (ped 16)
Sire: Skydiver of Lowglen (particolor)
                              Ch. Laguna Light Lagoon
              Crystal of Hardknott (particolor)
                              Summersway Sandmartin, Fleeting breeding

              Ch. Ravensdowne Bright Star (ped 16)
Dam: Flarepath Caprice
              Ch. Laguna Ravensdowne Astri (ped 16)
```

Among the most successful of Cavalier's offspring during the latter part of the 1970s were a trio from Frank Moore's Allgarth Kennels—champions Envoy (exported to Australia), Edelweiss (owned by Lowglen) and Deborah (a group winner). Mr. and Mrs. Moore's most successful dog, Ch. Ambassador of Allgarth (ten

CCs) was sired by Cavalier's previously mentioned uncle Astrinought out of a Shalfleet bitch.

Cavalier is the only whippet known to have sired two Best in Show winners in all-breed championship competition—Ch. Savilepark Summer Season, who won from some 10,000 dogs at the Ladies' Kennel Association show in 1977, and Samarkand's Skytrain, who in 1978 at just over eight months became the youngest-ever BIS winner at Darlington. Summer Season was handled to her win by Roger Stock, and Skytrain to his by Anne Knight.

Two kennels which dominated much of the 1970s were based mostly on Laguna blood from another source. Mrs. Anne Knight's Dondelayos and Mr. Arthur Badenach Nicholson's Glenbervies each have an easily identifiable "kennel type" but are very closely related through the great star of the mid-1960s, Ch. Samarkand's Greenbrae Tarragon. He first hit the headlines in 1962 when only ten months old; the great all-rounder judge Joe Braddon, famous for his ability to spot a future winner, saw enough star quality in the tall, gangly youngster to carry him right through all his classes to the Challenge Certificate and Best of Breed at Leicester.

During the next couple of years Tarragon left few records unbroken, always superbly handled by his owner Robert M. James, whose Samarkand kennel had been established several years earlier. With seventeen CCs, Tarragon equalled the all-time record for a whippet male, won Crufts in both 1963

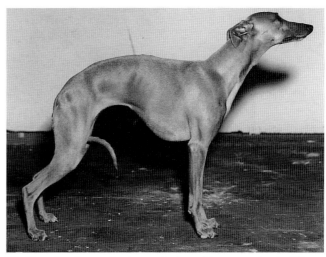

Ch. Greenbrae Laguna Lucia was the dam of three great sires in different countries: Ch. Samarkand's Greenbrae Tarragon in England, Ch. Coveydown Greenbrae Wayfarer in Canada and Ch. Greenbrae Barn Dance in the U.S.

and 1964 and each time went on to runner-up in the Hound Group. He was BIS at Chester in 1964 and won a third consecutive CC at Crufts in 1965; an achievement not surpassed in the breed since Ch. Manorley Moireen more than half a century before.

Tarragon's sire—the rawboned, hard and racy but not very glamorous Limelight—was litter-brother to Ligonier's dam, which means that two of the breed's greatest stud dogs were cousins (in fact even more closely related, since Tarragon's dam was also out of Ligonier's older sister). Runway Controller was from an early litter bred by Mrs. Argyle of the Harques, and Lucia came from one of the best litters ever bred at Laguna; she was a refined, rather long-cast

The famous Ch. Samarkand's Greenbrae Tarragon was a difficult dog to photograph; pictures hardly do him justice. He is shown (left) with owner Robert M. James in 1964, winning Best of Breed in Glasgow. Best bitch, right, is Ch. Harque Conneil Crown Jewel, one of Ann Argyle's first champions. Judge was Mrs. M. B. Garrish, in later years a Crufts Best in Show judge. Both Mr. James and Mrs. Argyle also judged BIS there — an honor few other breeds have seen bestowed on three of their own.

sister to Mrs. McKay's own great winner Ch. Laguna Linkway (who was rather overshadowed by Ligonier as a sire, however).

The breeder of Tarragon, in spite of her very brief time in whippets, had more influence than most big kennels can hope to achieve after several decades of breeding. In her first litter, Mrs. Alicia Yerburgh bred Tarragon; in her second (from the same dam bred to Ligonier) came the two great American and Canadian sires Barn Dance and Wayfarer. This means that three dogs bred in this tiny, two-litter kennel sired at least a hundred champions worldwide!

Mrs. Yerburgh emigrated from England with her musician husband in the late 1960s and has not been active in the breed since then.

Pedigree 18. Ch. SAMARKAND'S GREENBRAE TARRAGON, fawn dog, born 1961

Ch. Fieldspring Bartsia of Allways (ped 15)
Sire: Ch. Laguna Limelight (fawn)
Ch. Brekin Ballet Shoes (ped 8)

Ch. Allways Wingedfoot Running Fox (ped 11)
Ch. Runway Controller (ped 11)
Evening Mist
Dam: Ch. Greenbrae Laguna Lucia (fawn)
Ch. Bellavista Barry (ped 15)
Ch. Laguna Leading Lady (particolour), sister to Ch. L. Ligonier
Ch. Lily of Laguna (ped 15)

Tarragon eventually proved to be quite a revolutionary sire. There was some resistance at first, but eventually his importance was recognized and he sired some fifty registered litters. With hindsight it seems amazing that breeders did not flock to Tarragon immediately after seeing the first two champions he sired at an early age; the sound, substantial parti-colored dog Ch. Cockrow Tarquogan of Glenbervie and the racy, elegant brindle bitch Ch. Dondelayo Rue. Both were sensational winners, but the full impact of Tarragon blood was not apparent until Anne Knight in a stroke of genius bred the two together. Both were out of Laguna-bred bitches and therefore related on both sides of the pedigree.

The litter contained three Dondelayo champions which each made history in some way. The brindle Buckaroo became Britain's most popular sire of show stock, with 130 registered litters up to 1978 and a total of ten champions in Britain as well as several more in other countries. The brindle Ruanne was a

One of the most successful kennels of the 1970s and 1980s was Mrs. Anne Knight's Dondelayo, known for charismatic show dogs with sweeping lines and snakelike beauty. Ch. Dyanne Dondelayo, heavily inbred on Tarragon, was one of the kennel's last big winners; following Mrs. Knight's death, Dyanne was exported to Jim Burens in California.

the most conservative of the prewar breeders would have admired her.

Mrs Knight had started in whippets in the 1950s but did not exhibit regularly until she had Rue and her offspring. She embarked on an extremely tight inbreeding program, using Tarragon as the central figure; breeding Roulette back to her double grandsire resulted in the exquisite Ch. Dondelayo Duette, who made history for the breed by winning Reserve BIS at Crufts in 1972. This was one of the most exciting finales ever seen there, with the white bull terrier and the silver-fawn whippet contrasting and complementing each other in statuesque beauty. Duette also won BIS at Chester seven years after her sire had done the same thing. Her parti-colored litter-sister Ch. Courthill Dondelayo Tiara, taller, rangier and more extreme overall, won and produced extremely well for Roger Stock's Courthill Kennel—one of the few to combine successfully the almost unrelated Dondelayo and Shalfleet bloodlines. After several inactive years, Mr. Stock was back in the limelight again in 1993 with Ch. Courthill

Hound Group winner and, owned by Mr. and Mrs. Charles Dempster, the dam of three famous Charmoll champion brothers which proved influential in both Britain and America. The silver-fawn Roulette was the most famous of the three, equalled the breed record of nineteen CCs in 1971 and then, after almost three years' retirement, won her twentieth CC in 1974—thereby setting a new record for the breed. Roulette was also—like Lark and Astri—twice Best in Show at all-breed championship shows, won one reserve BIS and several Hound groups. She exemplified much of the "new" Dondelayo look—a snake-like elegance and extreme showmanship never seen before combined with classical beauty and ravishing long lines; even

Crown of Gold, a descendant on her dam´s side of Tiara twenty years later.

Later stars from Anne Knight´s stable included the fawn-and-white Ch. Dondelayo Statue, who after a short but sensational career in Britain went on to further fame in Australia. In failing health, Mrs. Knight was not able to exhibit consistently in later years, but in 1980 her brindle Ch. Dondelayo Reinette was Britain´s top-winning hound, with two all-breed championship Best in Shows; she was sired by Buckaroo out of a sister to Duette and was also exported to Australia. Anne Knight also gave the ageing Tarragon a home and showed the other Samarkand dogs when their owner´s extensive travelling and judging overseas prevented him from doing so; through the 1970s and 1980s Bobby James was one of the world´s most admired international all-rounder judges. The Dondelayo and Samarkand dogs were in effect two kennels in one; regardless of prefix, registered breeder or owner, the dogs were for all practical purposes of the same family.

One of the most illustrious eras the breed has known came to an abrupt end in 1988. Anne Knight died in June, shortly after returning from a judging trip to Australia and New Zealand, and Bobby James died even more suddenly just six months later. Both losses were felt far outside the whippet world and far beyond England, but is too early to say how much influence the Dondelayo breeding program will have for the future in England. A high percentage of the winners in the mid-1990s have at least some Dondelayo breeding, and the dozens of exports worldwide—especially to Scandinavia and Australia — may well prove to be even more influential. A bitch from the last litter bred by Mrs. Knight, named Firedance at Silkstone, was owned and shown to her title in 1990 by Roma Wright-Smith—a fitting conclusion, since she had also handled some of the Dondelayo winners during Mrs. Knight´s illness.

Meanwhile, Arthur Nicholson had been producing a long row of homebred champions in his Glenbervie kennel near the Scottish border. He successfully showed spaniels for many years before starting in whippets around 1962. The stud dog which brought him the greatest fame was the previously mentioned Tarquogan, acquired as a puppy from the Misses Hudsons´ small but extremely influential Cockrow Kennel in the Lake District. Tarquogan died prematurely at only six years of age, but sired nine champions in Britain and more overseas. Since he has only eighteen litters listed in the Kennel Club records, this is by far the highest percentage of top winners for any stud dog in Britain; had he lived longer he would almost certainly have sired even more champions.

Apart from his litter out of Ch. Dondelayo Rue, most of Tarquogan´s fame as a stud dog rests on the winners Arthur Nicholson himself bred out of his two foundation bitches—the silver-fawn Ch. Hillgarth Sun Star of Glenbervie, a great winner in her own right, and the virtually unrelated parti-colored White Gorse of Glenbervie. The latter might almost as well have been born in America, as her sire Am. Ch. Cockrow Grouse and both grandsires—Tantivvey Diver and Courtenay Fleetfoot—spent most of their mature years there. The offspring of these two bitches, when bred to each other or to the closely related Ch. Dondelayo Buckaroo helped to produce an impressive total of fifteen homebred champions in Britain. It speaks well for their quality that many of the champions were sold as youngsters to novice exhibitors—a good example is Ch. Gypsy Picture of Glenbervie, owned by R. Pye from Wales, who travelled with her to London to win Best of Breed at Crufts in both 1973 and 1974.

The most successful of the kennels based on Glenbervie stock was short-lived in England but has been a strong influence in South Africa as well as North and South America. In England Jack Peden´s Denorsi Kennel showed half a dozen champions, all heavy in Tarragon blood. Some were homebred, but the best-known were probably the two almost identically named full brothers Ch. Denorsi Moonduster of Glenbervie and Ch. Denorsi Moon Dust of Glenbervie. The former was a brindle-and-white who became a top sire after the move to South Africa, with champion Oldland sons in America as well during the 1970s; the latter was a blue-and-white Crufts winner. Both were bred by Arthur Nicholson, who died in 1984.

Variations on the basic Laguna theme proved consistently successful throughout the 1970s and 1980s. One of the best recipes was to use Tarragon blood on whatever was left of Tantivvey Diver´s descendants in Britain. A Tarragon son bred to a Diver daughter produced the brindle Ch. Baydale Cinnamon. He was a lovely mover who won a Crufts CC and has been influential on both sides of the Atlantic. In Britain his son, Ch. Charmoll McTavish, sired half a dozen outstanding champions in the 1980s, such as Ch. Hillsdown Tobique, Ch. Oakbark Middleman, Ch. Peperone Pepper and Ch. Novacroft Madrigal, which in their turn have proved excellent producers and are behind many of the top winners in the early 1990s—not just in England but in other countries as well. In the U.S. Cinnamon´s son Eng. Am. Ch. Charmoll Clansman and daughter Ch. Whitbarrow Parsley produced the top winning dog and bitch in the breed for several consecutive years at the Sporting Fields and Whippoorwill kennels respectively.

Another Cinnamon son, the striking Ch. Black Knight of Carmodian, sired the most outstanding stud dog of the late 1980s and early 1990s, Ch. Carmodian Tawny Knight of Hutaka. Bred in the Carmodian Kennels owned by Mr. and Mrs. George Carmichael, who for many years produced a line of glamorous champions, Knight was owned and shown to his title by Ann Beckett-Bradshaw.

Pedigree 20. Ch. CARMODIAN TAWNY KNIGHT OF HUTAKA, brindle dog, born 1980

Ch. Baydale Cinnamon (ped. 32)
Sire: Ch. Black Knight of Carmodian
        Highland Star, by Allgarth Careless Rapture
    September Girl
        Drabengro Petulengro, by Hillgarth Selector

Ch. Lowglen Newbold Cavalier (ped. 17)
Dam: Allgarth Countess Penelope
        Ch. Shalfleet Sultan of Sherrimere, by Shalfleet Skyliner
    Shalfleet Stylish
        Shalfleet Sinderella

Ch. Carmodian Tawny Knight of Hutaka (Ch. Black Knight of Carmodian - Allgarth Countess Penelope), photographed as a veteran, is one of several influential stud dogs from Mr. and Mrs. George Carmichael's kennel. Owned by Ann Becket-Bradshaw, he sired several top champions, including the record-breaking Ch. Tilegreen Tornado.

Fleeting Flamboyant (later exported to Sweden), produced the brindle Ch. Fleeting Fulmar, who in his turn sired the Crufts winner and excellent brood bitch Ch. Crysbel Skylark.

One of the most successful stud dogs in Britain since Ligonier's days has also been bred according to that formula. In the late 1960s, two litters combining almost all of the above dogs were bred by R. Pendleton and included Fleeting Akeferry Miss Emma (dam of Fulmar), Miss Clay's black brindle Ch. Tantivvey Akeferry Crusader and last but not least Ch. Akeferry Jimmy—sire of ten champions in Britain and several more overseas in the fifty litters by him recorded up to his death in 1982.

Jimmy's owners, Mr. & Mrs. Nev Newton and daughter Editha, have established their

Among his best champion offspring in England were Ch. Pennybeck Silver Sixpence and Ch. Tilegreen Tornado, the current alltime top winning whippet male in England. There was also an exquisite daughter, later exported to Norway, Ch. Sunsalve Hollidaze at Hutaka, who had a brief but spectacular career in England, including the Hound Group at Windsor and Best in Show at Bournemouth.

Another variation was provided by Diver himself when bred to a sister of Tarquogan's: from that combination came Ch. Cockrow Pheasant and the almost unshown Cockrow Partridge of Crawshaw, a top sire with several champions to his credit. One of his daughters, when bred back to Diver's son Ch.

One of the most influential English stud dogs of the 1970s and 1980s, Ch. Charmoll McTavish (Ch. Baydale Cinnamon - Ch. Dondelayo Ruanne of Charmoll). An older brother, Eng. & Am. Ch. Charmoll Clansman, founded his own dynasty in the USA.

Nevedith kennel on Jimmy blood. One of the first winners by Jimmy, Ch. Nutcracker of Nevedith, was actually bred by the Hillsdown Kennels which would have such a deep impact later on; he was BIS at both the Whippet Club and the National Whippet shows but died shortly after being exported to Italy. Those that remained in Britain included the racy dark brindle-and-white Ch. Crysbel Skylight of Nevedith (out of the previously mentioned Crysbel Skylark). When Skylight's daughter Ch. Houghtonhill Night Starry Sky of Chatwig won BOB at Crufts under the author in 1984 she was the third consecutive generation Crufts winners on her dam's side. Several of the Nevedith champions have been co-owned with Ray Hill of the Houghtonhill prefix. Other Jimmy champions carry the kennel names of Sakonnet, Mispickel, Zarcrest, Killigrew, Pardee and Baydale.

Pedigree 21. Ch. AKEFERRY JIMMY, red brindle-&-white dog, born 1969

```
                    Ch. Laguna Ligonier (ped 15)
       Eng. Am. Ch. Tantivvey Diver of Pennyworth (ped 29)
                    Fleeting Fancy Free
Sire: Cockrow Partridge of Crawshaw (brindle/white)
                    Ch. Samarkand's Greenbrae Tarragon (ped 18)
       Cockrow Taradiddle (fawn), sister to Ch. Tarquogan (ped 19)
                    Cockrow Lady Kate

                    Ch. Samarkand's Greenbrae Tarragon (ped 18)
Dam: Eegee Jane (brindle)
                    Ch. Laguna Ligonier (ped 15)
       Eegee Anita (fawn)
                    Harque To Dream Girl
```

The most outstanding show star in the British rings during the 1970s was the stunning brindle-and-white Ch. Beseeka Knight Errant of Silkstone. During his brief career in Britain he won fourteen CCs and the Hound Group at Crufts in 1975, shown by his owner Roma Wright. When exported to South Africa he did equally well for his new owners, Mr. and Mrs. Gary Kartsounis.

Pedigree 22. Ch. BESEEKA KNIGHT ERRANT OF SILKSTONE, brindle-&-white dog, born 1973

```
                    Ch. Ravensdowne Bright Star (ped 16)
       Eng. Am. Ch. Flarepath Tambillo Tarquin (fawn-white)
                    Ballagan Shining Star, by Ch. Laguna Ligonier (ped 15)
Sire: Oakbark Moonduster
                    Ch. Samarkand's Sun Courtier, by Ch. S. G. Tarragon (ped 18)
       Oakbark Ballerina
                    Laguna Lynda, by Ch. Laguna Ligonier (ped 15)

                    Ch. Ravensdowne Bright Star (ped 16)
Dam: Newbold Madelina
                    Samema King o'Diamonds, by Ch. Playmate of Allways
       Newbold Samema Queen o'Diamonds (white)
                    Snowden Fawn
```

In view of his excellent pedigree it was a pity that "Whiskey" did not get much opportunity to prove himself as a sire in Britain. The night before leaving for South Africa he was bred to Oakbark Miniver, a well-bred bitch whose litter included champions in several countries, notably the sensational fawn Ch. Jubilant Lady of Tygreen and Lowerdon. In the ownership of Mrs. Sandra Marshall she turned the British dog world upside down by winning Best of Breed, Best Hound and Best in Show with her first two CCs in 1979, each time in competition with several thousand other dogs! According to reliable sources, it hasn't happened for several decades that any dog of any breed has managed to pull off such a stunning debut, and Jubilant Lady confirmed the early rave reviews by winning the

Hound Group at Crufts in 1980 and a full dozen CCs. Specialist judges such as Mrs. Garrish, Anne Knight and Mary Lowe described Lady as one of the best ever; Mrs. Lowe in her critique wrote that "Every so often the breed produces something which is so close to the ideal or to the mental picture of the Standard which every judge must have in the mind's eye that recognition is instantaneous. For me this bitch is such an example."

Much of the credit for Lady's success should go to the Oakbark dogs which feature so prominently in her pedigree. Mr. and Mrs. Dennis Meakin got their first Oakbark champion from Dondelayo in 1968, and by incorporating Ligonier blood and Flarepath breeding have

Ch. Martinsell Wild and Lonely (Rystone Blue Magpie - Martinsell Wild Rose), probably the only really blue whippet ever to become a champion in England, gained his title in 1987. Owned and bred by Joanna Russell and Caroline Brown.

produced such an impressive line of champions in England as well as other countries that they felt justified in advertising Oakbark as "No. 1 in the World" in their Dog World Annual presentation in 1993!

An interesting feature in the late 1970s was the reappearance of blacks among the top winners. The early stud-book entries prove that blacks and black-and-whites were quite common in those days, but with few exceptions blacks have not had much show ring success since then. However, at the Whippet Club championship show in 1980 Best in Show went to a black dog, Poaching Black Jack, sired by the fawn Ch. Shalfleet Sailing Free but "color-bred" on his dam's side. Before his untimely death in an accident, Jack sired several outstanding daughters—the two fawn sisters Ch. Curlands Night Dancer and Ch. Curlands Night Alert, and the white-trimmed black Ch. Martinsell

Ch. Oakbark Middleman, a son of Ch. Charmoll McTavish, won 10 CCs and proved an influential stud dog: among his grandchildren are a Crufts BIS winner and a Crufts Reserve BIS winner! Bred by Mr. and Mrs. Dennis Meakin and owned by Mr. Phil Moran-Healy of the Hillsdown prefix.

Grand Slam. The latter, owned by Dog World's whippet columnist Joanna Russell and her sister Caroline Brown, repeated her sire's win as BIS at the Whippet Club show two years later.

Unfortunately history repeated itself; Grand Slam died in an accident shortly afterwards, but her breeders made history again in 1986 when their homebred blue Ch. Martinsell Wild and Lonely gained his title; the first of his color since Ch. Manorley Maori eight decades earlier if official registration records are to be believed; quite possibly the first ever. (There have been several blue-fawn and blue-and-white parti-colored champions, but previously none where the blue color was documented.)

Quite possibly these wins served as encouragement for fanciers of the reputedly "difficult" blacks and blues; at least a couple of blacks have become English champions in recent years, including Ch. Laurelcote Lady in Black who won half a dozen CCs in 1993 and may well be the top winner ever of this color in England.

The influence of British whippets and whippet people in other countries is well-known, but there has been fairly regular interchange of people and dogs in the opposite direction as well. As early as 1922, Z.J. Batten, president of the short-lived Whippet Club of America, was announced as the whippet judge at the Ladies' Kennel Association's championship show in London, and in later years several American breed specialists have judged at important whippet events in Britain. The great all-rounder judge Percy Roberts (who had shown Ch. Flornell Glamorous in the 1940s) judged at Windsor in 1951, and Julia Shearer of the Meanders judged in Scotland in 1966. Margaret Newcombe (Pennyworth) and Doris Wear (Stoney Meadows) have both been over several times; the late Ann Gallup Marsh of the Gallways judged at Blackpool in the late 1960s, Dr. Charles Billings at the Midland Whippet Club in 1986 and Isabell Speight of the Runner's judged the Whippet Club's open show in 1982. The author has also judged several championship shows since the 1970s.

In fact, more Americans have probably judged in Britain than the other way around. Two of the few exceptions are Barbara Wilton-Clark of the Shalfleets, who has judged in California several times, and Mary Lowe of the Nimrodels, who proved a very popular judge at the American Whippet Club's eastern specialty in 1984 and in Canada a couple of years later. It seems a pity that such breeders as Mrs. Garrish and Mrs. McKay, whose Fleetings and Lagunas have meant so much in the U.S., never had the chance to judge whippets there. Mrs. Knight of the Dondelayos had in fact accepted and been approved to judge the famous Santa Barbara show in California but died less than two months before this assignment.

Direct influence through imported dogs has been restricted to a minimum, due mostly to the six months' quarantine still required of most livestock imported into Britain (new regulations are in force since 1994 but are not expected to affect domestic pets in the foreseeable future). In the early 1960s British exhibitors had their first look at foreign whippets when Mrs. Wendy Howell moved her Great

Circle Kennels from California to Northern Ireland. Some of her dogs were at first boarded with Mrs. McKay at Laguna; I remember the attractively colored bitch Great Circle Wise Child with particular affection. She later became an Irish champion and a top racing dog in her new country, as did several of her kennelmates.

Only a few years later another American breeder came to live in England. Elizabeth Fell´s family has owned whippets in the U.S. since the 1920s and she herself judged them at the famous Morris & Essex show before the war. When her husband was stationed in Britain Mrs. Fell brought over several of her Badgewood dogs, including the fawn Am. Ch. Badgewood Michael of Meander. He was never shown in Britain, but daughters from his few litters there produced remarkably well. One of them, Badgewood Charlottesville, was the dam of the previously mentioned Ch. Crysbel Skylark, and another bitch of part Meander breeding produced Mrs. Fell´s own lovely Ch. Badgewood Sewickley. When the Badgewoods moved back to the U.S. again they took with them several youngsters of mixed Anglo-American parentage which became champions after arrival in the U.S. In later years Mrs. Fell has been more active as a judge than as a whippet breeder and was president of the American Whippet Club for several years.

Since the early 1960s there have been occasional imports to England from various other countries. A Canadian-born daughter of the famous American sire Ch. Misty Moor´s Chalmondoley, Gambit Penny of Phaedra, took some good placements at championship shows in 1979. A South African champion, Athene of Racour, even won a challenge certificate a few years earlier, but the first and only two imported whippets to become English champions were both brought in and shown by Barbara Wilton-Clark: the Dutch-born brindle Ch. Samoems Silent Knight of Shalfleet and the Canadian-bred particolor Ch. Lorricbrook Runaway at Shalfleet. Both were largely descended from Barbara´s own English stock, however. At least a couple of older American champions have also moved to England with their owners and have been incorporated in the breeding programs of some top kennels, and a few puppies have gone through the rigors of quarantine, but until quarantine restrictions are lifted the English whippet is likely to remain relatively unaffected by developments elsewhere in the world.

In 1974 the Whippet Club´s seventy-fifth anniversary was celebrated with a championship show in the Garrison Theatre at Bicester, outside Oxford. Entries compared with both the first postwar show and the anniversary in 1950 showed a big increase: 246 whippets, more than three times the 1950 number, made 368 entries. Dogs were judged by Mr. A. Chew (Heywood) from northern England and bitches by Barbara Wilton-Clark of the Shalfleets. Best in Show was awarded to the exquisite parti-colored bitch Ch. Deepridge Miniva, the result of a half-brother and sister inbreeding to Mintmaster. Best dog was the striking fawn Ch. Oakbark Merchant Prince and best puppy the bitch Newbold Sweet Martini.

The club´s eightieth anniversary was celebrated in 1979 with champagne, a special exhibition of racing and coursing champions, fanfare in the canine press and 289 whippets entered—probably an all-time world record at the time. Elsie Watson of the Towercrests judged dogs and Shelagh Thompson of the Walkabouts judged bitches. Barbara Wilton-Clark was still in the limelight, now an exhibitor—her classic fawn bitch Ch. Shalfleet Sequilla won BIS. The dog winner was a new name, Mr. and Mrs. Hempstock's Welstar Royal Mint, a stunning fawn with white trim. A son of Ch. Nimrodel Wiveton, he became a champion before the year was over and wound up with a total of nineteen CCs.

The decade from the mid-1980s onwards was dominated first for several years by one of the most outstanding winners at breed level which whippets have ever had. The practically unanimous admiration which English breed specialists felt for the fawn bitch Ch. Selinko Another Lady was something you have to go back many decades to find; she won Best of Breed at Crufts for three years in a row, won 25 CCs (more than any other whippet before her) and was Best in Show eight times at major whippet club shows, including the National Whippet Assocation in 1984 and 1985. It hardly makes the story less interesting that "Fern," although well bred (she was sired by Ch. Marlins Dusty Miller of Iniskhelltr), was the first champion of her owners, Carole and Barry Kennett, or that she was handled by her owner to all her successes.

Fern had some success in all-breeds competition as well, but she was primarily the choice of breed specialists and a superb example of what can be achieved even by a relatively new fancier with a really outstanding dog. It did not seem realistic to expect that another whippet would come along any time soon to achieve a comparable record, but that's what happened almost as soon as Another Lady had left the arena.

In 1988 Nev Newton brought out a young bitch which immediately attracted a lot of attention and within a few years managed to completely rewrite the record book for whippets in England. She became famous far outside the realm of whippet fanciers as Ch. Nutshell of Nevedith. A glamorous brindle and white, "Shelly" during her peak in 1989 and 1990 won more than practically any dog before her, regardless of breed; she was England's top dog in 1989 and runner-up to that title the following year, and although she only made occasional appearances after that (for one thing, it isn't considered good form to show a second time under a judge who has already awarded your dog a CC in England, and almost all the judges had already done so in Shelly's case), she had a grand total of 45 CCs by the end of 1993—at which point her puppies were already beginning to make names for themselves.

Shelly was bred by Mr. and Mrs. Barker, better known for Boston Terriers of the Chilka prefix, but a study of her pedigree shows the Newtons' foundation dog Ch. Akeferry Jimmy appears twice on the sire's side, the Charmoll/Baydale stud dogs several times on the dam's, and Cinnamon's son Ch. Black Knight of Carmodian on both the sire's and dam's side.

Pedigree 23. Ch. NUTSHELL OF NEVEDITH, brindle & white bitch, born 1987

```
                                            Nevedith Merry Monarch, by Ch. Akeferry Jimmy (below)
                          Ch. Nevedith Paper Weight
                                            Whitbarrow Minimist, by Cockrow Saturn
        Sire: Eng. Am. Can. Ch. Nevedith Uptown Guy
                                            Ch. Akeferry Jimmy (ped. 21)
                          Sakonnet Alfalfa
                                            Sakonnet Black Mustard, by Ch. Black Knight of Carmodian
                                            (below)

                                            Ch. Charmoll McTavish (as Ch. Charmoll Clansman, ped. 32)
                          Ch. Oakbark Middleman
                                            Oakbark Moving Picture, by Ch. Oakbark Armfield Joker
        Dam: Chilka Dairy Maid
                                            Ch. Black Knight of Carmodian, by Ch. Baydale Cinnamon
                          Pearl of Akonyte at Chilka
                                            Ch. Hillsdown Tobique, by Ch. Charmoll McTavish
```

Shelly´s sire in fact was exported to Pennyworth in the U.S., which means that Peggy Newcombe has had a hand in the only whippet to be No. 1 of all breeds in England as well as in the only one to take the same spot in the United States.

Records are made to be broken, but it isn´t likely that the breed will see another winner of Shelly´s caliber anytime soon. In spite of Best in Show victories in at least seven of the major all-breed championship, perhaps Shelly´s most important win was Reserve Best in Show at Crufts in 1990, and it speaks volumes for the high esteem in which the breed is held in England that only two years later a young dog came along which actually managed to go one step higher at that show.

The big star of 1991 was a brindle dog from Scotland, Ch. Pencloe Dutch Gold, who swept all before him to win thireen CCs in his first season (almost as many as Shelly in her best years) as well as Best in Show at the Hound Association show. Then at Crufts in 1992, every exhibitor´s dream came true for Dutch´s owner Morag Bolton, when together they conquered all at what is now the world´s biggest show. It must have made the victory even sweeter that the Best in Show judge was an internationally respected all-rounder who also happened to be a great breed specialist: Mrs. Ann Argyle, of the long-established Harque whippets.

Following this win, Dutch was retired from active competition, still only two years old. As his owner said, when you´ve won the best there is, what more could you ask? Not surprisingly, Dutch has proved a popular and dominant stud dog; young Dutch Gold puppies from Nevedith, Mithrandir, Courthill and Silkstone won their first CCs in 1993. His daughter Ch. Silkstone Jewel in the Crown ended the year as top whippet in the country and was BOB at Crufts in 1994.

Eng. & Ir. Ch. Hino Legacy (Eng. & Ir. Ch. Painted Pony - Barnesmore Blue Angel) won Best in Show at the Northern Ireland Whippet Club´s show in 1986, 1989 and 1990. Her owner Lucinda Thompson´s Barnesmore whippets have been successful in England as well as in their native Northern Ireland.

Pedigree 24. Ch. PENCLOE DUTCH GOLD, fawn brindle with white dog, born 1989

                                    Samarkand's Sea Leopard, by Ch. Dondelayo Buckaroo
                         Birkonbrae Coeur de Lyon
                                    Ch. Nicely Naughty at Birkonbrae, by Ch. Oakbark
                                    Middleman (below)
Sire: Hillsdown Fergal
                                    Ch. Black Knight of Carmodian, by Ch. Baydale Cinnamon
                         Siobhan of Hillsdown
                                    Ch. Hillsdown Tobique, by Ch. Charmoll McTavish

                         Ch. Oakbark Middleman (ped. 23)
Dam: Moonbeam of Pencloe and Kienford
                         Siobhan of Hillsdown (above)

It is interesting to compare the pedigrees of Nutshell and Dutch Gold. There are great similarities—the dams in fact are blood sisters, sired by the same dog out of full sisters. Dutch Gold is inbred since the parents are half brother and sister, both out of the important brood bitch Siobhan of Hillsdown. Much of the credit for Dutch Gold should in fact go to Phil Moran-Healy's Hillsdown Kennel which either owned or bred most of Dutch's close ancestors.

Ch. Tilegreen Tornado (Ch. carmodian Tawny Knight of Hutaka - Tilegreen Misty Morning) holds the all-time record for a whippet male in England with 25 CCs to his credit.

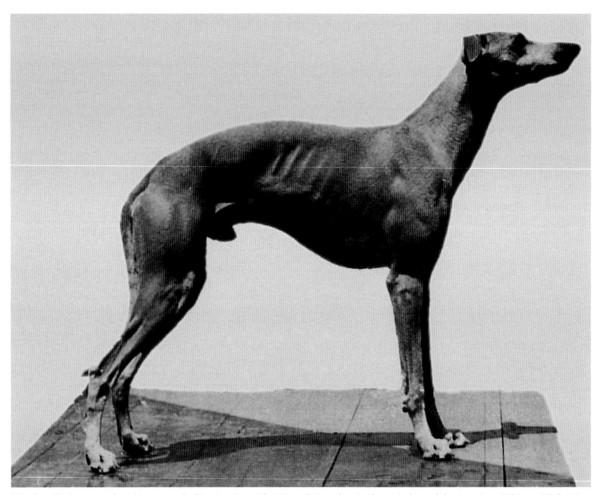

The dog which rewrote the whippet standard in America, Ch. Mica of Meander. In the early days of the American Whippet Club, Mica was used as a model for the revised breed standard. He was the most famous of fifteen champions produced by English import Ch. Sand-brilliant of Meander out of Ch. Syndicate of Meander, all bred by Julia and Judith Shearer. Sandbrilliant's sire was a grandson of Ch. Willesbeaux and Syndicate's dam, a granddaughter of Ch. Manorley Maori.

The Whippet in North America

The sport of pure-bred dogs was at first heavily British-oriented, but has long developed along different lines in the U.S. The main reason is geographical: in a country as large as the whole of western Europe it is not possible to concentrate all important activity into a small number of huge events like the championship shows in Britain. By the turn of the twentieth century there were already more championship shows in the U.S. than in Britain, and in the 1990s there are over a thousand officially approved American Kennel Club all-breed shows each year—about forty times as many as the equivalent in Britain. Most of the shows in America are much smaller, however; the average entry is just over a thousand exhibits in competition, and even the biggest shows are smaller than many of those in Scandinavia, England and Australia. Competition within each breed, naturally, is often not overwhelming (the average whippet entry is less than twenty), which has led to a deflation in the value of wins on the breed level, with a correspondingly greater importance placed on Group and Best in Show awards.

By far the most important shows for whippet people in the United States are the specialty events organized each year by the American Whippet Club; these receive nationwide support and employ almost exclusively specialist breeder judges. Entries at the annual national show have exceeded even those seen at whippet shows in England, and several times hit the 500 mark—a far cry from the average run-of-the-mill all-breed shows.

Another difference concerns the judges. In Britain almost nine championship shows out of ten are judged by breed specialists; in the U.S. nine out of ten are judged by all-round dog people whose personal experience seldom lies with whippets, so much greater emphasis is placed on soundness, showmanship and glamour, sometimes at the expense of the finer points of breed type. The different priorities, in addition to those in the American breed standard, have produced a somewhat different-looking whippet from the one seen in Britain; American show whippets are generally taller, often more brightly colored, almost always with elegant heads, dark eyes and well-folded ears;

many are higher on leg without corresponding greater length of loin and depth of body. The insistence on showmanship and the greater emphasis on professional grooming and handling also helps to produce a slightly different effect from that of the quieter, more relaxed shows in most other countries.

In view of the different breed standards, it is rather surprising that some of the top dogs in one country still manage to please fanciers from another. Although the British influence in America has been nowhere near as strong in the 1980s and 1990s as it was in the 1960s and 1970s, carefully chosen imports can still make a valid contribution. Even more amazingly, a few British breeders have begun to take a positive interest in the American dogs, even incorporated American blood in their pedigrees. As for the rest of the world, in spite of the fact that the English breed standard is officially recognized in almost all countries except the U.S., they seem to have no problem in importing and assimilating American whippets.

Approximately 2,000 whippets are registered annually in the U.S.—a much smaller percentage of the total number of dogs registered than in Great Britain. (Whippet registrations

The first American whippet champion, Bay View Pride, was born in 1902 of unregistered parents. In spite of a deluge of later imports, many whippets in the United States can still trace their pedigrees back to the Bay View dogs.

are only about 25% higher in the U.S., but the total number of dogs registered is at least four times as high.) The growth has been much faster in the United States, however; in the 1930s and 1940s only a few dozen whippets were registered each year, and as late as 1960 the total was still under 200 a year—about one-tenth of the figure in Britain at that time. By the mid-1960s the annual figure reached 500 and a few years later 1,000.

In spite of the comparable size of the whippet populations, there are at least ten times as many whippet champions in the U.S. as in Britain. Well over 150 whippets "finish" their titles every year in the U.S., and the championship is often regarded merely as a stepping-stone on the way to bigger and presumably better things in the all-breeds competition, instead of being seen as the ultimate goal it is Britain. The reasons are not only the far higher number of American shows, but also the fact that champions do not compete for these points—only for Best of Breed. Most dogs in the U.S. have not defeated a single champion when they become champions themselves, are moved up to the "Specials" class and then compete for Best of Breed only. A total of fifteen points is required for the title, and since the maximum number for any one win is five points, an outstanding dog can at least theoretically finish in only three shows.

The points system is fairly complicated and is revised by the AKC annually according to the competition in each breed and region. Lower points—or none at all—are awarded to the winners at shows with few competitors, but at least two "major" wins (3-5 points each) must be included in the total before the title is approved, as some sort of guarantee that each new champion must at least twice have defeated a substantial number of its peers. On the West Coast, the point score currently (1994) requires 2 male whippets and 4 bitches—not counting champions—to be present before any point is given to the winner; 12 males and 17 bitches are required for a "3-point major," 35 males and 52 bitches for a 5-point win. On the East Coast, the requirements are lower—2 whippets of either sex for 1 point, 9 and 12 respectively for 3 points, 18 males and 22 bitches for 5 points. Usually only a few shows in each region receive high enough entries for any 5-point major wins to be offered. There are various additional requirements for the champion title: the major wins must come under two different judges; if a dog wins 2 points as Winners Dog and a bitch at the same show gets 3 points as Winners Bitch, the winning dog will be awarded the same number of points as the bitch if he defeats her for the Best of Winners award; the winner over champions by going Best of Breed gets extra points, etc.

Despite Britain's early lead in the history of purebred dogs, the whippet was officially recognized in the U.S. earlier than in England;

in the AKC stud book, Volume V, 1888, listed as a whippet under the heading "Miscellaneous," is a white dog with "brown and yellow" markings registered as Jack Dempsey. (How could he be, when the famous heavyweight boxer of that name was not born until several years later? That's one of the little bits of trivia you pick up while doing whippet research; there was actually an earlier sports figure of the same name, less famous but obviously well known enough to inspire the names of both a whippet and a heavyweight boxer.) In 1893 a bitch called Boston Model became the first known winner by being placed first in a mixed class for various breeds at the first annual American Pet Dog Club show in New York. A total of 280 dogs were entered over four days, so judging must have been a lot more leisurely in those days.

In 1896 at least six whippets were shown at what was already the most important dog event in America, the Westminster Kennel Club show in February. First prize in the mixed class for dogs and bitches went to the male Endcliffe Rompaway. Amazingly, the show that year attracted over 1,400 exhibits and reached the 2,000 mark only a few years later. It has not been permitted to grow much since then: only a maximum of 2,500 dogs can be accomodated at Madison Square Garden. The Westminster Kennel Club show is now the second-oldest sporting event in America, surpassed only by the Kentucky Derby and much older than all but a very few dogs shows in Europe. Since the early 1990s it has been limited to champions of record and is by far the most prestigious dog show in America, receiving tremendous publicity through both the dog press and other mass media.

The first real whippet kennel, Bay View, appeared in 1903 with the impressively named dog Imperial Deodora Pride. The next year this kennel had the breed's first American champion, Bay View Pride, a male by unregistered parents, born in March 1902. No details of color are given. The first bitch champion, Northern Flyer, apparently fawn and owned by the Newton Abbott variety kennels, won her title only a few months later. In 1905 three more whippets won their championships, two of them owned by Bay View Kennels; at least one of them was almost certainly imported from Albert Lamotte's Shirley Kennels in England, although no details of breeder are given. One of the early champions apparently was black, but in contrast to the contemporary winners in England the majority of the first American champions seem to have been solid fawns.

Bay View was responsible for eight of the first twelve American champions and regularly entered as many as half a dozen whippets at Westminster during the first decade of the twentieth century. The kennel, in Rhode Island, must have been quite a sizeable operation; there were greyhounds and gundogs as well. The owner is usually given only as "Bay View Kennels," but the man behind it appears to have been Karl Bjurman (obviously of Swedish descent), later also an AKC judge and handler. Several of his dogs were English—at least one of the champions was sired by Ch. Shirley Wanderer and apparently imported in utero.

With the disappearance of the breed's strongest kennel around 1912, entries at the Eastern shows fell off. Practically the only breeder for several years seems to have been Ben Lewis of the Lansdowne Kennels outside Philadelphia. He finished five champions before 1920, but hardly anything is known about them, as they usually won their titles without being registered with the AKC—a fairly common occurrence in those days. Nor were whippets Mr. Lewis's main interest: he had a large variety and boarding kennel and ran a regular advertisement in the AKC Gazette.

There is evidence that the whippet established itself as a serious contender in all-breed competition, both on the East and West Coasts, far earlier than previously thought—in fact as soon as the Best in Show award was first offered on a regular basis in 1924. During that year, at least one whippet won the top award—the imported bitch Ch. Towyside Teasle at the Rochester show in New York of 14-15 May. Hounds were then still classified with the Sporting breeds—the next day Teasle was runner-up in the group to an English Setter! Teasle also won Best in Show in Canada that year. Her owner was Mr. McClure Halley, manager and handler for Geraldine Dodge's famous variety show kennel, Giralda Farms—one of the most lavish canine establishments ever conceived.

Another great winner around that time was Ch. Nomad Nancy of Oxon, also imported and the first of Henry E. Damon Jr.'s many Nomad champions from New Jersey; according to his advertisements Nancy was shown 38 times and won 34. Other kennels which started in the 1920s were the Freemanors of Felix Leser in Baltimore (where the Maryland Whippet Club would later be started), the Watlands of Mr. and Mrs. F. Addyman in New York and the Pocon Kennels of William Short, who did not show a great number of champions but helped popularize the breed through his whippet column in the AKC Gazette. Mae Bland in Columbus, Ohio, used her family name as a kennel prefix, and Ch. Bland's Althea in turn lent her own name to Howard S. Nielsen's kennel in Connecticut: Ch. Sept of Althea was sired by a son of Watford Bon, and like several of these old kennels has descendants today through the later Meander, O'Lazeland and Stoney Meadows kennels.

On the West Coast, the first champion was crowned in 1917, and California then remained a stronghold until the mid-1930s. Freeman Ford's Arroyo Kennel in Pasadena was obviously planned on the grand scale; with the help of Freeman Lloyd—of the "first whippet book" fame—James A. Young, a Canadian, was persuaded to move south and act as kennel manager. Arroyo housed numerous English and Canadian imports, obviously chosen as much

One of the first important show and racing kennels in America was Arroyo, located in southern California. Ch. Arroyo Miss Melody was photographed in 1921 with kennel manager James Young. His daughter Christine Cormany remains active in the breed with her own Strathoak prefix in the 1990s.

for their racing ability as their looks, and even included several wirecoated dogs, seldom shown but fast racers. Mr. Young had owned whippets in Canada since 1906, some of them from the earliest Watford breeding in England; since his daughter Christine Cormany is still active in the breed in the 1990s, the family kennel names of Strathcona, Corsian and Strathoak cover almost nine decades.

In the mid-1920s, the black imported English bitch Sidlaw Sloe Eyes of Arroyo won Best in Show at the big Los Angeles show in spite of being basically a racing dog. Show entries were quite large; three years later the Los Angeles Kennel Club had 1,000 dogs entered, nineteen of which were whippets. One was the famous Ch. Nomad Nancy's Papyrus, offered for sale in the catalogue for $1,000; it is not known if there were any takers. The Santa Barbara show even then worked closely with the breed clubs, and as early as 1934 had an amazing entry of 34 whippets out of a total of 530 dogs, with the now-defunct Whippet Association of California offering trophies and prize money. The great all-rounder judge Chris Shuttleworth showed his Ch. Chrisworth

Ch. Nomad Nancy of Oxon, a daughter of the famous Ch. Willesbeaux, won two CCs as a yearling in England before coming to the United States in 1922. Described as "an ideal whippet," she weighed 19 lbs. and became one of the first heavily campaigned show whippets. She also produced six champions for her owner Henry E. Damon's Nomad kennels.

Crosty King; other exhibitors were Freeman Ford, James Young and newcomer Donald Hostetter, whose O'Lazeland Kennel became an important force in later years, both in showing and racing.

During the depression, entries on the West Coast almost ceased and did not pick up again until the arrival of the Great Circle and Canyon Crest kennels in the late 1940s and early 1950s. For many years, Santa Barbara was the site for the American Whippet Club's annual West Coast specialty event, first held with the famous all-breed show and later independently on the same grounds. In the 1980s the show moved about an hour's drive north to be held in Lompoc together with the beautiful Western Sighthound Combined Specialties in late July each year. No matter what the location is, the entries have kept increasing: over 100 by the end of the 1960s, over 200 several times later.

The history of the whippet in America is much the story of four great kennels—first Meander and Mardormere from the 1930s to the 1960s, then Stoney Meadows and Pennyworth from the 1950s up into the present. In combination with a flow of later imports from England, these four names figure in almost all American whippet pedigrees.

The Meander Kennels were established in 1928 by the sisters Julia and Judith Shearer, in Locust Dale, Virginia. Their colonial-style eighteenth-century family mansion was to house some of the most famous whippets in America, but the sisters also had other breeds of dogs, racehorses and Aberdeen Angus cattle, and were as well-known in Lexington and Keeneland as at the dog shows; they even had their own family pack of foxhounds! One of the three dogs registered by the sisters in 1928 was the bitch Ch. Syndicate, sired by a Freemanor-bred dog out of the BIS- winning English bitch Ch. Towyside Teasle. When searching for a suitable mate an agent for the sisters went shopping in England and found a young silver fawn dog named Sandbrilliant. He had done some winning there and his breeder Miss Bramwell had already turned down a tempting offer for his dam, the brindle Ch. Tregear Fascination.

Sandbrilliant came to America in early 1930, had the Meander suffix added to his name and was an immediate success at the shows. In 1934 he was announced as the breed's top winner that year with four BOB wins, which tells us something about the change of pace in today's competition. (The top winning whippet in 1992, Ch. Sporting Fields Kinsman, won Best of Breed 121 times, 79 Hound groups and 21 Best in Shows in that year alone.) Bred together several times, the Syndicate-Sandbrilliant pair produced an amazing total of fifteen champions, surely still a world record for a breeding pair of whippets. Many of these were successful producers in their own right, but one stands head and shoulders above the rest: Ch. Mica of Meander was not just a great show dog and sire, but was used as a blueprint upon which the first American Whippet Club standard was based.

Pedigree 25. Ch. MICA OF MEANDER, fawn dog, born 1933

<pre>
                                    Mathew of Sion Hill
                 Sandblaze (fawn-white)
                                    Gracie's Pet, by Ch. Willesbeaux (ped 3)
Sire: Ch. Sandbrilliant of Meander, imp UK (fawn)
                                    Stopwheel
                 Eng. Ch. Tregear Fascination (brindle)
                                    Carn Brea Lassie

                                    Ch. Coolridge Flying Fury, by Ch. Freemanor Glencoe
                                    Supreme
                 Kissell's Buddie
                                    Patricia, by Ch. Freemanor Glencoe Supreme
Dam: Ch. Syndicate of Meander
                                    Towyside Smoke, by Ch. Manorley Maori (ped 5)
                 Ch. Towyside Teasle (slate fawn), imp UK
                                    Towyside Tingle, by Watford Bon (ped 2)
</pre>

The established Meander type was a fairly tall, racy dog with long lines and much elegance; the favored color was solid red fawn with very dark eyes. Julia Shearer shows two typical specimens of the kennel's later days, Ch. Meander Pickpocket and his son Ch. Meander Flip The Dip.

It was of course unusual to shape the standard after a dog, instead of the other way round, but the Shearer sisters for many years almost literally owned the American Whippet Club and could make their own ideal the officially recognized version. (According to Louis Pegram, who knew the sisters well and was president of the AWC long after their influence was over, they paid off some borrowed money in 1934 which had kept the club in existence during the early years of the depression and thereafter ran the club "virtually as a private organization" until after the war.)

Mica was registered as "cream and fawn" with Judith Shearer as breeder. His official Certificate of Winnings from the AKC shows that he became a champion in ten shows with five Bests of Breed, two group firsts and three other placings along the way. Over the next three years Mica won eighteen breeds, four more groups and eight more group placings, including one at Westminster in 1936—altogether an outstanding record for those years. Mica remains one of the most admired and most influential American whippets of all time.

Meander is often thought of simply as the Sandbrilliant-Syndicate cross, but the breeding program was much more complex than that. The Shearer sisters imported at least a

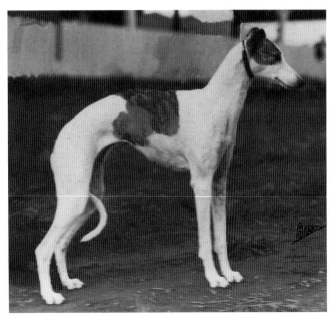

Ch. Dizzy Blond of Meander was one of the most important brood bitches of her day. She was a daughter of the English import Ch. Oldown Stormy out of the intensely linebred Mica descendant Question of Meander and produced several champions for Meander during the 1950s.

dozen whippets from England during the 1930s and early 1940s, most of them brindles or fawns, and these, when bred to each other, to the Sandbrilliant-Syndicate offspring and to older American lines, created several future generations of Meander champions. Meander type usually signifies a solid red-fawn dog with dark pigmentation, quite tall by contemporary American standards and beautifully proportioned—a true "greyhound in miniature" without any of the stumpy, cut-off look or exaggerated toplines often seen elsewhere.

Several of the Meander imports came from Stanley Wilkin in England, which is interesting since his Tiptrees were also used to found Meander's arch-rival kennel Mardormere: obviously these two kennels had more of a common background than is usually realized. As late as 1956 Julia Shearer even purchased a Pennyworth bitch of part Mardormere breeding. This bitch when bred to a Meander dog produced Pennyworth Sagebrush, bred by Miss Shearer and owned by the much later White Acres Kennels in Washington.

Harry T. Peter's Windholme Kennel is best remembered for its greyhounds but also imported several whippets at the time the Shearers were doing so. Among these was a red brindle dog from the Oldown Kennel in England, virtually unknown in its native country but important in the U.S. for its Meander and later Fleeting descendants and known principally for its brilliant colors and dark pigmentation. Ch. Oldown Stormy was later owned by Miss Julia, had one line back to Sandbrilliant's dam and when bred to a linebred

Mica bitch produced the two excellent brood bitches, Ch. Dizzy Blond and Ch. Snow Flurry of Meander—the latter one of the foundations for Mrs. Wear´s Stoney Meadows line.

<pre>
                          Ch. Manorley Manala
              Samema Snowflight
                          Oxted Dainty Maid, by Tiptree George
Sire: Ch. Oldown Stormy, imp UK (red brindle)
                          Downtrooper, by Ch. Boy Scrounger
              Oldown True Love
                          Downtitania, by Downtrooper x Sandbrandy

                          Ch. Mica of Meander (ped 25)
              Ch. Ptarmigan of Meander
                          San Benito Flash, by Eng. Am. Ch. Zanza Zoco O´Valleyfield
Dam: Question of Meander
                          Ch. Nimbus of Meander, by Ch. Mica of Meander (ped 25)
              Windholme Cloudy
                          Ch. Quiz of Meander, by Ch. Sandbrilliant (ped 25)
</pre>

Dizzy Blond was bred to Ch. Meander Robin, which takes us up to the 1950s through their son, the nearly all-white Ch. Meander Bob-White (sire of fifteen champions) and daughter Lorelei O´Lazeland (dam of eleven champions). These two are behind practically all later champions from Stoney Meadows, Whipoo, Seven League, Blue Beaver and many newer kennels.

In later years Meander did not import any dogs from England, although Miss Julia judged there during a visit in 1967. (She gave the top awards to the famous Ch. Harque The Lark and Ch. Oakbark Dondelayo Storming, which indicates that the views of British and American specialists did not diverge as far as sometimes assumed.) Meander remained a force

to be reckoned with during the 1960s and Ch. Meander Shakedown (owned by Calvin Perry´s Appraxin Kennel) took them into the 1970s through his two top producing sons Ch. Appraxin Mind Duster and Ch. Timbar´s Art-

The Meander and Mardormere kennels competed fiercely for top honors in the show ring, but irreconcilable differences were not apparent at the American Whippet Club show in 1958 where Miss J.R. Shearer judged and awarded Best in Show to Ch. Prima Donna of Mardormere, shown by Harry Murphy. Prima Donna was of pure Mardormere breeding for several generations.

ful Dodger. The last of Meander´s homebred whippet litters—around 150 of them—was born in the early 1970s; Miss Judith died in 1970 and Miss Julia in 1972, but the Meander ideals have been carried on by numerous other breeders into the present.

Of the early kennels which worked closely with Meander, the best known were Colin Studd's Birdneck Point and Mrs. Theodore Pedersen's Garden City. The latter included some stock which Mrs. Pedersen brought over from her native Belgium; its greatest star was the parti-colored Ch. Garden City Sleepy Mouse, who won a record ten BIS in the early 1950s.

Meander was already at the height of its fame when the other great kennel of this era appeared on the scene. Mrs. Margaret Anderson was a well-known breeder of cocker spaniels when she got her first whippet. In 1939 the Andersons toured the large kennels in search of suitable stock with which to found the Mardormere whippet kennels on Long Island, New York; they apparently even visited Meander, but after making up her first champion from a daughter of the original Sandbrilliant-Syndicate cross, Mrs. Anderson acquired two English bitches imported and shown by the famous Salmagundi poodle kennels: the parti-colored BIS winner Ch. Lady Bibi and her sister Ch. Madame Superb, sired by Tiptree Golddust.

Mrs. Anderson then enlisted the help of professional handler Percy Roberts, who had shown his imported bitch Ch. Manorley Marcia to group wins in the 1920s and later became one of America's foremost all-rounder judges. Mr. Roberts went to England and shortly before the outbreak of the war came back with a five-month-old bitch puppy. She would become famous as Ch. Flornell Glamorous but was originally registered as Tiptree Honey, bred by Mr. Wilkin and cousin to the great British sire Sapperly Tiptree Pilot. (I was curious to know where the Flornell prefix came from, as it also appears on two Westminster BIS-winning wire fox terriers of the 1930s. The late Mrs. J. Farrell, of the famous Foxden greyhound and terrier kennels, told me that Flornell was the prefix Percy Roberts used, not for any dogs he bred but only for those he imported from England and re-registered. Mr. Roberts won Best in Show at Westminster at least three times as a handler and is one of the few to have both won and judged the finale at this show.)

The first whippet ever to win the group at Westminster was Ch. Laguna Lucky Lad. He won in 1958, was an English import (Ch. Laguna Liege - Ch. Brekin Ballet Shoes) and exerted a big influence as a sire, although never at public stud outside the Mardormere kennels.

Pedigree 27. Ch. FLORNELL GLAMOROUS, particolour bitch, and Ch. TIPTREE NOEL, fawn dog, born 1938, both imported UK

```
                              Silians Tatters, by Ch. Towyside Tatters (ped 5)
              Tiptree Golddust (fawn)
                              Silver Phyllis, out of a Ch. Towyside Tatters daughter (ped 5)
Sire: Tiptree Monk (white-fawn)
                              Avonhill Supremacy
              Flemington Nun
                              Darky Queen

              Tiptree Golddust (as above)
Dam: Tiptree Ch. ristine
                              Zanza Zagreb, by Ch. Towyside Tatters (ped 5)
              Zanza Zorella
                              Ch. Zanza Zanita, by Ch. Towyside Tatters (ped 5)
```

Mrs Anderson purchased Glamorous, but Mr. Roberts remained her handler throughout a career which has never been equalled by any other whippet bitch: she won 21 BIS's, at least 70 groups and a Group second at Westminster. Her litter-brother Ch. Tiptree Noel was also imported by Mardormere; a stylish but rather short-coupled silver-fawn dog, he turned out to be an influential sire in both Britain and America. In one of the few outside breedings which Mrs. Anderson allowed for any of her stud dogs Noel sired Ch. Picardia Polkadot, winner of four BIS in California during 1946 and dam of Ch. Picardia Fieldfare, through whom some this blood was even brought back to Meander when he was used at stud there.

The rivalry between Meander and Mardormere for the position of top kennel was intense at this point. In fact their dogs seldom met in the ring; the difference in type was familiar to most judges, and those known to favor one did not get entries from the other. Both kennels were able to "carry their own points with them," which meant that since the number of points available at each show was dependent on the number of exhibits, a big kennel could create its own competition by filling the classes with young stock.

The most successful of Mardormere's later imports was the tall, stylish and extremely glamorous English dog Ch. Laguna Lucky Lad—too big for the show ring in his native country but ideal for American competition. He was very well bred by the Whippet Club jubilee show winner Ch. Liege out of Laguna's top brood bitch Ch. Brekin Ballet Shoes. After a show career which included at least nine BIS, three times best whippet at Westminster and the Hound Group there in 1958—a first for the breed—Lucky Lad was retired at stud, and although never used outside the home kennel sired eleven champions.

Mardormere at this time was virtually a closed operation, with no stud services and few puppy sales to outside breeders. This of course limited its later influence and is particularly regrettable as the few dogs which got away consistently reproduced their glamour and elegance in both the Stoney Meadows and Pennyworth kennels. After Margaret Anderson's death in the late 1960s some of the Mardormeres were used in other kennels and produced several top winners, such as the much-admired multiple AWC specialty winner Ch. Mare's Head Royal Blu Princess. Mardormere blood has also been instrumental in the background of some of the Ardencaple, Appraxin, Badgewood and Winterwhip pedigrees.

Robert Forsyth, the professional handler, now a judge, first came into contact with whippets through Margaret Anderson in 1949; he has since shown more whippets to all-breed wins than anyone else. In his opinion nobody deserves more credit for American whippets than Mrs. Anderson and Percy Roberts. In spite of the fact that Flornell Glamorous was a retired house-pet when he first knew her, Robert Forsyth feels that she could have held her own with the best today.

Margaret P. Newcombe of the Pennyworth Kennel was almost literally born into dogs. Her mother had a kennel of chow chows and won Best in Show at Westminster with a sealyham terrier in 1936. Peggy Newcombe started by managing her mother's kennel, bred some cocker champions and registered her own prefix in 1940. Soon afterwards she saw her first whippets at a show; they were from Mardormere, and Peggy was so taken with them that she managed to persuade Mrs. Anderson, in an almost unique transaction, to sell her some dogs. Mrs. Newcombe's first homebred BIS winner, Ch. Pennyworth Blue Iris, was sired by a Mardormere dog and turned out to be an excellent producer; this line can still be found far back in some pedigrees. Iris's dam was one of several Seagift imports from Britain which helped establish Pennyworth as a top show kennel in the early 1950s. Many of them had won before being exported—in fact Pennyworth through the years has owned about a dozen English champions—more than most kennels in Britain can claim.

Both the Seagift and later Wingedfoot imports produced champions, but a young brindle dog which Mrs. Newcombe judged in England and subsequently bought proved to be of more lasting value. Fleeting Falcon was less than ten months old when Mrs. Newcombe, in England on a judging visit, gave him the challenge certificate and Best of Breed at the Ladies' Kennel Association's show in 1957. After arriving in the U.S. he was an immediate sensation there too—first shown by John Hutchins of the Briarwyn Kennels in Texas, Falcon won at least a half dozen BIS and then went to Pennyworth for his final all-breed win. He was a grandson of the two best sires in England at this time, Pilot Officer Prune and Sapperly Tiptree Pilot of Mr. Wilkin's breeding. His dam came from the same Oldown Kennel as some of the Meander dogs; with his background he proved to be an excellent sire during his short life, with a long row of colorful dark-pigmented champions and top producers to his credit at Pennyworth as well as for the Briarwyn, Renpark, Sheldegren and Seyberne kennels.

In December 1962, following much excited cabling back and forth between Peggy Newcombe and her friend Martine Collings of the Winterfold Kennels, who was then living in England, there arrived in America what was to become the top winning import of all time. Mrs. Newcombe had heard of the sensational new champion Courtenay Fleetfoot—many British judges considered him to be one of the best ever, but he was up to size according to the British standard and might, Mrs. Newcombe thought, be suitable for American requirements.

She was right. "Ricky," after some initial problems in adjusting to his new surroundings, took the American shows by storm. Handled by Robert Forsyth he won eight BIS's during the first half of 1963, enough to make him top hound for that year. He then sailed into 1964 by winning Best in Show at Westminster under Len Carey—the breed's most prestigious win ever in America—and retired by winning the group at that show for the second time the next year. In between, Ricky had been shown a total of 36 times, won 21 Best in Shows, 32 Hound Groups, two group seconds and one group third, remaining undefeated in the breed every time except once—the occasion when Judith Shearer gave him Best of Opposite Sex to Ch. Stoney Meadows Snow Queen. This is one of the best records in the history of American dog shows, and Ricky appropriately was crowned Top Dog of all breeds in 1964—the only time this title has been won by a whippet in the U.S. Peggy Newcombe remembers adding up the distances she travelled with Ricky to the shows: over 24,000 miles by car and 6,000 by air.

Those of us who had the fortune to see Ricky remember him as one of the most beautiful whippets ever, reminiscent of his sire but with rather more bone and not so long-cast in body. Above all, Ricky had a touch of class which put him in a niche by himself, aloof and dignified with strangers. His nickname throughout his career was, appropriately, "The Golden One."

Pedigree 28. Eng. Am. Ch. COURTENAY FLEETFOOT OF PENNYWORTH, white-&-fawn dog, born 1960, imp UK

Sire: Ch. Bellavista Barry (red fawn-white)
    Ch. Pilot Officer Prune (ped 7)
    Brekin Bright Spark
        Ch. Balaise Barrie (ped 8)
        Ch. Brekin Spode (ped 8)

Dam: Myhorlyns Anita (fawn)
    Myhorlyns Shooting Star (fawn)
        Ch. Evening Star of Allways (ped 10)
        Myhorlyns Candy Kisses, by Ch. Allways Wingedfoot Running Fox (ped 11)
    Myhorlyns Silver Belle
        Ch. Allways Wingedfoot Running Fox (ped 11)
        Myhorlyns Lady Jane

As a sire Ricky repeated the pattern: top Hound sire in 1965 and top sire of all breeds in 1966 (in a tie with a Yorkshire terrier). About half of Ricky's 45 champions in America were bred at Pennyworth, many from Falcon daughters, but the most outstanding was out of the Meander-bred bitch Ch. Legend O'Lazeland— Ch. Pennyworth Mother Goose, according to many the best Pennyworth ever, and a multiple winner of AWC specialties.

Among the champions by Ricky were several from Jacqueline Q. Kubat's Dragonfly Kennel in California (later in Argentina), Mr. and Mrs. Willard Denton's Ardencaples and the great star from Canyon Crest, the BIS winner Bakara. The many Flying W and later Amigo champions in New Mexico were based on Ricky blood in combination with Canyon Crest and Whipoo-bred Blue Beaver lines, and Dress Circle's outstanding foundation sire Ch. Bettebrook Benchmark was a son of Ricky's. Most important of all was probably the combination of Ricky with the best Stoney Meadows bitches, which established the so-called "golden cross": English-bred sons or grandsons of

Bellavista Barry bred to "old American" bitches were to prove the most reliable way to success for many years.

The last important Pennyworth import of this era was Eng. Am. Ch. Tantivvey Diver of Pennyworth in 1966. The strongly colored brindle-and-white Diver had as distinguished a career in Britain as Ricky, but for various reasons the American show ring success predicted for him never materialized. For one thing Diver was a size smaller than Ricky, for another Mrs. Newcombe closed the Pennyworth Kennels in New Hampshire in 1968 and moved to Florida, bringing with her three children and only a small nucleus of breeding stock. As a sire, however, Diver proved his worth even with limited opportunities, and after getting a new lease on

life at Charles and Lillian Billings' Flyalong kennels increased his number of champions to over 25—several of them in Britain, Canada and Scandinavia.

Pedigree 29. Ch. PENNYWORTH WOULD YOU BELIEVE, dark brindle-&-white dog, born 1966

Ch. Laguna Ligonier (ped 15)
Sire: Eng. Am. Ch. Tantivvey Diver of Pennyworth, imp UK (white)
Eng. Am. Ch. Seagift Fleeting Fly Half
Fleeting Fancy Free (white)
Fleeting Fun of the Fair, sister to Ch. Fleeting Falcon

Eng. Am. Ch. Courtenay Fleetfoot of Pennyworth, imp UK (ped 28)
Dam: Ch. Pennyworth Burning Dream
Ch. Stoney Meadows Red Fox
Stoney Meadows Snow princess
Ch. Stoney Meadows Snow Queen (ped 31)

Ch. Pennyworth Would You Believe was probably the most influential stud dog bred in Mrs. Newcombe's famous kennels. He was a son of Eng. & Am. Ch. Tantivvey Diver of Pennyworth out of Ch. Pennyworth Burning Dream, owned by Carol Willumsen and sired over twenty champions in the 1970s.

Diver's best-producing American son has been the dark brindle-and-white Ch. Pennyworth Would You Believe, owned by Carol Willumsen's Willcare Kennel and responsible for at least as many American champions as his sire.

Other champions by Diver are from Flyalong, Appraxin, Beachward and Rolling, and through his English-born brindle son Ch. Cockrow Grouse he is also behind many champions from Kai Esa, Wheeling and Chehalem.

There was one more Pennyworth import in the 1970s, the ill-fated Eng. Am. Ch. Flarepath

Tambillo Tarquin who died just after beginning his show career in America; although he had no influence there, from a few litters born in Britain he is sire and grandsire respectively of top stud dogs in both Australia and South Africa.

Mrs Newcombe's last homebred litter before closing down the kennel for almost a decade was born in 1974; Ch. Pennyworth Better Watch Out went on to produce several Alcyon champions for Christine Hopperstad in Washington, and Ch. Pennyworth Watch Out Now lived out her retirement as Mrs. Newcombe's only whippet. Mrs Newcombe credits the British breeders who sold her so many top-quality dogs with much of her success: "I owe so many thank you's to all the marvellous whippet breeders in England who so willingly parted with animals they loved, so that Pennyworth could be built on a solid, firm foundation and without whose help none of it would have been possible. Pennyworth could not have done it without Diver, a great little dog whose heart was as big as he was—he loved everyone and was a dear dog in every way; Fleetfoot whose record speaks for itself and who will be remembered here simply as `the golden one,` or Falcon who broke the ice for English whippets in the American show ring with eight Best in Shows for John Hutchins and myself—`Tigger` will always be one of my darlings because after not having seen me in years he remembered me when he came home to stay for good. He in his own right was a top sire who is in many pedigrees here still. Then last but not least my darling `Skinny Brinnie,` Ch. Wingedfoot Fieldspring Bryony; she was constantly on a diet, hence her call name. A great show girl and a love, she helped raise my son Stanley and oldest daughter Rose Marie, was never too tired to play and they were always in her sight while she was alive. Thank you one and all for letting these lovely animals come to America and for all the others who have to go unmentioned."

This was by no means the end of Pennyworth, however; in 1985 Mrs. Newcombe returned as an active exhibitor with a young group winning bitch, Ch. Bo-Bett's Patty Whack Dandy. She also imported yet another top winner from England, Ch. Nevedith Paper Weight (sire of England's Dog of the Year in 1989, Ch. Nutshell of Nevedith). Paper Weight added American and Canadian titles to his English one and has sired several champions, but Pennyworth's chief success in the 1990s has come through a bitch who descends from the old Pennyworth lines: the exquisitely feminine Ch. Willcare's Aged in Wood.

In spite of her kennel name "Claire", in one of the arrangements which have become increasingly common in the U.S., was co-bred by Mrs. Newcombe with the Ringmaster kennels in California which had produced the dam (bringing in modern American blood from Ch. Delacreme de la Renta, Gold Dust, etc.). Claire was at first owned and registered by Carol Willumsen who bred her sire — and it is through him that the pedigree goes back quickly to the great Pennyworth winners of previous decades.

Pedigree 30. Ch. WILLCARE´S AGED IN WOOD, brindle & white bitch, born 1990

Ch. Pennyworth Would You Believe (ped. 29)
Sire: Ch. Willcare´s Believe You Me, CD
         Eng. Am. Ch. Charmoll Clansman, imp. UK. (ped. 32)
    Ch. Willcare´s Decoupage
         Ch. Willcare´s Collage, by Ch. Hound-Hill Constant, CD

    Ch. Delacreme de la Renta (ped. 38)
Dam: Ringmaster´s Reggae
    Ch. Gold Dust´s Limited Edition

Ch. Stoney Meadows Snow Queen (Stoney Meadows Epic - Ch. Snow Flurry of Meander) was handled by Mrs. Wear to Best of Breed at Westminster in 1960 under Mrs. P.S.P. Fell (Badgewood) but is best remembered as a brood bitch, producing nine champions by four different dogs. Her descendants fill the show rings across America.

Claire, when teamed with her namesake—Mrs. Newcombe´s daughter Claire—as owner and handler, has achieved numerous Best in Show wins in both all-breeds and American Whippet Club specialty competition. A superbly refined, feminine and elegant whippet of classical type, she is a true Pennyworth in all respects and an effective rejoinder to those who say that "they never come back." Whether any other kennel has managed an equally successful return to the top is doubtful, but in addition to Claire, Mrs. Newcombe can take credit for a number of other young home-bred champions in the 1990s.

The Stoney Meadows Kennel in Maryland was started more or less by accident when Mr. and Mrs. W. Potter Wear acquired a whippet as a family pet from the Shearer sisters in the 1940s. Meander Topaz was bred in 1948 "just for the fun of having puppies" to the proverbial next-door neighbor´s dog, and it was only later that Mrs. Wear found out that this dog was of the best Meander breeding and in fact a half-brother to her "Tilly´s" sire. That first Stoney Meadows litter contained the fawn Ch. Stoney Meadows Masquerade. He immediately put the kennel on the map by winning a BIS, the breed at Westminster twice (with second place in the Hound group both times) and twice best at the AWC specialty show.

Mrs Wear was then able to acquire Ch. Fashion of Mardormere, sired by Ch. Tiptree Noel; her daughter by Masquerade was bred to a half brother, also by Masquerade, and this combination of Meander and Mardormere blood resulted in the tremendously influential stud dog Stoney Meadows Epic. He was not, according to Mrs. Wear, a show dog himself; in fact he was sold to a non-show home while still a youngster, but he sired fifteen champions and is behind later conformation and racing champions from a vast number of kennels: Eyleland, Traymatt, Bardon, Wyndsor, Roving, Sheridan, Marial and Runner's.

Mrs Wear herself bred the newly acquired Ch. Snow Flurry of Meander (see pedigree in Meander section of this chapter) to Epic. From this combination stemmed the elegant white Ch. Stoney Meadows Snow Queen, pro-

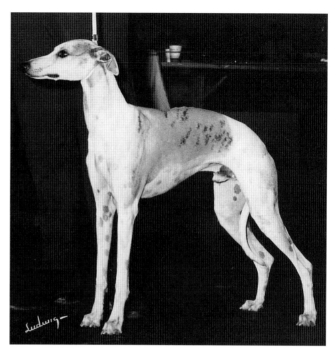

One of the most prolific kennels of the 1960s was Eyleland, owned by Ralph and Barbara Eyles. Based on old American lines, their dogs were successful in both the show ring and on the track. Among those most influential in later pedigrees was Ch. Eyleland Double Or Nothing (Stoney Meadows Epic - Meander Double Or Quits), born in 1962 and registered as "yellow brindle and white": through his daughter Ch. Runner's Our Own Charisma he had grandchildren winning in the 1980s and is still close up in many American pedigrees of the 1990s.

Ch. Stoney Meadows Masquerade, of mainly Meander breeding, was the first in a line of over a hundred champions from Stoney Meadows over four decades. Owner Mrs. W. P. Wear handled Masquerade to Best in Show in 1950 under judge Mrs. Wm. Long. Trophy presenter is Margaret Newcombe of Pennyworth whippets.

genitor of what Mrs. Wear considers her best line and the only whippet to defeat the great "Ricky" in his prime.

Snow Queen was "a show girl with a grand outgoing temperament" according to Mrs. Wear, won several groups and the breed at both Westminster and the AWC specialty show, but above all she was a brood bitch supreme. She was the dam of nine champions by four different Stoney Meadows dogs, but her most important daughters were the brood bitches Can. Ch. Stoney Meadows Snow Princess and Stoney Meadows Bold Queen. The former produced well for Pennyworth, the latter gave Mrs. Wear her top stud dog of the 1960s, Ch. Stoney Meadows Royal Flight, and also became the dam of half a dozen Winterfold champions in Canada.

Snow Queen´s full brother Ch. Stoney Meadows Monocle was important through his son Ch. Lysander of Briskway, a top stud dog with 22 champions to his credit, a record which Lysander´s strongly line-bred descendant Ch. Humble Acre Williemakit equalled in the early 1980s. Owned by the Lyca Kennels in Kentucky, Willie—in spite of his premature death—sired such classics as the lovely Ch. Dublin´s Dancing Lights, winner of one of the largest breed events up to that time—221 whippets entered at the AWC Midwest specialty in 1982.

In order to establish several different lines which could be combined to produce homebred champions, Mrs. Wear added new stock

The most successful of all the Stoney Meadows whippets, as a show dog and sire, lived on the West Coast: Ch. Stoney Meadows Royal Fortune, owned by the Terrace Hills Kennels of Joan Frailey and Julie Holm. Shown by Bob Hastings, "Gridley" won five all-breed Best in Shows and sired 34 champions in the late 1960s and 1970s.

from different sources in the 1950s. She soon established the "Stoney Meadows type"—a substantial yet elegant, very eye-catching dog, often high on the leg by European standards and not over-long in loin, more often parti-colored than solid fawn or brindle. A small black dog of pure Meander breeding was acquired in 1954, and in 1957 the Wears brought in two important dogs from England: the inappropriately named Chanctonbury Hercules (one of the smallest whippets of correct type Mrs. Wear had ever seen) was well bred from Tiptree and Fleeting lines and has gone down in posterity through his daughter Ch. Stoney Meadows Golden Apple. The rose-fawn bitch Laguna Leonie (sired by a Marksman son) is credited with giving the Stoney Meadows whippets their depth of body and strong running gear, but Mrs. Wear says that it took her years to get the old beautiful heads back. Bred to two different Meander dogs Leonie produced Ch. Stoney Meadows Red Fox and Ch. Stoney Meadows Rufus, both excellent sires; a sister to Red

Fox also founded Ralph and Dorothea Eyles´ successful 1960s Eyeland Kennel of bench champions and working whippets.

The most important of all the home-based stud dogs was probably a son of Rufus and Golden Apple, the light fawn-and-white Ch. Stoney Meadows Bold Venture. He sired fourteen champions in the 1960s, some in the home kennel and some out of Pennyworth, Eyeland, Seven League and Hollypark bitches. Of his sons, Ch. Stoney Meadows Bold Chance sired as many champions as his father. Out of the great Snow Queen came a litter which included both the previously mentioned Bold Queen and the top winning dog ever bred by Mrs. Wear, Ch. Stoney Meadows Royal Fortune. "Gridley" was sold as a youngster to two new fanciers starting out in California—Joan Frailey and her sister Julie Holm of the Terrace Hills Kennel. Less active as exhibitors than judges in recent years, the sisters received a unique vote of confidence in that both are American Whippet Club national specialty judges: Mrs. Frailey in 1994 and Mrs. Holm in 1996.

Shown by Bob Hastings, "Gridley" won five BIS´s, an AWC specialty and exactly 100 Best of Breeds before retirement, and also turned out to be one of the top American sires up to that time.

Pedigree 31. Ch. STONEY MEADOWS ROYAL FORTUNE, white-&-red brindle dog, born 1964, also showing pedigree of STONEY MEADOWS BOLD QUEEN

Ch. Meander Bob-White
Ch. Stoney Meadows Rufus
Laguna Leonie, imp UK
Sire: Ch. Stoney Meadows Bold Venture (white-fawn)
Chanctonbury Hercules, imp UK
Ch. Stoney Meadows Golden Apple
Ch. Stoney Meadows Fairy Tale, half-sister to S. M. Epic (below)

Stoney Meadows Madrigal, by Ch. Stoney Meadows Masquerade
Stoney Meadows Epic (fawn)
Stoney Meadows Make Believe, by Ch. Stoney Meadows Masquerade
Dam: Ch. Stoney Meadows Snow Queen (white-fawn)
Ch. Snow Flurry of Meander (ped 26)

The best known of Gridley´s 34 champions was probably Ch. Hollypark Honey Bee, the top whippet of 1970 and at twelve years of age BOB at the AWC specialty show in 1979 from an entry of 160 whippets!

Stoney Meadows has continued to turn out champions over six decades, using variations of the basic few combinations and carefully adding some of the newer British lines. One of the most admired descendants of Stoney Meadows breeding in later years was the 1989 national specialty winner Ch. Roving Roulette; she was sired by the Canadian dog Ch. Swiftsure Happy Daze, ARM out of Ch. Stoney Meadows Miss Julia and has Meander blood close up in her pedigree. The two most successful Stoney Meadows sires of the 1980s —the full brothers Ch. Stoney Meadows Magnet and Ch. Stoney Meadows North Star—represent homebred lines on their dam´s side; their sire is Ch. Hound Hill Constant from Cora Miller´s small but extremely influential kennel, founded on

Stoney Meadows and Kirklea stock. The famous Rimskittle poodle kennel has also maintained a successful small whippet breeding program in close cooperation with Stoney Meadows and Hound Hill. Owner Mrs. James E. Clark is one of the world's most respected all-rounder judges and was therefore doubly qualified to judge the American Whippet Club national specialty, an assignment which she fulfilled in 1991.

Peggy Newcombe's success with imported dogs inspired other breeders to turn their eyes to England. In the west, "Ricky's" halfbrother Ch. Ringmore Finisterre was top hound for 1965, and a few years later the imported Ch. Leatty Court Marshall won at

Ch. Morshor's Majestic Dell (Ch. Plumcreek Walk On Water - Ch. Morshor's Royal Bid), owned and bred by Dianne Bleecker, has continued the kennel's tradition of top sires into the 1990s.

One of the most admired whippets ever in America, Ch. Gold-Dust's Twenty-Four Karat (Ch. Morshor's Bold 'n Courageous - Ch. Gold-Dust's All That Glitters), won four American Whippet Club specialties, owner handled by Joan Goldstein. "Kerrie" is behind many of the top winners in the early 1990s.

least eight BIS's for John Hutchins in Texas.

The Eastern breeders remained the most British-influenced. Mrs. Margaret Hodge brought in Ch. Selbrook Highlight in 1961, a fawn-and-white daughter of the famous Stargazer, and in order to find a suitable mate for her Mrs. Hodge imported the strikingly beautiful Ch. Greenbrae Barn Dance three years later. He was by England's bright young sire Ch. Laguna Ligonier and had already placed at Crufts as a puppy. However, like "Ricky" he was felt to have a better future in the U.S. on account of his size.

With these two Mrs. Hodge founded her Highlight Kennel. The original pair produced eight champions, which when bred back to their sire, each other or newer imports, resulted in numerous other winners. One of "Barney's" best daughters was Ch. Highlight's Legacy; she, her sire, her dam Ch. Stoney Meadows Moon Mist, old Highlight, the English import Ch. Dondelayo Shaun and Ch. Hound Hill Highbrow constitute an impressive line of Best in Show winners all owned by Mrs. Hodge. Through a much later Surrey Hill´s breeding to one of the latest Highlight dogs, Barn Dance blood has been brought all the way up into the 1990s.

Barn Dance sired a new record of 63 champions in the U.S. and was the subject of close and successful inbreeding, both at Highlight and at Virginia Almonrode´s Briarwyke Kennel in Washington. The latter´s top brood bitch Ch. Edenfield Flaming Rose (of Farvel and Eyleland breeding) was bred back to various Barney-bred dogs for a total of eleven champions. Other kennels for which Barn Dance sired more than a single champion were Stoney Meadows, Morshor, Elan, Lenwal, Renpark, Cresswood and Whippoorwill.

In 1965 Barn Dance was bred to his own daughter Ch. Hill´s Harvest Moon Dance, a black-brindle-and-white bitch owned by Diane Bleecker. There were five champions in the litter, one of which was Ch. Morshor´s Whirlaway—the top whippet of 1967 when campaigned by Bob Forsyth. A car accident ended his show career, but Whirlaway soon became one of the breed´s most popular stud dogs, as seen by the number of litters recorded by him in the AKC stud books, as well as one of the most successful. The top sires in America of those years were generally less often used than those in Britain; Whirlaway has only 50 recorded litters, his sire Barn Dance 41 and his great-grandson Ch. Misty Moor´s Chalmondo-

ley 39; the older "Ricky" and Royal Fortune both had less than 30 recorded litters.

Of the 57 champions sired by Whirlaway, seven were out of Mrs. Bleecker´s great brood bitch Ch. Stoney Meadows Imp of Satan. Several others were out of Ardencaple and Pennyworth bitches—the Falcon daughter Ch. Pennyworth Betony alone had eight champions by Whirlaway for the Seyberne Kennel in California, and at least four other Pennyworth bitches produced Appraxin champions by him, including the top sire Ch. Appraxin Zachariah. Other kennels with Whirlaway champions were Canterbury, Carousel in Canada, Grovenor, Sheldegren, Folquin, Itsme and Farvel (where Whirlaway even stood at stud for a while to accommodate breeders in the West).

In 1968 Dianne Bleecker acquired a young bitch from Canada which during the next decade became one of the most admired whippets of all time. Ch. Winterfold´s Bold Bid, sired by Barn Dance´s litter brother Wayfarer out of a Stoney Meadows bitch, took her first BIS victories when shown by Bob Barlow for Morshor. She was then bred to a Whirlaway son and produced the two important stud dogs Ch. Morshor´s Bold N´ Courageous and Ch. Morshor´s Appraxin Ariel. The short-lived Bold N´ Courageous sired seventeen champions, including the top sire Ch. Sporting Fields Bold Imp and the classical winner Ch. Gold Dust´s Twenty Four Karat—one of the most beautiful whippets this writer has seen and the winner of a record four AWC specialty shows. Ariel became a popular stud dog in his old age and will forever live in breed history as the sire of the top whippet sire of all time, Ch. Misty Moor's Chalmondoley.

Mrs. Bleecker has the distinction of having owned at one time or another not only several of the all-time top sires of the breed but also three of the all-time top dams: Ch. Stoney Meadows Imp of Satan, Ch. Winterfold's Bold Bid and her half sister Morshor's Cicada, unshown due to a broken leg but dam of the BIS winners Chs. Morshor's Jai Baba and Run for the Roses. In recent years, Dianne Bleecker continued the tradition of influential stud dogs through the much admired black-brindle-and-white Ch. Morshor's Majestic Dell, sired by Ch. Plumceek Walk On Water but bringing in the old Morshor and Stoney Meadows lines through his dam Ch. Morshor's Royal Bid (a daughter of Jai Baba). "Davin" was himself a successful show dog, going BOS to his own daughter at the first AWC National Specialty in 1987, and has been even more successful as a sire, with an equally prolific son, Ch. Morshor's Majestic Prince, to follow in his footsteps. Among the kennels which have presented several champions of this line are Whippletree, Alerek, Ripshin, Hamrya, Locar, Norika, Heatherlane, Karasar, Raybar, Carbeth, and Claymar all the way up in Alaska.

Many of the Morshor champions have been bred in close co-operation with Calvin Perry's Appraxin Kennel. Cal Perry had the distinction of showing the Best in Show winner at the first AWC National Specialty show, the exquisite brindle Davin daughter Ch. Morshor's Majestic Ball O'Fire.

When Mr. and Mrs. James E. Butt purchased Bold Bid from Dianne Bleecker around 1970 it was not so much a start for their Sporting Fields Kennel as a new beginning. The kennel name had been registered as early as in 1945 for spaniels, and whippets were added in the late 1960s. The first champions were of Meander and Badgewood breeding—notably the top sire Ch. Sporting Fields Charter Oak, who was repeatedly and successfully bred to Bold Bid for a total of eight champions.

In spite of her busy motherhood "Hettie," as Bold Bid was known throughout the breed, also resumed her show career at an age when most other bitches would have been retired, and continued to win groups and BIS's, now handled by Robert Forsyth. When she won her last BIS at nine years of age in 1976 the Butts' young daughter Debbie showed her; this win made Hettie the top winning bitch in the breed since Flornell Glamorous more than thirty years before.

The Sporting Fields dogs dominated the top awards in the breed with remarkable consistency throughout most of the 1970s and early 1980s. With Bold Bid retired from the arena, the imported Eng. Am. Ch. Charmoll Clansman took over as top whippet in the country for three years in a row. He was a rich red brindle with white markings, bred from top-class brindle British champion parents and sired over twenty champions in the home kennel as well as at Alpine, Ardencaple, Willare and other kennels.

After one Clansman came another: through Ch. Sporting Fields Clansman, alias

"Buoy," the Butts continued to dominate the annual charts for several more years. Bred in California by Richard Sufficool and Bruce Tague out of a bitch carrying a double dose of both Barn Dance and older American breeding, Buoy started his career under Robert Forsyth´s guidance with a first few BIS´s in 1977. He won ten more in 1978 and a record 27 in 1979, making him one of the top show dogs in America that year. Although less frequently campaigned in 1980 Buoy remained among the top hounds, and his occasional appearances in 1981 and 1982 left him with the grand total of 59 all-breed BIS wins, around 165 Hound Groups and several hundred Best of Breeds—far more than any whippet before him. In 1984 Buoy made a spectacular comeback as a veteran by winning the AWC Western Specialty at nine years of age.

Pedigree 32. Ch. SPORTING FIELDS CLANSMAN, red fawn-&-white dog, born 1975

	Eng. Ch. Samarkand´s Sun Courtier, by Tarragon (ped 18)
Eng. Ch. Baydale Cinnamon (brindle)	
	Cockrow Merle, by Ch. Tantivvey Diver of Pennyworth (ped 29)
Sire: Eng. Am. Ch. Charmoll Clansman, imp UK (white)	
	Eng. Ch. Dondelayo Ruanne of Charmoll (brindle) (ped 19)
	Ch. Greenbrae Barn Dance, imp UK (ped 34)
Ch. Briarwyke´s Moonshine Boy (white)	
	Ch. Briarwyke´s Night Song, by Ch. Stoney Meadows Royal Fortune (ped 31)
Dam: Dadaelis Cerulea	
	Hollypark Page Mall, by Ch. Stoney Meadows Royal Fortune
Hollypark Spirit	
	Hollypark Tiger Tail, by Ch. Terrace Hill El Cid of Suntan

Buoy also became the third whippet—and the first American-born—to win the Hound Group at Westminster; this occurred in 1980 under breed specialist Louis Auslander. Like his sire and namesake, the younger Clans-

man has also become an influential sire, in just a few years eclipsing his sire´s record of more than twenty champions, almost all carrying either the Sporting Fields prefix or that of Elaine Usherson´s kennel, Usher´s.

An act like Buoy´s was difficult to follow, but his son Ch. Sporting Fields Windjammer was a Best in Show winner and America´s top whippet in 1981, and his grandson Ch. Sporting Fields Strider took several all-breed Bests in 1983. There was also a new import, Eng. Am. Ch. Hillsdown Repique (by Buoy´s brother Ch. Charmoll Mctavish) who sired several champions and the big-moving Best in Show winner Ch. Sporting Fields Troy. Following the death of Mr. Butt, and the departure of Sporting Fields handler Robert Forsyth to pursue a judging career, the future of the kennel seemed uncertain in the mid-1980s. Daughter Debbie had matured from junior showmanship to become a topflight adult handler — every bit as good as the professionals she competed with and frequently defeated, but I remember her saying in 1989, when introducing a particularly lovely puppy, that he probably never would have a career like Buoy´s.

Well, she was wrong; the puppy grew up to become Ch. Sporting Fields Kinsman, the most successful whippet for three consecutive years in the early 1990s, and for part of that time one of the most successful hounds in the country as well. At the time of writing "Luke" is younger than Buoy was at the time he retired, yet has won some 50 Best in Shows and could conceivably top his great-grandsire´s record. Most importantly, from his owner´s point of view, "Luke" has been shown since he was a puppy by

Pedigree 33. Ch. SPORTING FIELDS KINSMAN, white & fawn dog, born 1989.

```
                              Ch. Sporting Fields Clansman (ped. 32)
                  Ch. Sporting Fields Windjammer
                              Ch. Sporting Fields Opening Bid, by Ch. Morshor's Bold 'n
                              Courageous
  Sire: Ch. Sporting Fields Strider
                              Ch. Sporting Fields Clansman (ped. 32)
                  Ch. Sporting Fields Oh My
                              Ch. Morshor's Kissimee, by Ch. Sporting
                              Fields Bold Imp

                              Ch. Delacreme de la Renta (ped. 38)
  Dam: Shilo's Avia of Sporting Fields
                              Ch. Misty Moor's Chalmondoley (ped. 34)
                  Ch. Shilo's Miss Independence
                              Ch. Baywood Renaissance, by Ch. Fenwick of Whippoorwill
```

his owner; together they constitute one of the most admired teams in dogdom, seldom failing to thrill spectators through an almost uncanny rapport between owner and dog. If ever there was a born showdog, it is Luke; one judge compared him to a particularly hammy stage actor who just could not bear to have the audience's eye stray to anyone else on center stage…

Luke's pedigree goes back to Buoy twice through his sire but also incorporates Shilo, the ubiquitous "Oscar" and a double dose of Chalmondoley, even some Whippoorwill blood on the bottom side. Co-bred by the Butts with M. and C. Baldwin, Luke has proved a tremendously popular stud dog, making him the top whippet sire of 1993. Proving that Luke was no fluke, his sire Strider is also responsible for the delicious-looking little Ch. Sporting Fields Winsome Won (possibly the only whippet ever to win Best in Show, Best in Specialty Show and Best in Lure Coursing Trial). Although the breeding program at Sporting Fields is more complex than appears from the above, all these dogs are typical Sporting Fields in so far as they are mostly white, of sensible size and have a great sense of showmanship. They have helped establish Sporting Fields as the top breeding and show kennel in America—perhaps the world — with over 125 champions to its credit.

The title as most successful whippet sire of any time still remains with Ch. Misty Moor's Chalmondoley, however. His total of over a hundred recorded AKC champions—mostly in the 1970s and 1980s—constitutes a record seldom achieved by a stud dog in any breed.

"Chummy" was bred by Jerry Edwards, who had been given the eight-year-old Moon Dance by Dianne Bleecker on condition that he should breed only one more litter from her. Moon Dance had of course already made her mark as the dam of Whirlaway, and Mr. Edwards wisely took her back to this dog's young grandson Ariel. The pedigree, apart from doubling-up on Moon Dance herself, involves strong linebreeding to the Laguna-bred imports from Britain. There is also a heavy dose of Stoney Meadows and even some Meander blood close up on the dam's side.

Chalmondoley's pedigree is also interesting because it incorporates most of the top producers of the breed in America; at the time he himself became the number one sire of champions, Barn Dance was number two and Whirlaway number three; Imp of Satan and Bold Bid were the two top-producing dams.

```
                              Ch. Morshor´s Whirlaway, by Barn Dance x Moon Dance
                              (see below)
              Ch. Morshor´s Bold N´Brave
                              Ch. Stoney Meadows Imp of Satan, by Ch. Stoney Meadows
                              Bold Chance
Sire: Ch. Morshor´s Appraxin Ariel (white)
                              Ch. Coveydown Greenbrae Wayfarer, imp UK, litter brother
                              to Barn Dance
              Ch. Winterfold´s Bold Bid
                              Stoney Meadows Bold Queen, by Ch. S. M. Bold Venture
                              (ped 31)

                              Ch. Laguna Ligonier (ped 15)
              Ch. Greenbrae Barn Dance, imp UK (white)
                              Ch. Greenbrae Laguna Lucia (ped 18)
Dam: Ch. Hill´s Harvest Moon Dance (dark white)
                              Solar System O´Lazeland, by Eng. Am. Ch. Ravenslodge
                              Solitaire
              Seven League Snowscape
                              Ch. Seven League Songbird, by Ch. Meander Bob-White
```

The top whippet sire of all time, Ch. Misty Moor´s Chalmondoley (Ch. Morshor´s Appraxin Ariel - Ch. Hill´s Harvest Moon Dance), has over a hundred champions to his credit in the U.S. and added great refinement, style and elegance to the breed. He was linebred on the Greenbrae brothers and shown by Jerry Edwards, who co-owned "Chummy" with Roberta Russ.

In the ownership of Roberta Russ´s Misty Moor Kennel, and handled by his breeder, Chalmondoley has had a stud career which somewhat overshadows his own wins, but he was in fact the first male whippet ever to win three AWC specialty shows. In 1982, when I first saw him, the elegance, refinement and "class" with which he stamped his progeny were still much in evidence; he was also considerably more masculine and substantial than his not always flattering photographs might indicate.

A son and daughter won specialty shows themselves—Ch. Runner´s Creme de la Creme on the West Coast in 1978 and the BIS winner Ch. Plumcreek I Am in the Midwest in 1983. More than a half dozen Chummy children have won all-breed bests—apart from I Am, also Ch. Misty Moor´s Royal Huntsman, Ch. Khiva´s Show Stopper, Ch. Braemar´s Fife and Drum, Ch. Norika´s Wild Flower, Ch. Raybar´s I´m Rim, Ch. Shilo´s Houdini V Hasue and Ch.

Misty Moor´s Oh Julie. Of the many kennels which have had champions by him, apart from his owners´ and breeders´, Plumcreek and Greyfriars are outstanding, with about ten each; others with several include Vagabonded, Patric´s, Runner´s, Winterwhip, Snowflight, Raybar, Khiva, Folquin, Gambit (in Canada), Rimskittle, Whippoorwill, Colonial Acres, Knolland, Coronation, Herloutam, Free Wynd, Tamerlane, Shilo, Baywoods, Ondega, Jaguar and Imperial.

Chalmondoley blood has been carried on by many sons and daughters; among the top producers by him so far have been the previously mentioned Royal Huntsman in the home

Pedigree 35. Ch. PLUMCREEK WALK ON WATER, brindle dog, born 1982

                    Ch. Misty Moor's Chalmondoley (ped. 34)
Sire: Ch. Plumcreek Chimney Swift
                              Ch. Marial's Phoenix, by Limited Edition O'Lazebrook
                    Plumcreek Black Ternstone
                              Larel Traymatt Camass (below)

                    Ch. Laguna Ligonier (ped. 15)
          Eng Am Can Ch. Laguna Leisure, imp. UK
                              Laguna Ravensdowne Faerie Queen, by Ch. Ravensdowne
                              Bright Star
Dam: Plumcreek September Romance
                              Caledonia Big John, by Lucifer O'Lazeland
                    Larel Traymatt Camass
                              Traymatt Spinning Wheel, by Ch. Traymatt Rooster Boy

Ch. Plumcreek Chimney Swift was one of several influential sires from the same Midwest family in the 1980s. A Chalmondoley son, he contributed strength, substance and driving movement to his many champion children. Breeder Linda Larson showed Chimney Swift to win the American Whippet Club specialty in Ravenna in 1985. Australian breeder judge Brian Doherty put Chimney Swift to the top from the veteran class in an entry of 281 whippets.

kennels and Show Stopper in California, Ch. Plumcreek Chimney Swift, Ch. Plumcreek Chase Manhattan in the Midwest and Ch. Folquin Snowflight in Kansas.

The Plumcreek dogs of Linda Larson deserve a special mention; the black-brindle-and-white Chimney Swift and his younger full brother, the fawn and white Chase Manhattan, between them sired more than fifty champions in a wide variety of kennels, but Chimney Swift's son Ch. Plumcreek Walk On Water did even better and single-handedly has sired almost as many champions as the other two together.

There is much more to the Plumcreek dogs than the Chalmondoley ancestry, however; Linda Larson's bitch line goes back to strong, substantial dogs of old American blood, crossed with Chalmondoley for elegance and later also with the small, refined import Eng. Am. & Can. Ch. Laguna Leisure. Plumcreek's particular hallmarks seem to have been great angulation in both front and rear, excellent substance and powerful driving movement.

In later years Mrs. Larson has focused more on her Saddlebred horse activities than on the dogs, but the bloodline is continued in many kennels. Among the most successful with numerous Plumcreek-sired champions are Carbeth, Barchet, Elysian, Patric, Saxon Shore, Greycott, Morshor, Topnotch, Tripletime, High Flyer, Lidemara and Heatherlane. Walk On Water's most outstanding winning son is a striking brindle dog from the south: Ch. Elysian A-Few Perrier, who has won several AWC specialties during the early 1990s.

The number of important kennels in the U.S. is now so large that it is hard to cover everyone—at least if by important one means a breeder who has been responsible for a sizeable number of champions. While in Britain any kennel with more than a handful of champions must be considered important, the AKC system which allows for 100-200 new whippet champions per year means that you have to multiply that requirement several times in order to prevent a chronicle of this type from becoming completely unwieldy. Many dedicated, intelligent and successful breeders who are responsible for scores of champions or even more can be mentioned only in passing. It doesn't mean that their dogs are less outstanding than others, but although show wins are not necessarily the best measure of success, they are the only ones available. National recognition in the form of all-breeds or specialty Best in Show, top producer or top breeder status are what a breed historian has to base assessments on.

Most breeders with at least a couple of dozen champions have already been mentioned. Pat Dresser's Dress Circle Kennel was started in the 1960s and was notable for a particularly strong bitch line as well as for two excellent sires: Ch. Bettebrook Benchmark (by Courtenay Fleetfoot) and his son Ch. Cricket Hearth Bristol Cream. Although less active as a whippet breeder or exhibitor in recent years, Mrs. Dresser has remained active in AWC affairs and also for many years (probably more than she would like to remember!) served as editor of the American Whippet Club's monthly newsletter—the glossy, richly illustrated annual is produced by Wendy Clark (Dunberry). The Terrace Hills and the Ardencaples have been mentioned before, while Mr. and Mrs. Louis Auslander during a brief but spectacular appearance with their Alpines bred many champions. Mr. Auslander is now best known as a judge and has periodically occupied the key position of Chairman of the Board of the American Kennel Club. His top winner in the 1970s was the mostly British-bred Ch. Alpine Ski Bum, sired by Eng. Am. Ch. Laguna Leisure out of the top producing bitch Ch. Unmitigated Gallway, a daughter of the imported Ch. Roanbar Son of Cachalong.

The dual-purpose Marial kennels in the Midwest are co-owned by Mr. and Mrs. Douglas Arthur with Mrs. Arthur's mother Mrs. Bernice Strauss, and have produced champions in both field and conformation since the early 1960s. In the early 1980s a dog from Dr. John Shelton's long-established Sheridan line in California added further laurels—the glamorous Ch. Sheridan Marial's Nikita, one of the most successful sires of this period. Both the Arthurs and Dr. Shelton are judges and have officiated at AWC specialty shows—Dr. Shelton since the 1970s and in 1995 at the National Specialty show. Nikita is a son of the beautiful specialty winner Ch. Sheridan Bianca, one of the whippets I remember admiring in the pages of the late Gazehound magazine in the 1970s.

In Oklahoma, Mrs. Jean Ueltschy founded her Wheeling Kennel on a combination of Alpine blood with direct English imports from Cockrow and Barmaud. The late Pat Speight had great success in California with her Pathens dogs in the 1970s; she established a line by breeding Pennyworth bitches to the top sire Ch. Pinetop's Chatterbox, grandsire of Nikita and owned by Dr. Shelton and through two of Norman Ellis's Madcap dogs going back to old American breeding from Meander and Great Circle. The Pathens blood was later combined with Kai Esa and Kindochaline stock to found the successful Chehalem Kennels of Janet van Wormer in Oregon.

Pathens in combination with more Pennyworth breeding was behind the Westgate dogs in California, which figure prominently in contemporary kennels such as Summerwind (Rosemary Sutton) and Merci Isle, owned by Iva and Jeffrey Kimmelman in Maryland but started by Iva on the West Coast; their breeding program later achieved great success in the early 1990s when both Ch. Merci Isle Meridian and his young son Ch. Merci Isle Burncoat Babylon won AWC specialty shows within a few months of each other. One of the all-time top-producing bitches, the beautiful Ch. Westgate The Enchantress, was owned by Phoebe Booth's Shamasan Kennels—less active in recent years since Phoebe's turning to a successful career as a professional handler.

The Cyrano and Rafina whippets in the Midwest, owned by Donna Kelley and Barbara Pendergrass respectively, share a common ancestry, descending from a combination of Pennyworth, Alpine and Misty Moor breeding, with the excellent brood bitch Ch. Bee Jay's Cassandra as a focus. Rafina breeding proved important in California through Dan Lockhart's amazing little bitch Ch. Rafina Rhianda of Kamara, a granddaughter of Cassandra; as the dam of at least seventeen Saxon Shore champions in the 1980s "Zinger" became one of the most successful brood bitches the breed has ever known.

Two of the most successful kennels of the 1970s and 1980s were founded mostly on British lines, although sometimes in a roundabout way. Mrs. Christy Gordon-Creed started her Oldlands Kennel on Denorsi and Glenbervie blood while living in South Africa; moving back to her native United States she had great success crossing her imported dogs with American stock from Highlight, Dress Circle and Seyberne. Oldland dogs also had great success in South America but disappeared almost completely from the scene in the U.S. in the 1990s.

The opposite has been true of Barbara Henderson's Whippoorwill Kennel, increasingly recognized over the past couple of decades as a breeding establishment of world importance. Her first champions were sired by Greenbrae Barn Dance; one of them was bred to the substantial, brilliantly colored English import Ch. Whitbarrow Parsley, which resulted in the brother and sister pair of Chs. Fenwick and Lady Blair of Whippoorwill. The former had a low-key show career but big success as a sire and was the first in a line of four tremendously influential stud dogs: Fenwick's son Ch. Rolling's Viktor sired Ch. Saxon Shore Amber Waves who in turn sired Ch. Delacreme de la Renta. Lady Blair was bred to her cousin (doubling up on the Barn Dance sons) and produced a sensational "gem" litter which included two Best in Show winners—Chs. Whippoorwill Tanzanite and Diamond—as well as one of the greatest producing bitches ever, Ch. Whippoorwill Precious Gem.

Herself an AWC specialty winner, Gem was bred to a young English import, Ch. Hard-knott Maestro of Bohem, for her most memorable litter, one of the best this writer has ever seen. (It was difficult picking a favorite when seeing them at two months; in retrospect it wouldn't have mattered much which one I chose although I'm certainly not sorry it turned out to be Ch. Whippoorwill Bohem Aria.) Seven of the eight puppies became champions, and at least six of these (Chs. Whippoorwill Sonatina, Fanfare, Aria and Overture, Unicorn's Encore and Crescendo) have in turn produced Best in Show winning offspring in different parts of the world.

Whippoorwill breeding was also partly responsible for one of the most admired whippet males ever, the smooth-moving Ch. OBailee's Britannia (sired by the Chalmondoley son Ch. Greyfriar Captivator out of a Whippoorwill bitch of part Nevedith breeding), who won a record four AWC specialty shows in the mid-1980s. The two kennels which have achieved the most success breeding on similar

The Whippoorwill Kennels has experienced great success by blending British and American bloodlines. Owner Barbara Henderson, VMD, holds the English import Ch. Hardknott Maestro of Bohem (far right) and a 1987 group of his champion children: from right, next to his sire, is Ch. Whippoorwill Overture, Ch. Whippoorwill Rum Toddy, Ch. Whippoorwill Suave, Ch. Unicorn's Encore and Ch. Whippoorwill Sonatina.

lines are Surrey Hill and Chelsea; their two most important stud dogs are half brothers, sired by yet another dog from the "gem" litter. Whippoorwill Moonstone could not be shown due to an early accident but managed, in spite of limited opportunities, to sire three spectacularly successful stud dogs: Ch. Patric´s Quotation in St Louis, Ch. Chelsea Drakkar of Oxford in California (twice BOS at the National), and—the oldest and so far the most prolific — Ch Surrey Hill´s Houston in the South (sire of the exquisite National Specialty winner Ch. Allerei´s Ain´t Misbehavin).

Ch. Chelsea Drakkar of Oxford has been one of the most consistent winners at specialty shows in the early 1990s and was twice Best of Opposite Sex at the AWC National. He is also a field champion and a successful stud dog. "Drake" was sired by Whippoorwill Moonstone out of Ch. Chelsea Saffron and cobred by Dianne Bowen with Lee and Deann Christianson.

Fawns seldom win as much as the flashy brindle-and-whites at American shows. An exception was provided by Ch. Allerei´s Ain´t Misbehavin (Ch. Surrey Hill´s Houston - Allerei´s Shaharizad), who won three American Whippet Club specialties, including the 1990 National. Bred by Si & Jean Simonsen, "Ava" is owned by Carolyn & Karen Bowers.

Pedigree 37. Ch. SURREY HILL´S HOUSTON, fawn brindle & white dog, born 1985

	Ch. Misty Moor´s Thornwood Dondi (ped. 36)
Sire: Whippoorwill Moonstone	
	Ch. Lady Blair of Whippoorwill (ped. 36)
	Ch. Blue Fox of Whippoorwill (ped. 36)
Dam: Ch. Whippoorwill Surrey	
	Ch. Misty Moor´s Chalmondoley (ped. 34)
	Ch. Whippoorwill Red Poppy
	Ch. Whitbarrow Parsley, imp. UK (ped. 36)

Along different bloodlines but equally successful have been Carol Curry´s Locar dogs in northern California during the past decade, breeding along mostly old American lines from Madcap, Roving, Sheridan, Kindochaline and

America's top whippet in the early 1980s was Ch. Runner's He's The Continental (Ch. Misty Moor's Royal Huntsman - Ch. Runner's Our Own Charisma), bred and owned by Isabell Stoffers and usually shown by Michael Dougherty.

Marial, and notable for a long line of top-producing bitches. The most successful stud dog, Ch. Locar's Dressed to Kill, is a half brother to Chalmondoley with Hound-Hill and Sheridan breeding on his dam's side.

Less active today is the Runner's prefix in southern California, started by Isabell Stoffers in the 1960s and for many years the most successful of all the smaller kennels in the country. Her beautiful bitch Ch. Runner's Our Own Charisma took BIS at the biggest show ever won by a whippet in America, at Ventura during the Santa Barbara weekend in 1974, with some 3,800 exhibits entered. Charisma was a combination of the best old blood from Flying W and Eyeland and became a key bitch for future whippet breeding. In one litter (by Chalmondoley) she produced Ch. Runner's Creme de la Creme, foundation bitch for Delacreme, and in a later litter (by a Chalmondoley son) came the classically handsome Ch. Runner's He's The Continental, the country's top whippet for two years and himself a sire of many champions. Several of them were out of Runner's brindle Australian bitch Ch. Martinique SS Shamrock, a specialty winner and one of the most successful whippet imported to the U.S. in the 1980s.

Both Carol Curry and Isabell Speight, incidentally, have fulfilled the highest honor an American whippet judge can recieve: judging the National Specialty.

Mary Dukes was barely more than a teenager when she won her first AWC specialty and Best of Breed at Westminster with Creme de la Creme. In spite of these wins, it is as the dam of three outstanding sires that "Darcy" is best remembered; in one litter, sired by a dog of old California breeding, Ch. Sea Wind Yankee Clipper, came Ch. Delacreme Avant Garde (a BIS and AWC specialty winner); in an inbred litter by Avant Garde came Ch. Delacreme Dragonslayer (a top sire in Australia); and in a litter by the previously mentioned Ch. Saxon Shore Amber Waves came Ch. Delacreme de la Renta. These three dogs between them have sired well over a hundred champions, but there is no question that "Oscar" is the most important. His pedigree is shown in four generations since both his parents, even apart from the breeding which produced Oscar, are extremely influential producers.

Just as in the case of the breed's other great sire, Chalmondoley, Oscar's influence as a stud dog has tended to overshadow his own show career. He won a number of Hound Groups and two specialties and was one of the most beautiful whippets this writer ever laid eyes on, more reminiscent of distant English relatives such as Ch. Deepridge Mintmaster than anyone else—all long sweeping curves with a beautifully carried long neck and a distinctly aristocratic aura about him. But it is as an immensely popular and dominant sire that Oscar's real importance has been.

By the early 1990s Oscar's total number of champions in the U.S. exceeded 80,

The top American whippet sire of the 1980s, Ch. Delacreme de la Renta (Ch. Saxon Shore Amber Waves - Ch. Runner's Crème de la Crème), has over 80 champion sons and daughter in the U.S. "Oscar" has consistently stamped his get with his long neck, elegance and carriage.

making him the top living sire and second only to his grandsire Chalmondoley among all whippets. Five of his children are specialty winners: Ch. Oakhurst Astin, Ch. Ringmaster's Gold Fever, Ch. Sonsteby's Smooth Character, Ch. Bohem Delacreme Demoiselle and Ch. Merci Isle Meridian—the two latter both won the National Specialty and Demoiselle became the first bitch ever with multiple wins in both all-breeds and specialty competition; she was the country's top whippet in 1988-1989. The kennels which—in addition to those above — have been responsible for the most "Oscar" champions are Rafina, Gold Dust, Saxon Shore, Shilo, Antares, Lyons and Waybroke. Oscar is also a grandfather par excellence—most of the top winners in the early 1990s are his grandchildren, including Ch. Sporting Fields Kinsman, Ch. Willcare's Aged in Wood, Ch. Starline's Claim to Fame and Ch. Sporting Fields Winsome Won. It is too early to say which of Oscar's sons will carry on the family tradition; his top producing offspring so far is a bitch: Ch. Cygnet Watch Me Ms. Whitney.

The most successful combination of all was that of Oscar with Ch. Gold Dust's Limited Edition, a daughter of the famous Twenty Four Karat: a full dozen Ringmaster champions, of which Gold Fever won the most and also excelled as a brood bitch. Her son Ch. Starline's Reign On is one of the most promising young sires in the 1990s and his litter sister Claim to Fame was one of the top winning bitches for several years.

Pedigree 38. Ch. DELACREME DE LA RENTA, brindle & white dog, born 1983

```
                                       Ch. Blue Fox of Whippoorwill (ped. 36)
                        Ch. Fenwick of Whippoorwill
                                       Ch. Whitbarrow Parsley (imp. UK, ped. 36)
            Ch. Rolling's Viktor
                                       Ch. Rolling's Pepper Shaker, by Ch.
                                       Dondelayo Buccaneer
                        Rolling's Rosanne
                                       Ch. Rollings Going Strong, by Ch. Stoney
                                       Meadows Bold Chance
Sire: Ch. Saxon Shore Amber Waves
                                       Ch. Misty Moor's Chalmondoley (ped. 34)
                        Ch. Misty Moor's Royal Huntsman
                                       Marial's Mystic, by Ch. Forest Slim Jim/ Ch.
                                       Eyleland Paisley
            Ch. Rafina Rhianda of Kamara
                                       Ch. Alpine Applejack, by Ch. Charmoll
                                       Clansman (ped. 32)
                        Ch. Cyrano's Rafina Ms Demeanor
                                       Ch. Bee Jay's Cassandra, by Pennyworth
                                       Splash Down


            Ch. Misty Moor's Chalmondoley (ped. 34)

Dam: Ch. Runner's Creme de la Creme
                                       Stoney Meadows Epic (ped. 31)
                        Ch. Eyleland Double or Nothing
                                       Meander Double or Quits, by Ch. Meander
                                       Bob White
            Ch. Runner's Our Own Charisma
                                       Ch. Tonto of Flying W, out of Ch.
                                       Homestead Cinderella (below)
                        Ch. Tesuque of Flying W
                                       Ch. Homestead Cinderella, by Ch.
                                       C. Fleetfoot of P. (ped. 28)
```

Reign On's sire was a dog who in spite of his premature death lived up to the deeper implications of his name, Ch. Hamrya's Lucky Charm. In his short lifespan "George" sired more winners than most other dogs do in twice as long. Himself a son of Ch. Morshor's Majestic Prince, with Plumcreek and Bitterblue on both sides of his pedigree, he was a striking brindle-and-white whose general look and genes were carried on in the 1992 National Specialty winner Ch. Sporting Fields Chosen One as well as in two of the potentially most influential stud dogs of the 1990s—Reign On on the one side, on the other Ch. Broadstrider's By George, a dramatic big-moving specialty winner, owned by the successful and long-established Raybar Kennels of Ray and Barbara Parsons in New Mexico. It is obviously too early to predict their future influence, but chances are that these two dogs will appear in a great number of pedigrees in the future.

Ch. Locar's Martini On The Rocks (Ch. Morshor's Majestic Prince - Ch. Locar's Show Off), handled by his owner and breeder Carol Curry, won the American Whippet Club's Southern specialty in 1991 under breeder judge Nubby Errickson (Amigo).

With two of the country's most successful sires of any time standing at stud in southern California, this area developed into one of the most hotly competitive in the country. Oscar had the higher profile show career, but he also helped attract attention to his own sire, Amber

Waves, and it is difficult to say if either would have experienced more or less success if the other had not been around. Many breeders sent bitches to both and took advantage of the obvious opportunities for linebreeding; some kennels which had exceptional success through Amber Waves champions not already mentioned were Stargazer, Summerwind, Nasusa in Canada, Patric and Halstan, Bob´N, Skeedoodles and Crestfield.

In view of the hotbed which California has become for whippet fanciers, it is worthy of note that several of the recent Western specialties have been won by dogs from other areas: one from the South, Ch. Elysian A-Few Perrier, won the 1993 summer specialty, and one born in the Midwest, Ch. Carbeth Pretty Boy Floyd, won the winter specialty in Los Angeles the same year. On the other hand, California dogs have gone out of the area to win major shows in other parts of the country. In spite of distances which exhibitors in other countries can only faintly imagine, there is now so much interchange between distant areas that the emergence of regional types within a breed are much less likely to occur than in the past.

One more kennel must be mentioned. Just a few years after first appearing in the early 1980s, the Bo-Bett Kennels in Florida—another highly competitive area of the country—shattered most records and became firmly established as one of the most successful in the country. It probably helped that owner Carol Harris was already a leading breeder of quarter horses and experienced with dogs as well, although not in whippets. When Mrs. Harris decided to get involved in whippets she simply employed the same principles which had worked so well in horses, one of which was obviously not to deal in half measures; Bo-Bett even from the start had its own handler, Davin McAteer, and a breeding program which seemed quite extensive compared to most other whippet kennels. This impression was at least partly caused by the fact that Bo-Bett frequently carried a large show string and won with what seemed like an endless stream of champions, but many of them were littermates. Quite quickly, employing a consistent breeding program, Carol Harris established an easily recognizable family of dogs—usually correctly sized, elegant and appealing, often subtly colored in cream fawn and white, and invariably with attractive heads and expressions.

Among the most memorable dogs at Bo-Bett is a bitch who has produced an almost unimaginable total of 23 champions, Ch. Misty Moor´s Divine Pleasure—which of course means that both the all-time top sire and the all-time top dam of champions in America come from Roberta Russ´ now dormant breeding program. Divine Pleasure was sired by Chalmondoley´s half brother out of his daughter and produced most of her champions by different Bo-Bett males—several of whom have become top sires in their own right, such as Ch. Bo-Bett´s Luke Skywalker, CD. On the show bench, the kennel hit a home run almost from the start with a line of Best in Show winners such as Tina Ballerina, Wild Waylon, Starman, and above all Snow Bunny, whose record of sixteen all-breed Best in Shows is the most achieved by any bitch since the days of Ch. Flornell Glamorous half a century before.

Pedigree 39. Ch. BO-BETT'S SNOW BUNNY, brindle & white bitch, born 1986

```
                              Ch. Bo-Bett's Luke Skywalker, CD (below)
               Ch. Bo-Bett's Wild Willie
                              Bo-Bett's Mighty Millie, by Ch. Montalba's Red Barron x
                              Marla (below)
Sire: Ch. Bo-Bett's Wild Tobiano
                              Grovenor's Pillar of Fire, by Ch. Grovenor's Bold N' Brassy
               Ch. Grovenor's Marla of Morshor
                              Stoneleigh Star of Grovenor, by Ch. Tantivvey Diver of P.,
                              imp. UK (ped. 29)

                              Ch. Flippet's Appraxin Marshall, CD, by Ch. Appraxin Mind
                              Duster
               Ch. Bo-Bett's Luke Skywalker, CD
                              Ch. Appraxin's Kampfer Nicole, by Ch. Truly A Windance
                              Triumph
Dam: Ch. Bo-Bett's Divine Dessert
                              Ch. April's No Fooling Around, by Ch. Morshor's Appraxin
                              Ariel (ped. 34)
               Ch. Misty Moor's Divine Pleasure
                              Ch. Misty Moor's Ravendune Alwyn, by Ch. Misty Moor's
                              Chalmondoley (ped. 34)
```

The most influential of the relatively few dogs coming from England since the 1970s has been a dog which wasn't even born when the author "found" him; the beautiful orange brindle and white bitch Ch. Belinda of Hardknott could have had a fantastic career in the U.S. if given half a chance, and when she was bred to the classic winner Ch. Novacroft Madrigal it seemed like a match made in heaven, especially in view of how well English dogs of similar breeding had done in America before; further back in the pedigree are famous names such as McTavish, Cinnamon, Diver and a whole row of old Laguna champions. Their son Ch. Hardknott Maestro of Bohem, in Barbara

Henderson's loving care, had a successful show career which in addition to a number of wins in Breed and Group competition included BOS at the National Specialty in 1988 under Mrs. Isabell Stoffers. (Like Ch. Morshor's Majestic Dell the year before him, Maestro was defeated by a young descendant for BOB; in this case his granddaughter Ch. Bohem Delacreme Demoiselle.) Maestro has sired over 40 champions, mostly for Whippoorwill and mostly in the U.S. but others as far apart as Scandinavia and South America.

One of the top winning whippets ever to leave England came to California in the mid-1980s. Ch. Dyanne Dondelayo had a shining career behind her in the UK; if nothing comparable materialized in the U.S. it was mainly because her owner Jim Burens felt that a dog of Dyanne's stature should not be exposed to the whims of the average all-rounder judge. Although hardly glamorous by American standard and in spite of approaching middle age, Dyanne would no doubt have been able to break through in any case; she was to my knowledge only shown once in America, at the 1988 AWC National Specialty, where she created a great deal of interest and took a meritorious placement in a big Open Bitch class. The Burens' Samarkand and Dondelayo bred dogs have champion offspring in their own Paws 'N Oaks Kennel, in the primarily old American based Kindochaline Kennels in northern California, and in Canada. Other English-born champions have come from Chatwig, Walkabout and Barmoll.

While the influence of English dogs has

diminished since the 1960s and 1970s, there have been additions—frequently of basically English-bred dogs—from other parts of the world. Whippoorwill breeding also combined successfully with some Scandinavian blood; the half brothers Ch. Terra Whisetta Brian Bohem came from Norway and Ch. Bohem American Way was imported utero from Sweden. Both won at AWC specialties and both sired champions, including the prematurely deceased specialty and BIS winning American Way daughter Ch. Bohem Moonshine Lullaby.

The Australian influence has been mentioned elsewhere. One import from France, the charming little Ch. Beautiful Dreamer du Sac à Malices, was brought over by Sharon Sakson´s appropriately named Paris Kennel after a visit to Europe and has sired several champions.

Ch. Bohem Delacreme Demoiselle, by Ch. Delacreme de la Renta and Ch. Whippoorwill Sonatina, won three American Whippet Club specialties as well as several all-breed Best in Shows. She was handled by Phoebe Booth.

The most important development in American whippets over the past decade was the development of a national specialty show in 1987. Ever since the foundation of the club in 1930, the American Whippet Club has orga-nized specialties—at first on an irregular basis (during the first sixteen years there were only eight shows) and only in the East, but from 1947 annually and beginning in 1954 with an additional show in California. The Midwest specialty came just a year later, and for the next 30 years the club established a tradition of three AWC specialties per year: one in the East, one in the Midwest and one in California. It was a tradition which served the breed well and assured that specialty wins in whippets, if not in other breeds, really counted.

Entries at the first shows in the 1930s do not seem to have attracted more than a couple of dozen entries—exact figures are unavailable even in the American Kennel Club archives. The first AWC specialty was held with Greenwich Kennel Clun on June 7, 1931, was judged by F.H. Addyman and won by Ch. Sandbrilliant of Meander. In 1952 the great all-rounder (and sometime whippet handler) Winifred Heckman had a record entry of 60 whippets in Pikesville, Maryland, with Best of Breed going to one of that year´s most famous winners, Ch. Garden City´s

Sleepy Mouse. After that, entries dropped off again and did not reach higher figures until the early 1960s. The first show with more than a hundred whippets was Santa Barbara KC in 1969 when Mrs. Cynthia P. Schmick awarded Ch. Hollypark Honey Bee her first specialty win. At the same show in 1977, whippets for the first time surpassed the 175-dog limit which AKC then imposed as the maximum for one single judge; Ch. Gold Dust´s Twenty Four Karat won under the author. From then on AWC frequently assigned separate judges for dogs and bitches, with either of these—or even a third person — judging the specials class for champions only. In 1981 the 200 figure was first reached by the Midwest specialty, held with Western Reserve Kennel Club´s all-breed show in Ohio; Anthony Gutilla of the Lazebrook whippets awarded BOB to that year´s top winner Ch. Delacreme Avant Garde. The Midwest remained a mecca for whippet lovers for many years, but entries rose all across the country, and by 1985 the AWC added a fourth regional show, in the South, to the annual schedule. Held with the Classic City Kennel Club in Georgia, the first Southern specialty attracted 123 entries and saw

After many years away from dog shows, Pennyworth made a comeback in top competition with the ultra-feminine Ch. Willcare´s Aged in Wood (Ch. Willcare´s Believe You Me, CD - Ringmaster´s Reggae), a multiple specialty and Best in Show winner, owned and shown by Peggy Newcombe´s daughter Claire.

Mrs. W.P. Wear of Stoney Meadows award the top spot to the classic brindle beauty Ch. Whippletree´s Icy Hot.

Unlike most other breeds, few of the local whippet clubs which at various times have sprung up around the country seem to have had a ambition to host an official specialty show. (Most other breeds have many more specialty shows than whippets do in the U.S.—popular breeds such as German Shepherds and Poodles may have close to a hundred specialty shows in a year, allowing exhibitors to forsake the all-breeds scene altogether.) Many whippet clubs focus on racing or coursing and some of them hold matches, but not until the Southern California Whippet Association´s first show in 1984 was there an additional official specialty show for whippets. Held each year in January, it has provided a bright spot in the calendar and attracted judges and exhibitors from across the country. In 1993 another West Coast club, the Western Washington Whippet Association, held its first specialty show, with Mrs. Isabell Stoffers awarding Best of Breed to Ch. Sonsteby´s Smooth Character.

While these and possibly other future regional club shows are positive developments, offering a chance for large numbers of whippet fanciers to gather and compare notes, nothing in recent years has been more important than the instigation of an American Whippet Club national event. The original reason was simply to attract more members to the club's annual meeting, which according to the bylaws must take place in April — and what better way to convince whippet people from around the country to get together than to offer them a chance to show their dogs, to each other and to a knowledgeable judge? The first AWC National Specialty took place in Columbus, Ohio on 18 April, 1987, with an all-time world record of 340 whippets entered under whippetdom's grand lady Mrs. W.P. Wear. One of America's most experienced sighthound specialist judges, Mrs. Betty Stites, of the Hullabaloo Afghan hounds and whippets, took over part of the huge assignment, and Phoebe Booth (Shamasan) judged the sweepstakes classes for young stock which (alternating with a futurity) have been a feature of most AWC specialties for many years. When the dust settled, Mrs. Wear awarded BOB over a field of 69 champions to her Winners Bitch, Morshor's Majestic Ball O'Fire, handled by Calvin Perry, with Best of Opposite Sex to "Lisa's" sire Ch. Morshor's Majestic Dell. Winners Dog under Mrs. Stites was Oakhurst Astin, and best in sweepstakes—as well as best puppy in the regular classes—went to Norman Ellis' fawn youngster Madcap Master Key. Lisa as well as Astin and Master Key all became champions later.

It was obvious that the National Spe-cialty would become an annual feature, moving around the country from one region to another each year, and later shows have continued to improve, offering far more than just the annual club meeting and the conformation judging which is at the core of a national specialty. In fact, there are now so many different events taking place at the same time as the National Specialty that you need a week to attend them all — but given the scarcity of truly interesting shows for whippets, breed fanciers from all across America and foreign countries as well gather in increasing numbers each year; the figures obviously vary depending on many factors, mainly location, but more than 500 whippets have been entered on more than one occasion.

At the 1994 American Whippet Club National Specialty, the schedule included three days of official conformation judging, a gala Top Twenty tournament to which the top whippets of the previous year are invited (to be judged by three separate judges — one breeder, one handler, and one official AKC Hound Group judge), obedience competition, a tattoo clinic, an agility demonstration, junior showmanship, a futurity, veteran sweepstakes (both judged by a breeder who need not necessarily be an officially approved AKC judge), an eye clinic, two board meetings and an annual members' meeting, a round table discussion, a Parade of Honors limited to the great winners and producers of the past, a judges' study group, a race meet, two lure coursing meets, and of course the Annual Awards banquet where the winners are honored and the club's Register of Merit certificates to outstanding producers are awarded.

Many people are responsible for the success of the National Specialty, none more so than Cathy Gaidos, whose position as show chairman for the first few years meant that she had to forsake her own Konza whippet activities for the sake of the club. The importance of having one person who remains in charge for several years should be obvious, especially with a show which moves from one part of the country to another each year. In later years when this position has been taken over by Cindy Scott (Brookwood whippets), Cathy Gaidos has remained president of the club and as its delegate to the American Kennel Club provides the breed's most visible window to the world.

Whippets in Canada

It is a difficult task to condense Canadian activities due to the fact that both the human and the canine population are more thinly spread out over a vast area than in the United States. There has been less intermingling of whippet bloodlines than south of the border, records are more difficult to compile as even the Canadian Kennel Club does not have all the answers, and until recently there was no national breed club.

Whippets in Canada are affected by the sometimes contradictory influences of Britain and the United States. The Canadian official standard is identical to neither, and the top breeders use American lines at least as often as direct imports from Britain. The National Whippet Club of Canada was not founded until 1993, but there have long been a number of regional whippet clubs—Canada in fact has more whippet specialty shows than the U.S., although the entries are lower. The most important events prior to the first national specialty in 1994 have been specialty shows hosted by organizations such as the Whippet Club of Eastern Canada, the Central Canada Whippet Club, the Stampede Whippet Club, the Lower Mainland Whippet Club, etc.

Although some of the early American fanciers and their dogs came from Canada—such as James Young—registration figures were low and could sometimes be counted on the fingers of one hand. Two of the first all-breed wins for whippets in North America occurred in Canada; a little fawn bitch named Ch. R.A.F. (named for the Royal Air Force) won the Grand Challenge Cup at Winnipeg in 1924, "getting best of all breeds, defeating many of the most noted champions of other breeds of both Canada and the United States," according to Whippet Club of America records, and the famous English import Ch. Nomad Nancy of Oxon was best in show in Toronto, apparently in the same year.

Interest did not start to grow until the 1960s with the arrival of kennels such as Pamela Arthur's Rock-A-Bye in British Columbia and Martine Collings' Winterfold. Mr. and Mrs. Collings had moved back and forth across the Atlantic several times before finally settling in Canada; Mrs. Collings had then already been partially responsible for the importation of Courtenay Fleetfoot to Pennyworth and even registered a separate kennel

Canada's greatest contribution to the world of whippets was no doubt Ch. Winterfold's Bold Bid (Ch. Coveydown Greenbrae Wayfarer - Stoney Meadows Bold Queen), one of the most admired whippets of all time and a great producer. "Hettie" is shown taking one of her Best in Shows in 1971 under judge Mr. William Brainard, shown by Robert Forsyth.

name—Coveydown—while living in England. That name was added to a puppy which later became famous across North America as Ch. Coveydown Greenbrae Wayfarer. He was from the same litter as the illustrious Barn Dance—Mrs. Collings remembers that "Barney" was offered to them as company for their puppy, but she felt that one male from the litter was enough, and Barney had to wait a few more months before he too crossed the Atlantic.

After the move back to Canada in 1963, Mrs. Collings registered a new kennel name, Winterfold. Wayfarer's daughters in particular both won and produced well on both

sides of the border; two of them, Ch. Winterfold's Bold Bid and Morshor's Cicada are among the most outstanding champion producers since records started in the U.S. When the time came to purchase a brood bitch Mrs. Collings managed to acquire Stoney Meadows Bold Queen from Mrs. Wear. Her offspring by Tantivvey Diver of Pennyworth soon topped the shows in Canada, but it was left to a daughter by Wayfarer to conquer the United States. Recognizing the quality in the young Ch. Winterfold's Bold Bid, and not herself having time to campaign her extensively, Martine Collings let her go to Dianne Bleecker of the Morshor Kennels. "Hettie" became one of the most successful show whippets of all time in the U.S. and is regularly mentioned by experienced breeders as one of "the best ever." Hettie also produced no less than fourteen champions in the U.S. for Morshor and for the Sporting Fields Kennel by which she was later owned.

Many of the later breeders in the U.S. and Canada started with Mrs. Colling's stock. Pat Miller's Woodsmoke Kennel began with two Winterfolds; her foundation bitch, the obedience and racing winner Ch. Sirhan Great Expectations, CD was a granddaughter of the Ligonier sons Wayfarer and Eng. Ch. Deepridge Mintmaster. Great Expectations was bred to Barn Dance in the U.S. and produced the great star Ch. Night Talk of Woodsmoke—winner of thirteen all-breed BIS winners for the home kennel. Night Talk was the top winning Canadian-bred whippet of for many years. Heavy linebreeding to Night Talk resulted in the BIS winning brood bitch Ch. Woodsmoke's Winter Moon: she was bred to Pat Miller's stylish Australian import Ch. Rothbury Replica and produced, among other winners, the beautiful Ch. Woodsmoke's Share A Moment, winner of seventeen Best in Shows in the late 1980s. One of Share's daughters was then bred back to Replica, doubling up on his all-English Dondelayo and Allgarth blood, which resulted in Ch. Woodsmoke's All Ablaze, sire of top winners in both Canada and the U.S. in the early 1990s.

The Alery Kennels were started by Allan Pepper and Terry Taft with a Winterfold bitch of Diver and Stoney Meadows breeding. When mated to Ch. Morshor's Whirlaway she produced the top whippet of 1971, Ch. Alery White Warlock, and he in turn sired the stylish Ch. Astrologer of Alery—top whippet of 1980 and the first Canadian-owned whippet ever to win an AWC specialty. His young son Ch. Alery Astrologer's Antares was the top winning whippet in Canada for 1982. Alery has been less active in later years, but Terry Taft embarked on a successful breeding program of his own under the Baccarat prefix. His imported brood bitch Ch. Bohem Delacreme Chevrotain (litter sister to Demoiselle in the U.S.) is responsible for at least ten champions, including the 1993 top winner Ch. Baccarat Bon Chance (sired by Ch. Woodsmoke's All Ablaze).

More direct influence from British imports is evident in the Lorricbrook Kennel owned by Max Magder. The superbly bred fawn import Ch. Dondelayo Buccaneer (by Buckaroo out of Duette) lived up to his illustrious parentage by taking a long line of all-breed wins and was responsible for an even longer line of champion offspring (including nine in the U.S.). A

Dr. John Reeve-Newson from Canada awarded top placements at the American Whippet Club's Eastern specialty in 1985 to (left to right) Ch. O'Bailee's Brittania (Best of Breed, shown by Kim Strong), Ch. Surrey Hill's Goldenrod (Best of Opposite Sex, with Joy Brewster), and Lasma's Continental Divide (Best of Winners, with Christy Nelson-Evans). Brittania won a record four AWC specialties, Goldenrod was the country's top whippet in 1985 and 1986, and Continental Divide became a champion on this day and won the AWC Western specialty a few weeks later.

later import, Ch. Shalfleet Statesman, also produced well and helped make Lorricbrook into one of the world's most international breeders of whippet champions; dogs exported from Mr. Magder's kennel have won champion titles in England, central Europe, South America and of course in the U.S. and Canada as well.

The top sire in the U.S., Ch. Misty Moor's Chalmondoley, produced some of his best puppies in Canada. His granddaughter Ch. Gambit's Vitesse won the "Champion of Champions" contest for all-breed BIS winners in Canada in 1980 shortly before her premature death. Other kennels which exerted a major influence were Carousel (now in the U.S.), Sirhan (of borzoi fame), and Denroc in Calgary, Alberta—the only western kennel to win Top Whippet in Canada for many decades.

Several British whippet breeders have emigrated to Canada and brought with them some of the best native bloodlines. The Sakonnet prefix was prominent in Canada for a few years before being transferred to Bermuda and back to Britain. Mispickel, Boarley (now both back in England), Ringdove and Padneyhill are other names well known on both sides of the Atlantic. The last-mentioned kennel bred Ch. Marial's Padneyhill Illusion, top racing dog in the U.S. for 1979. On the other hand, whippets from the U.S. have had even more influence in recent years; three different Sporting Fields dogs have occupied the No. 1 spot in Canada since 1983, and the top winning Canadian-bred bitch Ch. Nineveh Royal Denby was bred to Ch. Saxon Shore Amber Waves in California, producing a line of Nasusa champions which have been successful on both sides of the border.

Racing in Canada comes under the auspices of the American Whippet Club and greatly expanded in the late 1970s; meets often include as many as 40 or 50 whippets. The winner of the first race meet in 1965 was Urray Chieftain, an early representative for the enormously successful racing kennel "of Course" owned by Bill and Margaret Turpin in Vancouver. Their Ch. Rockabye Ember of Course was the first of her sex to win the AWC's Award of Racing Merit and for three years was never outranked by any other bitch. Bred to the top show dog Ch. Stars & Stripes of Suntan she produced Ch. Emberson of Course who was one of the top racing whippets in North America, dominating the scene for three years. Linda Buchholz of the Swiftsure Kennels imported Ch. Marial's King Arthur from the U.S. and exerted much influence through him, both in showing and racing. His son Ch. Swiftsure Happy Daze must be one of the most titled whippets in Canada—a show champion with the ARM in racing and the American-Canadian Field Champion title as well—while Happy Daze's son, Ch. Swiftsure Out of Africa (out of a sister to the top U.S. sire Ch. Surrey Hill's Houston) was Canada's top whippet in 1990.

Lure coursing started in 1976 and has seen many show winners take top awards—Ch. Fraserfield Silverheels, Ch. Marial's Swiftsure Phantasy, etc. Lure coursing, as opposed to racing, is organized independently from the American clubs, but the Canadian Sighthound Field Association was patterned after the already-existing ASFA south of the border.

A classic example of Anglo-Scandinavian breeding from the late 1970s: Ch. Colt´s Alouette (Ch. Bohem Lekain - Ch. Gårdsjöns Carolina). The great English breeder Anne Knight considered Alouette the best whippet bitch she ever saw; she also proved to be an influential brood bitch.

Around the World

Though tradition-
ally whippets have
been especially popular in the English-speaking
world, they now prosper in every country where
dogs are kept for companionship, showing, racing or coursing. Over the past few decades, an
increasing number of countries have managed
to produce whippets of high international standards. In fact, one of the most interesting trends
in the 1980s has been the unprecedented degree
of international cooperation involving countries which only a few years ago would have
been considered at best of peripheral interest.
Instead of the one-way traffic of exports from
England to the rest of the world, a trend which
has influenced the breed´s development since
the beginning of the century, top class whippets
are now exported from Australia to Scandinavia
and vice versa, from America to France and and
back again — just to mention a few of the most
active countries. The dogs in most cases are of
English breeding a few generations back, and in
some parts of the world a British-bred whippet is
still the only possible option, but the absolute
monopoly which the British breeders once had
in the export market world-wide is now past.

Although regional
differences exist,
due as much to local idiosyncracies as to actual
differences in the breed standards, all whippets
in the world are related to some degree, often
within a few generations of their pedigrees. Now
that international cooperation in the world of
dogs is ever more easily available and quarantine restrictions are gradually being eased out
between most countries, some knowledge of
conditions and breed development around the
world will prove increasingly useful.

Australia

For cultural as well as quarantine reasons, Britain´s canine influence has been
stronger in Australia than almost anywhere else.
The quarantine laws have made importing from
Britain easier than from the rest of the world,
and although the restrictions were lifted to some
extent in the 1980s (and may be further eased in
the 1990s), they are still the strictest in the
world and make traffic between Australia and
most other countries difficult for dog breeders.

The general development of the dog sport in many respects mirrors that of the U.S. in the early days. Activity is heavily concentrated on the densely populated eastern and southeastern coasts, with a later movement towards the west. Australia has long been governed not by a national kennel club but by the canine section of the Royal Agricultural Society (RAS) in each state, held together by a national council with limited responsibilities. In recent years there has been a move towards independence from the RAS and more cooperation between the different states, but there is still no single national body which issues registrations, championships, etc. This is done independently in the different states.

The show system is a combination of the British and the American styles. Both champions and non-champions compete for Challenge Certificates (here usually just called "Challenges"), but these carry a different number of points depending on the number of dogs defeated. A total of 100 points is required for the Australian title, and since the maximum number of points per challenge is 25 it takes at least four shows to complete the championship. On the other hand, without any competition in the breed the challenge is worth only 6 points, so great persistence is needed to "make up" a champion in some breeds or areas.

By far the biggest and most important canine events in Australia are the "Royal" shows held annually in each state. These huge, week-long exhibitions of livestock and agricultural products are organized by the RAS, and are among the biggest dog shows held anywhere outside Britain. The Melbourne Royal show in September on occasion hsd had over 6,000 dogs; the Sydney Royal at Easter (which limits its entry for space reasons) usually has between 4,000 and 5,000 dogs, and the Brisbane and Adelaide equivalents attract only slightly fewer. Since only a handful of judges are employed for each Royal show, they are usually all-rounders and have to be prepared to work their way through a couple of hundred dogs per day for more than a week. There are regional whippet clubs but no nationwide organization and no national specialty.

Whippet racing was recorded in Australia as early as 1869, and it is quite likely that whippets were exhibited at the very first Australian shows—starting in Hobart on Tasmania in 1862. No doubt some early settlers brought whippets with them from Britain, but not until well into the twentieth century are there any records of whippets being bred specifically for show purposes. One of the first major wins came when the brindle Ch. Calpin Bartic Coquette won Best in Show at Brisbane Royal show in 1951. In spite of many outstanding wins at the top shows in recent years, this is by all accounts the only Royal BIS win ever recorded for the breed. The Calpin Bartic whippets were entirely British in origin and based on the well-known Bolney line. Coquette's son Ch. Flashing Cyclone was a multiple BIS winner, owned by the influential Amersham Kennel of Messrs. I.M. Payne and K.L. Karas in Sydney, where he sired a large number of champions. Amersham later imported a son of the great Eng. Am. Ch.

Courtenay Fleetfoot of Pennyworth from England; Briarcliff Rameses could not be shown due to an accident but was an exceptional sire and turns up over and over again in older Australian pedigrees.

Some of Amersham´s first champions were bred by Miss Marie Waddell of the Waddellie Kennels. Her foundation bitch was sired by the imported Eng. Ch. Response of Ballymoy, a golden brindle of pure Tiptree breeding who must have been responsible for the fact that so many of the early Australian champions were brindle. Response also sired Ch. Brucebeen Babee, best bitch of all breeds at Sydney Royal in 1958. Miss Waddell later imported a series of dogs of the Marksman line, notably the powerful parti-colored Eng. Aust. Ch. Playmate of Allways, and bred dozens of champions from these well into the 1960s.

Most of the activity at this time was concentrated in the Sydney area, and when a breed club was formed in 1959 it was named the Whippet Club of New South Wales. It had a nationwide list of members, however, and by 1967 became simply the Whippet Club. It was long the only single-breed club for whippets in Australia and has held regular championship shows in Sydney since 1964, sometimes with overseas breed specialist judges and frequently over a hundred entries. The Easter show is held during the same week as the Sydney Royal show and the newly founded Sighthound Association´s event, offering whippet fanciers three major shows in the same area within a few days of each other.

Since the mid-1960s there has also

been another specialist club, the Whippet & Greyhound Club of South Australia, which holds well-attended shows in the Adelaide area. The leading kennel in that state was Allstar, based on strong Marksman blood through his imported son Ch. Wingedfoot Crackerjack. Later a different line was added through Eng. Ch. Laguna Limelight, whose son Ch. Allstars Audacity—imported in utero—sired champions both for his breeder and for the Wingstar kennels. (With the arrival of later imports descended from Audacity´s halfbrother Eng. Ch. Samarkand´s Greenbrae Tarragon, the opportunities were there for some interesting line-breeding, but this does not seem to have materialized.) The advent of newer names—Allswell, Skyeway—strengthened competition in this area considerably. David and Carolyn Mudge´s Allswell Drummer Boy in fact won Best Puppy in Show of all breeds at the 1993 Melbourne Royal show.

In the Melbourne region the Whippet Club of Victoria now hosts an annual championship show. The most important breeder in this part of Australia was for a long time Mrs. Dot Stewart of the Rosiel Kennel. Her foundation bitch was Ch. Amersham Ability of the old Calpin Bartic breeding; she won several BIS and when bred to Briarcliffe Rameses started a whole line of champions which form the basis for most later breeding in Victoria. Mrs. Stewart´s best dog was probably the classic parti-colored Ch. Rosiel Royal Sign, best puppy in show at the Melbourne Royal in 1972. When I judged him he was already old, but he combined the best features from the famous dogs in

Australia's top sire in the 1970s was Ch. Lowglen Oakbark Masterminde, owned by the Martinique kennels of Brian Doherty and Terry Crowley. He was imported from England, sired by Eng. & Am. Ch. Flarepath Tambillo Tarquin out of Oakbark Ballerina, and had already established himself as a show dog and sire in his native country before going to Australia.

his pedigree—substance and power from two lines to Ch. Robmaywin Stargazer of Allways, glamour and "class" from a double influence of Ch. Bellavista Barry on his dam's side.

In later years competition has again been strong in the Sydney area. The Martinique Kennels, established in 1962 by Brian Doherty and Terry Crowley, has probably bred more champions than any other in Australia. Their first champions were of Miss Waddell's breeding and included the light brindle Ch. Waddellie Lancer, winner of the Hound group at Melbourne Royal in 1961 under Col. E. Ferguson, U.S. The homebred fawn Ch. Martinique My Fair Lady took the same award in Sydney in 1967, under Robert Waters from Canada, but

Martinique's most important dog did not arrive from England until 1972. The fawn-and-white Lowglen Oakbark Masterminde had a successful career behind him, including one Challenge Certificate and several litters which were to prove important in Britain as well as elsewhere. (Masterminde's son Eng. Ch. Flarepath Astrinought of Lowglen was a Crufts winner and successful sire.) In Australia, Masterminde became a champion himself and sired over 30 champions at Martinique and other kennels, setting a new standard for the breed. In the early 1990s Martinique added new blood by importing the colorful, mostly American-bred young male Ch. Airescot Chaconne from Sweden.

In the 1970s competition was intensified with the arrival of the first of several top-winning imports owned by Frank Pieterse. The parti-colored Eng. Ch. Allgarth Envoy was closely related to Masterminde on his sire's side but out of a Shalfleet bitch. He was shown to many all-breed victories by Brian McCowage, who later bred Envoy to an imported Dondelayo bitch and from those two produced the top-winning Ch. Andiamo Sabreur in New Zealand.

Probably the best known whippet ever to come to Australia was the young English star Ch. Dondelayo Statue, owned by Frank Pieterse and usually shown by Graham Bailey. Statue made a deep impact when he arrived in Australia in 1977, took several major BIS and won the Whippet Club show no less than four times. He sired 43 champions, an amazing number particularly in view of the few bitches he bred. In 1980 Statue offspring were in the Hound Group finals at all the three biggest Royal shows, and his famous daughter Ch. Martinique Papier Mache was Best Bitch of all breeds at the Sydney Royal show under the great British all-rounder Catherine Sutton. Papier Mache has also won the Whippet Club show and several times competed with her sire for Best in Show at that event.

***Pedigree 40.** Ch. MARTINIQUE PAPIER MACHE, fawn-&-white bitch, born 1978*
                           Ch. Samarkand's Greenbrae Tarragon (ped 18)
              Dondelayo Mosaic (brindle-white)
                          Dondelayo Nicola - 7 lines to Tarragon
Sire: Eng. Aust Ch. Dondelayo Statue, imp UK (fawn-white
                           Oakbark Pyramid, by Tarragon son (ped 18)
              Eng. It. Ch. Denhills Delectabelle (fawn-white)
                           Rasaday Alisa, by Ch. Deepridge Mintmaster

                           Ch. Waddellie Mighty Atom
              Ch. Martinique El Cordobes
                         Ch. Waddellie Candy-Bar
Dam: Ch. Martinique Sombrero
                           Ch. Lowglen Oakbark Masterminde, imp UK
              Ch. Newbold Vanity, imp UK
                         Newbold Samema Queen o'Diamonds

His owner's most successful Statue offspring no doubt has been the magnificent, multiple Royal group winner Ch. Statuesque Res Anibrow. Statue was used not only in Frank Pieterse's own Statuesque Kennel and by Martinique, but also by most of the other successful breeders in the same area. Bellendene, Dachlah, Deerfoot and Kylebay were just a few of the kennels which bred champions in New South Wales during the 1980s, usually from a combination of Masterminde and Statue blood. Most of them remain in some way involved in the breed in the 1990s, although more often as judges than as active breeders or exhibitors. Other current kennels include Calahorra which in recent years has focused as much on whippets as on their world famous Afghan hounds, and Meilandina which has brought Rosiel breeding into the 1990s, in addition to their Martinique and New Zealand breeding.

The history of top-class British imports in Australia continued with Martinique's acquisition of Ch. Solotown Simon, imported in 1980. He carried both Tarragon and Ligonier blood on his sire's side, and his dam was a daughter of Knight Errant. In his first litters Simon sired several all-breed winners; visiting American breeder Phoebe Booth acquired an Australian son of his, Stormbay Flin, who later became a champion in the U.S. (BOB at the show which Mrs. Booth judged, however, went to a young Statue daughter, Ch. Stormbay Thisbe.)

Ch. Dondelayo Statue (Dondelayo Mosaic - Ch. Denhill's Delectabelle) won the CC at Crufts as a youngster and was exported shortly afterwards. In Australia he was largely undefeated but is best remembered as an outstanding sire. Bred by Mrs. Anne Knight, Statue was owned by Frank Pieterse.

Frank Pieterse meanwhile had imported the brindle English top winner Ch. Dondelayo Reinette, who soon added several all-breed wins in Australia to those in England. Even more important was the parti-colored Ch. Cottonmere Monty of Oakbark, whose Australian-born son Ch. Statuesque Personalised brought English blood to Scandinavia in a roundabout way. Swedish breeder Nenne Runsten Fodstad organized a lease which meant that "Person" came to Scandinavia for a long enough time to allow him not only to become a top show winner—with back-to-back Skokloster wins as an apex—but also to

sire several extremely successful litters there. Person's pedigree incorporates Mr. Pieterse's earlier imports Envoy and Statue as well.

Pedigree 41. Ch. STATUESQUE PERSONALISED, fawn & white dog, born 1987

```
                              Moonstorm of Oakbark, by Ch. Oakbark Dondelayo Storming
                Oakbark Mr Blue
                              Flarepath Aquaria, by Aust. Ch. Lowglen Oakbark
                              Masterminde
Sire: Eng. Aust. Ch. Cottonmere Personality of Oakbark
                              Bunnyridge Gypsy Baron
                Ribblesmere Xmas Carol
                              Thurma My Love

                              Ch. Lowglen Newbold Cavalier (ped. 17)
                Eng. Aust. Ch. Allgarth Envoy
                              Shalfleet Stylish, by Ch. Shalfleet Sultan of Sherrimere
Dam: Ch.Statuesque Sundancer
                              Eng. Aust. Ch. Dondelayo Statue (ped. 40)
                Ch. Zipity Tartan Statuet
                              Ch. Glenbervie Sky Belle, imp. UK
```

Ch. Rothbury Replica exemplifies the modern cosmopolitan whippet: born in Australia of English breeding (Ch. Dondelayo Statue - Andiamo Columba), he had great success when imported to Canada by Pat Miller's Woodsmoke kennels and has sired winners on both sides of the North American border.

Frank and Lee Pieterse's most recent import does not come from England but from New Zealand; on a judging trip on the other side of the Tasman Sea, Mr. Pieterse was so impressed by the brindle Ch. Noholme Beauling Alli that he arranged a temporary lease. His grandsire from the same kennel, Ch. Noholme Pepper Mill, is already a successful sire in Australia, owned by Molly Rule-Steele's Taejaan Kennels: her two half sisters by Pepper Mill, Ch. Shalique Satin Layce and Ch. Taejaan Tia Maria have won particularly well under international judges (including an impressive Hound Group at the Sydney Royal show in 1993 for Satin Layce).

One of Australia's most successful whippet kennels since the mid-1980s has been Pauline and Iven Affleck's Rothbury in Victoria. With a background in Bedlington terriers, the Afflecks quickly got to the top in whippets, breeding from mainly Dondelayo lines via Statue and the Andiamo litter; the elegant, oddly marked parti-colored Ch. Rothbury Hotlips and the brindle Ch. Rothbury Rust Bucket were just two of the most noticeable early winners from this kennel. International recognition came in the form of a Statue son who was exported to Canada, Ch. Rothbury Replica, where he has become a strong influence. Even more important for breed development in Australia was the importation of a dog from California, Ch. Delacreme Dragonslayer—an inbred son of Ch. Runner's Our Own Charisma (sired by her own son, Ch. Delacreme Avant Garde). Dragonslayer added an Australian title to his American one but had his most important influence as a sire of a whole line of Rothbury champions—Snow Chief and Storm Boy are among the best known. One of them, the white dog Ch. Rothbury Bonecrusher was exported to Norway and became a top winner at the Scandinavian shows in the early 1990s.

Up north in Queensland, the leading breeders for many years were Mr. and Mrs. Len Bright, whose first top winner Ch. Zipity Wonder Lad was by two Waddellie dogs of pure Allways blood. Later the Brights imported the British CC winner Skybelle of Glenbervie. She soon became an Australian champion and in an outcrossed litter by Lad gave the Brights several champions; when later bred to Statue they provided Queensland with a younger generation of Zipity champions. The most successful newer kennels in this area are Oakway and Ryeford, who have cooperated successfully both with each other and with the Statuesques in Sydney.

One of the top wins ever for whippets in Australia was recorded in 1987 when the brindle dog Ch. Acaiza Jokers Wild was reserve Best in Show at Melbourne Royal show. Bred in Tasmania, he was sired by Ch. Allstars Fine Liquer out of Ch. Martinique Calico Sea. In Western Australia, Anne Mitchell's Keheilans won Royal show awards for many years, and in the sparsely populated Northern Territory the Famoustee prefix is one of the few to keep the breed going. Other modern English blood is represented by many well-bred imports, including the beautiful Crufts CC winner Ch. Denhill's Deligate who has sired several champions and a line of successful Nevedith champions—Ruegeto Nikki of Nevedith, Nevedith Apple Scrumpy and Nevedith Call Me Dash, all of whom have also produced Australian champions.

New Zealand

New Zealand came late to whippets, but activity has increased dramatically during the 1980s; there is now a thriving breed club which encourages both racing and showing. A dual champion title can be awarded to whippets which excel in both areas, as well as a Grand Champion title for dogs with wins beyond that of the average winners. (At least two all-breed BIS's and about 50 CCs are reported to be required.)

Whippets were rare in New Zealand until Mrs. Marilyn Reynolds arrived there from

Britain in 1969. She purchased several dogs from Australia and after many difficulties managed to import two very well-bred Nimrodel dogs from England. One of these became a champion and both produced champions, including Ch. Tynchewick Gueldor Rose—the first whippet ever to win the group at New Zealand´s National Tux show in Wellington. In the late 1970s more Australian blood was added, with the already mentioned Ch. Andiamo Sabreur winning a record number of all-breed bests. The Windswift kennel of Alan and Cheryl Wise imported the fawn-and-white dog Laguna Lussac from Dorrit McKay´s famous line in England and soon made him a champion, with several good wins in group and BIS competition.

Among the many other kennels which have shown champions over the past decade are Highlife, Dash, Pennant and the Woollahras of Mr. and Mrs. P. Kersey (who have also judged whippets in England and Sweden), and most importantly the Noholmes of Mr. and Mrs. Brian Wilson. Based on mostly Australian Martinique breeding—directly or through Allstars and Skyeways champions — and with several lines back to the English-born top sires Statue and Masterminde, they have produced a line of champions which have been successful in both their own country and in Australia.

Scandinavia

Percentage-wise, purebred dogs are more popular in Scandinavia than anywhere else in the world. In spite of the relatively small human population, the number of dogs annually registered by the four national kennel clubs in Denmark, Finland, Norway and Sweden totals over 150,000 per year. Some of the shows are among the biggest in the world; the international winter event in Stockholm can attract as many as 5,000 exhibits, and Finland became one of the wonders of the canine world in the 1980s when several different shows began to receive 4,000, 5,000 or even more entries on a regular basis. Quarantine laws have long kept all or parts of Scandinavia sealed off from the rest of the world, but with the arrival of new regulations in 1994 it is likely that breeders and exhibitors will become even more a part of the European community.

There are records of whippets being shown in Scandinavia as early as 1900, and the breed received a boost in popularity through the support of Queen Maud of Norway, who imported two whippets around 1917. Annual registration figures remained in the two figures until the 1950s, however. Even now only a few hundred whippets are registered per year— about half of these in Sweden. Norway and Finland have smaller breed populations, and Denmark, after a good early start, had almost no whippets until the end of the 1960s. Breed clubs were a long time in coming, but in 1976 the Swedish Whippet Club (Svenska Whippetklubben) was formed and has been followed by similar organizations in the other countries. It holds several well-supported regional shows every year and a national specialty event every summer at the old castle of Skokloster outside Stockholm. Entries there have reached the 300 mark, and a huge sighthound show is held on the same grounds during the same weekend—all of which has helped Skokloster become recognized as a world-class event for whippet people.

The first important whippet kennel in Scandinavia was founded in 1937, when Madeleine Rieber Salvesen started her Brenna line in Norway, based on a dog of Willes breeding, a bitch from England, Ch. Tiptree May, another from Sweden and a third from Denmark. The latter introduced the blue color which remained a common denominator for many of the Brenna dogs up through the 1960s. In 1952 Ch. Brenna´s Blue Pixie won BIS at the international Oslo show, then the largest dog show in Scandinavia, the first such win recorded for a whippet in these parts. After breeding exclusively down from its foundation quartet for the first few decades, Brenna successfully outcrossed to Ch. Spinning Lariot of Allways in 1962. After Mrs. Rieber Salvesen´s death in 1965 the kennel was transferred first to her widower, then to Mrs. Hjørdis Espeland, who had started helping with the dogs as a teenager and still carries on the line. In 1994 it is 57 years since the first Brenna litter was born, resulting in 43 homebred champions—quite possibly making it the longest-running whippet breeding establishment in the world.

Around 1970 the brindle-and-white

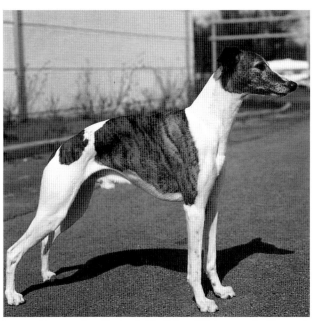

Imported in utero from England, Ch. Bohem Filipin was a double grandson of Nevedith´s foundation sire Ch. Akeferry Jimmy. Like him, Filipin was an exceptional sire, with more than twenty champions in relatively few litters during the 1970s and 1980s, mostly in Scandinavia but some as far apart as South Africa and the United States.

brother and sister pair Int. Chs. Brenna´s Sheik and Shirin (sired by Sweden´s top sire Int. Ch. Laguna Leader) were among the foremost all-breeds winners in Norway, and in 1974 Mrs. Espeland added her own outcross—an imported white-and-brindle puppy from England named Dondelayo Jonty. He was intensely inbred with a dozen lines back to Ch. Samarkand´s Greenbrae Tarragon, soon became an international champion and turned out to be an outstanding sire with nineteen champions to his credit. Jonty opened the door for a whole series of successful Dondelayo exports to Norway, which in turn helped start several new kennels. The top winner was probably the smooth Skokloster winner Ch. Doriel Dondelayo, but the most outstanding long-term results so far have been achieved by Målfrid Baasnes´ Incarvill´s prefix which is responsible for about twenty home-bred champions, including the all Dondelayo-bred Ch. Incarvill´s Brilliant Pearl.

Over the past few years imports have arrived from other countries: from Australia came the previously mentioned Ch. Rothbury Bonecrusher and Ch. Statuesque Personalised, from France a half brother/sister duo bred by the Manoir de la Grenouillière Kennels, Chs. Emotion and Diorissimo. These, together with other imports, older Norwegian-bred dogs and offspring from the frozen semen technique which Norwegian veterinarians pioneered, make up a small but very cosmopolitan whippet population in Norway.

Sweden´s first major kennel was Fleet Foot, started in the 1940s and of short duration. However, both the top kennels of the next two decades began with Fleet Foot stock—usually parti-colored and often sired by the English import Ch. Warrior King of Sagaland, a half brother to the great British sire Ch. Pilot Officer Prune.

One of the homebred Fleet Foot champions, Ginni, served as foundation for the largest whippet breeder Scandinavia has known: the Tundran Kennel of Mrs. Tony Hörberg. In its prime, it raised as many as seven or eight litters per year, at first by inbreeding strongly to the older Swedish lines but by 1956 adding a fawn Marksman son from England, Int. Ch.

Wingedfoot Cream Cracker, and later several other imports. One of the most notable was the fawn-and-white Bellavista Barry daughter Ch. Treetops Jenny Wren, an excellent brood bitch and the only whippet known to have carried this world-famous greyhound prefix.

The last Tundran litter was born in 1969. All told, Mrs. Hörberg bred 22 champions in a little over 50 litters; both figures long stood as records for the breed in Sweden. Several kennels have carried on with Tundran blood, none more successfully so than Walter Åkerström´s High Speeds Kennel in the far north of Sweden. His BIS winner Ch. High Speeds Blue Sheik was one of the top sires of the 1960s. In the 1980s High Speed added new British blood and won BIS with the imported Statue daughter Ch. Dondelayo Delia.

The Per-Mobile Kennels of Tina and Tommy Permo is based mostly on old Tundran lines and is known especially for racing winners, although later imports and additions have also become champions. Straight-track racing with whippets was introduced in Sweden by the Permos in the early 1970s and is now the most popular form of whippet activity there besides showing; over a hundred whippets race each year. There is also round-track racing, but lure coursing is still in its infancy, and field coursing is illegal in Scandinavia.

The other leading old kennel in Sweden, the Bojar Kennels of Mrs. Märta Zetterström, was founded in the 1950s with a Fleet Foot bitch, but its breeding program soon turned towards new British bloodlines. In one of the English dog annuals of 1957, Mrs. Zetterström saw a picture of the young black dog Tinribs Tophat and persuaded his breeder to part with him. "Hatty" became a champion in his new country and was the first of several imports from Mrs. Stancomb's colorful Tinribs line which produced champions for Bojar.

Mrs. Zetterström also used outside stud dogs such as the imported Ch. Robmaywin Starshine of Allways and the superb BIS-winning silver-fawn Ch. Spinning Lariot of Allways, brother and son respectively of the famous Stargazer in England. Bojar's most important stud dog was another Stargazer son, the fawn Int. Ch. Tinribs Trap of Allways, who sired an even dozen champions in Sweden. Mrs. Zetterström also imported the substantial brindle bitch Samarkand's Dragonfly of Test, tightly bred to the best Wingedfoot dogs (and the only brindle from these lines that I have known). She produced eight champions when bred in turn to Trap, to Bellavista Super Flash and to Int. Ch. Laguna Leader. In the 1970s the fawn import Int. Ch. Shalfleet Starbuck (initially imported and shown by Bohem) was acquired and as a sire added to Bojar's record of seventeen home-bred champions from about 25 litters.

Many later kennels have been founded on Bojar dogs. Mary Ansell's Seeberga started with two bitches by Ch. Tinribs Tophat and maintained a line noted as much for its brilliant colors as for insistence on ideal size, later adding newer English blood from Baydale and Waycross as well. Ann-Stin Willman's Zätaäng prefix was started at the same time and along the same lines; both kennels bred numerous

champions and were fairly sizeable operations with at least 50 homebred litters each over the past twenty years.

Of shorter duration in the 1960s were Enebo and Rayo de Sols, both based on Bojar—the latter in combination with Dutch imports of the old Wingedfoot breeding.

In 1961, following an encounter with Ch. Laguna Ligonier in England, I wrote to Mrs. McKay and after some correspondence a puppy arrived in Stockholm in 1961. Laguna Locomite was superbly well bred (by Tarragon's father Ch. Limelight out of Ligonier's sister Leading Lady), but he was not a conventionally "pretty" puppy and—compared with the dogs then existing in Sweden—appeared to have too much of almost everything, particularly size. After a few rough first shows he matured and hit his stride; in retrospect he was probably simply way ahead of his time. At the 1962 Stockholm show Locomite won Best of Breed as a yearling in a then-record entry of 37 whippets under Mrs. Judy de Casembroot of Treetops greyhound fame. Locomite soon became an international champion and the next year his sensational BIS win at the same show under Fred Curnow was one of the highest ever recorded for the breed in Scandinavia.

Locomite had almost no influence as a sire; I had no bitches and he looked too "different" for most breeders at the time. This changed with the next import: Laguna Leader was purchased as a puppy from Mrs. McKay's kennels in 1963 and was far prettier than Locomite, smaller and with attractive brindle-and-white markings, although not as good in front angulation and bone. He won well in group and BIS competition, however, and the breeders loved him—from a wide variety of bitches he sired a record 25 champions all over Scandinavia during the 1960s. Leader was sired by Ligonier out of a brindle litter sister to Ch. Laguna Lucky Lad in the U.S., making him closely related both to the Mardormere dogs and to the later Barn Dance/Whirlaway offspring in America.

With no facilities for breeding puppies, it seemed best to import stud dogs for more active breeders to use. A visit to Mr. and Mrs. Philip Fell´s Badgewood Kennel—originally from the U.S. but at that time located in England—resulted in the acquisition of the mostly white Int. Ch. Badgewood Mark Twain. He was by Locomite´s and Tarragon´s sire Laguna Limelight out of a Ligonier daughter, with Meander blood on the bottom side of his pedigree, and had won well in England, including the puppy class at Crufts. "Freddie" was rather short-coupled but extremely stylish, with one of the best heads ever and perfect ears. He was co-owned with Seeberga, did some very nice winning and sired quite a few champions.

Always having admired the sterling soundness and basic correctness of the Shalfleet whippets in England I also purchased a fawn puppy from an outcross litter when Ch. Shalfleet Starstruck had been bred to Ch. Laguna Leisure. The latter later sired Ch. Alpine Ski Bum in the U.S. and was the grandsire of Ch. Plumcreek Walk On Water, but neither of them looked anything like Starbuck—a small solid fawn who favored his dam´s

side almost completely and later, when owned by Mrs. Zetterström, sired several champions.

The most important import arrived in 1971. Throughout most of his career in England, I had admired Ch. Fleeting Flamboyant and never missed an opportunity to impress on his owner and breeder Mrs. Molly Garrish what an asset such a dog would be to Scandinavia. With a show record of eleven CCs, two Hound Groups at championship level and the status as top CC winning whippet of 1967, it did not seem realistic to hope that Flamboyant would ever leave England. However, in spite of being quite well-bred—by Ch. Tantivvey Diver, then long since emigrated to the U.S,. out of a bitch of Peppard and old Fleeting lines—Flamboyant was hardly used at stud in England and Mrs. Garrish finally agreed to let him go. (With great generosity she would not even accept payment for him; as she said, it would be impossible to pay what he was really worth anyway.) It was perhaps some compensation that shortly before he left England, Flamboyant sired a litter for Mrs. Garrish which included the brindle Ch. Fleeting Fulmar and his parti-colored litter-brother Fleeting Flamingo (who later came to Sweden also and became an international champion there in the ownership of Magnus Hagstedt).

Flamboyant was more than six years old when he arrived in Sweden, but he remained undefeated in the breed that year and was one of the top dogs of all breeds in Sweden for 1971. He was quite similar to his sire Diver, with the same spectacular "chocolate tortoiseshell" kind of brindle-and-white color. He sired both more good ones and more bad ones than Leader, but the good ones were very good and they in their turn, when closely linebred through their sire, managed to produce even better puppies. Robert M. James summed it up in Our Dogs by stating that Flamboyant "to a certain degree revolutionised the breed in Sweden." Credit for this should go to the breeders who used him so wisely and well.

The breeding program, if it can be called that, at Bohem was limited to little more than a dozen litters in as many years. By Flamboyant out of a Leader daughter came the colorful and quite large Ch. Bohem Flamous, still behind many Scandinavian whippets through the few litters he sired before leaving for Mexico, and by Flamboyant out of a sister to Laguna Leisure came Int. Ch. Bohem Lekain, one of the most popular and successful sires of his era. Lekain´s owner Ingela Kyrklund also bred his daughter Ch. Colt´s Alouette, one of the most admired winners in many years, described by Anne Knight as the best whippet bitch she ever judged.

In a 1974 litter by Mark Twain out of the pretty little imported bitch Cockrow Starmist (daughter of the Crufts winner Ch. Towercrest Flarepath Taurus and Ch. Cockrow Pheasant) came Int. Ch. Bohem Mome Rath, a classic beauty but rather wasted as a sire, as well as the all-white Int. Ch. Bohem Cheshire Cat, one of the foundation bitches for Siv Ögren´s successful Bokella´s Kennel. A third puppy, Bohem Tiny Alice, became a top producer as foundation bitch for Margareta Mårtensson´s Equus Kennel.

A year later, the brightly colored little bitch Baydale Bronze Bracelet was imported from England in whelp to the ill-starred Ch. Nutcracker of Nevedith (who died in Italy not long afterwards). Both parents were by Ch. Akeferry Jimmy, and in this litter came the dark red brindle-and-white Int. Ch. Bohem Filipin, a tall and substantial, extremely sound dog who was an extremely dominant and successful sire, with at least twenty champions to his credit— some as far apart as the U.S. and South Africa.

Most Swedish breeders of the 1970s based their breeding on some or all of these dogs. The Memoar Kennel of Mayvor Olsson started with a Mark Twain daughter from Seeberga; her daughter in turn was bred to Flamous and then produced the great little stud dog Ch. Memoars Elit, who may well have exceeded his great-grandsire Leader´s record of champions.

Catharina Östring´s Gårdsjöns Kennel is probably the most consistent of all, responsible for a long line of homebred champions of the same attractive type. She started with a Memoar bitch by Leader, which first produced the wonderful parti-colored Int. Ch. Gårdsjöns Aslög by Flamboyant, then the brindle Int. Ch. Gårdsjöns Beathe-Christine by Flamous. These bitches bred to Ch. Memoars Elit produced extremely well, and the next generation when bred to Lekain, Filipin or their progeny also had great success. For several generations Catharina Östring bred entirely from homebred stock with excellent results; the well-matched brindle-and-white Gårdsjöns teams were for many years almost undefeated in the Breeders Group competitions which are such an important feature at

Scandinavian shows. (The teams have to consist of four homebred exhibits and should be as well matched for both type and quality as possible.) In the 1990s several outcrosses to English, Australian and even American blood have been added with great success.

Top whippet in Sweden 1984, Ch. Bokella's Marilyn Monroe (Ch. Bokella's Spectrum - Ch. Bokella's San Black Coat) was Best in Show at the Skokloster specialty in 1983. She was owned by Magnus Hagstedt and produced several Signum champions in Sweden and Denmark.

Elit's most important son was the pale brindle-and-white Ch. Amiant (out of a High Speeds/Dondelayo-bred bitch), who sired one of the most classic winners ever seen in Sweden— the exquisite Ch. Accent's Akela. She was Top Whippet of the year three times, won the national specialty twice and notched up a record number of wins, with BIS at the Skokloster Sighthound show in 1983 under Mexican judge Robin Hernandez as her crowning achievement. Her dam goes back to Shalfleet, Laguna and the old Bojar dogs.

Other imports of different bloodlines include several from the Harque Kennel in England—all successful in the ring but too little used at stud. One daughter of Harque To Beaumont had lasting influence, however, as the foundation for Kerstin Rönne's Freeline kennel.

Several Oakbark, Glenbervie and Falconcrag-bred imports also produced champions. The full brothers Ch. Waycross Star Performer and Int. Ch. Waycross Wayward Star (by Shalfleet Spanish Hawk) both sired champions, while the solid brindle Ch. Houghtonhill Orbit (sired by Ch. Novacroft Madrigal out of Ch. Crysbel Skylight of Nevedith) became a Skokloster winner and one of the top sires of the 1980s.

Imports from a number of different British lines founded Anita and Leif Wounder's highly successful Blue Crazy kennel in the northern part of Sweden: Int. Ch. Puddledock Starry (by Eng. Ch. Flarepath Astrinomical) when bred to Ch. Crawshaw Poem (by Cockrow Partridge of Crawshaw) produced the lovely parti-colored Int. Ch. Blue Crazy Pia, and she in her turn was bred to the fawn import Int. Ch. Cornwater Comet (litter brother to the great winner in England, Ch. Jubilant Lady of Tygreen and Lowerdon). The Blue Crazy whippets have not been active in recent years, but the Wounders' son and daughter-in-law have continued the tradition along different lines; their Ch. Memoars Cineraria is the most successful of the "frozen semen" litter born by the English-born Am. Ch. Hardknott Maestro of Bohem out of a Swedish bitch in Norway in the late 1980s.

It is impossible to catalog all the imports which have arrived in Sweden over the past decade. After years of linebreeding mainly to the same Anglo-Scandinavian lines, the trend has changed decisively towards imports from other countries. One reason was no doubt the tremendous success achieved by Magnus Hagstedt when he brought in a French dog of part American breeding from France, Int. Ch. So Proudly We Sail du Sac à Malices. A small dog with tremendous charisma and great movement, "Kiwi" caught the imagination of the Scandinavian judges and in 1987 was one of the top show dogs in Sweden, with numerous Group and BIS wins—including runner-up to BIS at the big Stockholm show.

Kiwi helped open the door for other imports from France and also sired several top winners. One of his best litters were bred by Nenne Runsten Fodstad, who turned her attention to whippets in the mid-1980s after great success in Scottish deerhounds and terriers. Blazing new trails at the time, she decided to import a whippet from the United States, and after spending several months in English quarantine, Bohem Callas of Whippoorwill arrived in Scandinavia in 1987. She later became the first American whippet champion in Scandinavia and won back-to-back Best in Show at Skokloster under judges Max Magder and Hans Lehtinen. Bred to Kiwi, "Maria" produced champions in Norway, Finland and Sweden; Ch. Airescot Waistcoat was top whippet in Sweden for two years and is the result of a mostly American pedigree the likes of which are seldom seen in the United States, combin-

ing Whippoorwill and Plumcreek with some English Dondelayo breeding.

Pedigree 42. Ch. AIRESCOT WAISTCOAT, particolor dog, born 1989

```
                                    Denhill's Implacable, imp. UK
                    Pub Crawler du Sac à Malices
                                    Dondelayo Chorale, imp.UK
Sire: Ch. So Proudly We Sail du Sac à Malices, imp. France
                                    Ch. Plumcreek Chimney Swift (ped. 35)
                    Wilpat French Connection, imp. USA
                                    Ch. Wilpat Strawberi of Rosewood, by Ch. Appraxin
                                    Raspberry

                                    Ch. Greenbrae Barn Dance, imp. UK (ped. 34)
                    Ch. Proud Fox o Whippoorwill
                                    Jessica of Whippoorwill, by Ch. Highlight's Eidolon
Dam: Ch. Bohem Callas of Whippoorwill, imp. USA
                                    Ch. Hardknott Maestro of Bohem, imp. UK, (ped. 45)
                    Ch. Whippoorwill Bohem Aria
                                    Ch. Whippoorwill Precious Gem (ped. 36)
```

Waistcoat's litter sister was then bred to the Australian visitor Ch. Statuesque Personalised, a combination which resulted in the young cream fawn bitch Ch. Airescot Teenager, Sweden's top winner of 1993 and the latest in a line of some half dozen Skokloster winners for this kennel. There have been other champions: Kiwi's French-born grandson Int. Ch. Bas les Pattes du Sac à Malices, the Dondelayo-bred Ch. Moscow's Anastasia, and even puppies born from frozen insemination by America's top winner Ch. Sporting Fields Kinsman.

There have been other American influences in Sweden—Ch. Hi Tor's Baryshnikov and Ch. Rippleton Whitney Bay spring to mind —but at least one of the most successful and popular dogs of the early 1990s represents British blood. Ch. Play A While at Peperone is a strikingly handsome fawn-and-white of a type which would appeal to

Ch. Play A While at Peperone (Ch. Hardknott Quadrille - Mithrandir Gazelle) was top whippet in Sweden for 1989 and has become an influential sire in Scandinavia in the early 1990s. Imported from Jessie McLeod's kennels in Scotland, "Kim" is owned by Henrik Härling.

American breed specialists as much as to British, and he does of course descend from bloodlines which are popular the world over.

Pedigree 43. Ch. PLAY A WHILE AT PEPERONE, imp. UK, fawn & white dog, born 1987

Sire: Ch. Hardknott Quadrille
- Ch. Gainscliffe Renown
  - Ch. Oakbark Mr Magic at Silkstone, by Ch. Oakbark Armfield Joker
  - Solera Summer Rose, by Ch. Lowglen Newbold Cavalier (ped. 17)
- Hardknott Marietta
  - Ch. Novacroft Madrigal, by Ch. Charmoll McTavish
  - Ch. Belinda of Hardknott, by Cockridge Partridge of Crawshaw (ped. 21)

Dam: Mithrandir Gazelle
- Hardknott Neptune of Mithrandir
  - Ch. Oakbark Middleman, by Ch. Charmoll McTavish (ped 23)
  - Ch. Belinda of Hardknott (above)
- Peppermint of Peperone
  - Benroy Rikitik, by Troutburn Silver Sabre
  - Kienford Apache Girl, by Denorsi Imp

Whippets in Finland were long dominated by a series of solid fawn imports of Allways and Wingedfoot breeding. One of the most outstanding winners from these lines was the bitch Ch. Kiitäjä Astarte, who won BIS in Helsinki in the late 1950s. Later came the beautiful fawn Tarragon son Int. Ch. Bocachica Arapahoe and several black, blue and brindle winners from the Boughton Kennels.

The top breeder in Finland through the 1970s, Mrs. Hannele Takkinen of the Flaming Hill prefix, bred her first champions while still a schoolgirl in the mid-1960s. They were by the excellent mover Ch. Boughton Buy British out of a Finnish bitch from the older Streamline kennel. The next generation was bred to another Boughton dog and resulted in the dam of Finland's top whippets for 1976 and 1977—the glamorous parti-colored sisters Chs. Flaming Hill Taijka and Tekiitta. These two were sired by the Swedish stud dog Int. Ch. Bohem Lekain, and Mrs. Takkinen next purchased a Swedish puppy of similar bloodlines: Int. Ch. Colt's Better Be Good who was top whippet in Finland for three years in a row and won BIS at the Helsinki international show in 1979 over 2,000 dogs. Her pedigree sums up the breeding of many of the Scandinavian top winners at the time.

Better Be Good has the same dam as Ch. Colt's Alouette—bred to two different dogs Ch. Gårdsjöns Carolina therefore produced two of the all-time top winners in Scandinavia.

Tekiitta, when bred to Ch. Memoars Elit, produced one of the brightest stars of all breeds in Finland for 1980, Ch. Jakias Adimir, and two Jakias dogs were also behind the top kennel of later years, Woodbrook.

Pedigree 44. Ch. COLT'S BETTER BE GOOD, dark brindle-&-white bitch, born 1977

```
                              Eng.  Ch. Akeferry Jimmy (ped 21)
              Eng.  Ch. Nutcracker of Nevedith (white-fawn)
                              White Bud of Glenbervie, by Am. Ch. Cockrow Woodchuck
Sire: Int. Ch. Bohem Filipin (red white)
                              Eng.  Ch. Akeferry Jimmy (ped 21)
              Baydale Bronze Bracelet (red white)
                              Kilmarie of Baydale, by Ch. Baydale Cinnamon

                              Ch.  Bohem Flamous, by Int.  Ch. Fleeting Flamboyant
              Ch.  Memoars Elit (white-brindle)
                              Memoars Belizza, out of Int.  Ch. Badgewood Mark Twain
                              daughter
Dam: Ch. Gårdsjöns Carolina (white-brindle)
                              Int. Eng.  Ch. Fleeting Flamboyant, imp UK
              Int. Ch. Gårdsjöns Aslög (white)
                              Ch.  Memoars Astarte, by Int. Ch. Laguna Leader
```

In the mid-1980s whippets, like most other breeds, were affected by the tremendous upsurge in interest which made Finnish dog shows among the biggest in the world, and as usual when a population explosion occurs it was difficult for the quality to remain stable. Obviously aware of the problems, the Finnish breeders embarked on an import program which has been quite amazing, incorporating not just the best from the neighboring countries but also several glamorous Peperone champions from Scotland with the Hardknott background already popular in Finland. They also, most amazingly, have a whole series of American dogs.

By far the most successful, in fact among the top winners of all breeds in the first part of the 1990s, is a red fawn-and-white bitch of exceptional quality. Bred by Virginia Huffman in the United States, Ch. Autumn Terra Bella I'm Redee has been one of the top two or three dogs of all breeds in Finland for both 1992 and 1993, shown to a long series of group and Best in Show wins by her owner Unto Timonen.

Pedigree 45. Ch. AUTUMN TERRA BELLA I'M REDEE, imp. USA, red & white bitch, born 1990

```
                              Whippoorwill Moonstone (ped. 36)
Sire: Ch. Chelsea Drakkar of Oxford
                              Ch. Whippletree's Raisin Cain, by Ch. Fenwick of
                              Whippoorwill
              Ch. Chelsea Saffron
                              Ch. Spectre White Hot, by Ch. Runner's Notorious of Aryal

                              Ch. Novacroft Madrigal, by Ch. Charmoll McTavish (ped. 23)
              Ch. Hardknott Maestro of Bohem, imp. UK
                              Ch. Belinda of Hardknott (ped. 21)
Dam: Ch. Whippoorwill Fanfare

                              Ch. Whippoorwill Precious Gem (ped. 36)
```

Redee is by no means the only American winner in Finland. Her predecessor and half sister Ch. Autumn Terra Bella Cedar (by Ch. Chelsea Mesmorize) is a top winner and producer in her own right, and her litter brother Ch. Autumn Terra Bella Red Wine during a brief visit in Finland sired several litters and was BOS to his sister at the Finnish Whippet Club specialty under American greyhound specialist Pat Ide. Different bloodlines are represented by the Amber Waves daughter Am. Ch. Showtimes Classic Autumn and by several Sporting Fields and Seaspell winners—the most successful of whom has been the Kinsman daughter Ch. Seaspell's Blue Mesa.

Finland is one of the few countries where a working championship is available for whippets. After a certain number of racing wins the dog is officially recorded as a Working Champion. Not many have achieved this title, but the Boughton-based Black Pearl Kennel and the Dondelayo-bred Sopisco whippets have done very well both on bench and race track.

Denmark has old traditions in whippets, but since some of the first stock around the turn of the century were officially registered as "Italian Greyhounds" it may be as well that they left no modern descendants. In the 1950s the Midtfyn Kennel was going strong with mainly Wingedfoot blood, exporting breeding stock to Norway, Sweden and even the U.S., where a Danish bitch provided the foundation for Jacqueline Kubat's successful Dragonfly Kennel.

By the mid-1960s virtually no whippets were bred in Denmark and the few seen at shows were imported from Sweden. In the early 1970s several English dogs from Dondelayo and Crawshaw had great success for a few years, and Birgit Wamberg started her prolific Fairway Kennel which has imported stock from England, France, Holland and Sweden. Her greatest success has been with the brother and sister Chs Topall Snowy Owl and Linnet—very well bred by English Ch. Topall Newbold Miguel out of a Beseeka

Finland has hosted some of the biggest dog shows in the world since the late 1980s and Ch. Autumn Terra Bella I´m Redee (Ch. Chelsea Drakkar of Oxford - Ch. Whippoorwill Fanfare) has been a contender for the top spot of all breeds with numerous Best in Show wins in 1992, 1993 and 1994. She is an American import, owned and shown in Finland by Unto Timonen.

Knight Errant daughter. Birgit Wamberg has also become the leading international Danish judge for the breed, officiating at Skokloster as well as in England.

Of the new kennels which started in the 1980s, the most successful has been Vibeke Vamberg (no relation to the above) and her Vibes dogs. Her first big winner was bred by Magnus Hagstedt in Sweden, Ch. Signum Bournonville, and later the white English import Ch. Oakbark Snow Queen was one of Denmark's top winners of all breeds in late 1980s. Several other breeders have imported dogs from both England as well as other countries, and although entries are still low compared to the other Scandinavian countries, they have increased greatly.

Continental Europe

Whippet activities on the European continent are difficult to summarize. In spite of close geographical proximity, similar basic rules and no quarantine restrictions, the scene differs considerably from country to country.

All dog activities on the continent are governed by the Fédération Cynologique Internationale (FCI), a Belgium-based organization to which some fifty kennel clubs in Europe, Scandinavia, Mexico, South America, Australia and Japan, belong. At FCI shows judging is more complicated and time-consuming than the simple "one-two-three-four" procedure in the English-speaking countries. Each exhibit is given a detailed written critique and a "grade" which can vary from Excellent to Very Good, Good, Fair, and Insufficient. The best are then placed in order of merit, and the best of the non-champions in each sex may be awarded a national certificate. Champions usually compete in a class of their own and are only eligible for Best of Breed and—at international shows—the CACIB (Certificat d´Aptitude au Championnat International). No dog under fifteen months old can be awarded the CACIB (not even if it should win Best of Breed). Four CACIBs over a period of at least one year, won in three different countries under three different judges, are normally required for the official FCI title of International Champion, but there are some minor differences and additions to this rule depending on breed and country. The FCI also organizes a World Dog Show in a different country every year—usually in Europe but held in Mexico once in the 1970s and again in 1984, in Japan in 1982, in Peru in the late 1980s and in Argentina in 1993. Entries vary but can approach 10,000 dogs when the show is held in central Europe.

In many parts of Europe the emphasis was long more on producing ideal size according to the FCI standard than anything else. The FCI officially accepts the British whippet standard, but the size paragraph has frequently been

Ch. Statuesque Personalised was born in Australia but achieved spectacular wins during an extended visit in Scandinavia. Sired by Eng. & Aust. Ch. Cottonmere Personality of Oakbark out of a Ch. Dondelayo Statue granddaughter, "Person" won Best in Show at Skokloster in 1990, handled by Petter Fodstad. Behind them are three whippet specialist judges: from left, Lorraine Groshans (Loral) and Isabell Stoffers (Runner´s) from the U.S., and Dennis Meakin (Oakbark) from England.

adjusted to suit local requirements. The maintenance of racing ability has been strongly encouraged. For many years the international union of sighthound clubs in Europe, the UICL, awarded a special certificate for beauty and performance to any dog which met certain exacting requirements for excellence both in the show ring and on the race track. Since this award was first introduced in 1960 and up to the end of the 1970s less than a hundred sighthounds had been awarded it, 24 of them whippets—mostly from West Germany but others from Holland and even one import from America. UICL was officially disbanded in the early 1990s.

Whippets enjoy greater popularity in France than anywhere else in continental Europe. The poet and statesman Lamartine—candidate for the presidency in the mid-1800s, defeated by Napoleon III—is said to have been one of the earliest fanciers. The French whippet club was formed in the late 1940s, has several hundred members and can attract over 200 exhibits to its annual show. Registrations have increased so much that in the 1980s approximately 1,000 whippets were registered per year, but most of these remain pets only.

The title of French champion is extremely difficult to obtain, as at least one of the three certificates required must be won at one of four annual international shows designated by the whippet club, which also selects the judges. Certificates won at the breed club's own show count towards the title only if more than fifty exhibits are entered. Furthermore, a new champion may have its title revoked unless the dog also qualifies on the race track within two years after the show win!

Racing is quite popular in France. The whippets are divided into "small size" 43-48.5 cm. (roughly 17-19 in.) for dogs, 40.5-46 cm. (16-18 in.) for bitches, and "large size" 48.5-51 cm. (19-20 in.) for dogs, 46-48.5 cm. (18-19 in.) for bitches. For the top honors of a maximum 100 points only 40 can be awarded for speed; 60 are for "comport" (deportment).

In spite of the stringent rules on size, English and later American imports have made big inroads into French whippet breeding. Peggy Stancomb brought some English whippets with her to live in France during the 1960s and 1970s, and her Tinribs dogs are still behind some French-bred winners. One of the most popular stud dogs of the 1970s, the blue Int. Ch. Illion de Pic-Ardent, was sired by the imported Laguna Loganberry, and Martinsell blood has also produced well. Mme. Comtesse de Saint-Seine, whose Grillemont Kennel is one of the oldest in Europe for greyhounds, has also imported whippets—notably the top racing and show bitch Int. Ch. Laguna Leonora and the tricolor male Int. Ch. Sunsalve Heatwave of Hutaka. The Fulminante and Alleles kennels were founded on old British blood via Dutch imports; the Dillwyn kennel of Mme. Mather combined English lines from Nimrodel and Silkstone, while M. Cappi used mostly imported blood in his kennel Enfants de la Tramontane—notably the English CC winner and Jimmy son Int. Ch. Neon of Nevedith.

In the 1980s French breeders became increasingly cosmopolitan. American expatriate

Karen Mesavage of the Sac à Malices ("bag of tricks") Kennels broke new ground; she started with a French bitch, had great success with Silkstone imports from England and in 1981 won the breed from an entry of 93 whippets at the FCI World Show in Germany with her American bitch Int. Am. Ch. Itsme Autumn's Copper Glow. Mme. Mesavage also imported a daughter of the top American sire Ch. Plumcreek Chimney Swift, incorporated some Gold Dust blood from Twenty Four Karat and has combined her Anglo-American-Continental lines with great success. In the 1990s she imported the well-bred brindle dog Am. Ch. Paris Panther from Sharon Sakson; he has won at many of the top shows, and with his obvious quality and breeding (his sire is a litter brother to Ch. Sporting Fields Kinsman) is proving a valuable stud dog. It's been a two-way street: one of Mme. Mesavage's French-born bitches when exported to the U.S. became the dam of Am. Ch. Itsme Pardon My French, and more recently Ch. Beautiful Dreamer du Sac à Malices has sired several champions in the United States. The success of homebred Sac à Malices dogs in other countries, especially Scandinavia, has also been striking.

Only a few years later, another equally international and successful French kennel emerged—Jackie Bourdin and her Manoir de la Grenouillère (approximately, "frog-pond") dogs. Her first important stud dog was an English son of Ch. Newbold Muffinman, Int. Ch. Sandlena Astronomer, and the most important brood bitch was Hillsdown Mollie—closely related to the English top winners Nutshell and Dutch Gold. Mme. Bourdin also imported an American dog,

Ch. Normandy Social Standing (sired by "Oscar" and strongly line-bred on Ch. Saxon Shore Amber Waves), and different configurations of these and other breeding stock have resulted in a seemingly endless string of champions in most of the central European countries and Scandinavia.

During the 1980s, France emerged as a leading producer of top winning whippets. Ch. Emotion du Manoir de la Grenouillère was a winner in her native France, Spain and Belgium before being exported to Norway, where she was top whippet in 1992 and 1993. Sired by Ch. Beau Mec du Manoir de la Grenouillère out of an English bitch, Hillsdown Mollie, Emotion is owned by Espen Engh and Åge Gjetnes.

Pedigree 46. Ch. EMOTION DU MANOIR DE LA GRENOUILLERE, brindle & white bitch, born 1989

                    Ch. Newbold Muffinman
           Ch. Sandlena Astronomer, imp. UK
                    Oakbark Merry Maid
Sire: Ch. Beau Mec du Manoir de la Grenouillère
                    Ch. Almaglo Foreman
           Ch. Adorable Chipie du Manoir de la Grenouillère
                    Ch. Promesse des Chataigniers d´Argent

                    Ch. Oakbark Middleman (ped. 23)
Dam: Hillsdown Mollie, imp. UK
                    Siobhan of Hillsdown (ped. 24)

In Belgium, one of the first major victories for the breed came through a British-born Laguna dog which won Best in Show at the Brussels show in the mid-1950s. The English-oriented "du Panisel" kennel of Jean Cartier won numerous championships with imported champions such as Glenbervie Steelsword, Garnstones Marna and their offspring. In Austria the St. Barbara kennels of Mrs. Leonie Uibeleisen was founded in the 1950s with the fawn Int. Ch. Dreamland of Test but carries on today with newer English blood from Newbold and Courthill. Switzerland seems to have a high concentration of old-established breeders: Gertrud Brunner´s Whirlwind Kennel was started in the 1940s; the Lac des Cygnes (Swan Lake) Kennel of Mrs. Helmy Ranft was founded in 1950 and is now carried on by her daughter and son-in-law. One of the most admired of Mrs. Ranft's champions was the stunning white Int. Ch. Shalfleet Pollyanna from England, but Mrs. Ranft also used Laguna blood with great success. Lea Gut's Lightstep Kennel was of short duration but her gorgeous pair of imports Int. Chs. Laguna Lancelot and Laguna Lady Lightfoot had much success in the 1960s (and were full siblings to Leader and Locomite in Sweden). Miss Gut also started off Mrs. Eva Holz whose Fleetwing Kennel included imports from Laguna, Courthill and Dondelayo.

The largest and most important kennel in Switzerland, perhaps in central Europe, was long owned by Miss M. Wettstein (now Mrs. Haueter). She started with English imports from Molember, Vahlay and Boughton around 1960, all with Marksman background, and produced numerous champions—first under the Tierlipark, then the "of Liberty" suffix.

Whippets were first registered in Germany as early as 1903, when a bitch named Fidel, born in 1899, found entry into the German sighthound stud book. In those early days it was not uncommon for oversized Italian Greyhounds to be shown and bred as "whippets" in Germany. Quite a number of English whippets were imported before World War I, most going

A stream of imports began to flow into Scandinavia from "new" areas in the 1980s — central Europe, Australia and the United States. The French dogs have been particularly successful: Ch. So Proudly We Hail du Sac à Malices was one of Sweden´s top dogs in 1987, shown by Magnus Hagstedt.

back to Ch. Manorley Maori. Gradually the type changed, but the German standard diverged from the English one until the 1960s, when the FCI standard, an exact translation of the English one, came into to be used.

For many years German whippets remained isolated from the rest of the world. Int. Ch. Martyn of Allways (a litter brother to the famous Marksman in England) not only finished his international title but also won the federal track racing championship twice and although largely overlooked as a sire is responsible for one of the top show and racing whippets ever in Germany, his white-trimmed fawn daughter Ch. Fatme v. Schlesierland. One of the few other English imports, Atom´s Flash of Allways (by Ch. Fieldspring Bartsia of Allways) was influential mostly through his son Olaf v.d. Cloppenburg, who is behind numerous later race winners.

One of the few internationally known German whippet kennels of the early years was Baroness von Watzdorf´s Burgfried; older American fanciers remember Lars vom Burgfried who is behind many Kirklea and Hound Hill champions. The Baroness was the only German breeder ever to have awarded Challenge Certificates in the breed in England. Her kennel dominated the rings from the 1930s until well into the 1950s.

During the 1960s and 1970s the leading breeders were respectively Mrs. Lilo Consbruch´s Kollau and Mrs. Kleineberg´s Kleinen Berg, both based on old German, English and Dutch breeding, with an added dash of North American blood via Samoem dogs in recent

years for the latter. The Black Magic whippets of Mr. and Mrs. Senkbeil are based on pure dual purpose dogs of German breeding.

New lines were introduced by Marianne Kiack-Knöfel´s Superfly whippets; the almost white English dog Int. Ch. Bredand Percy Vere (Ch Gunsmith of Glenbervie - Hillgarth Sunkist), owned by Mr. and Mrs. Kiack, was one of the most significant winners in the early 1980s. Thomas Münch made his mark with the FlicFlac prefix a few years later; his mostly English-bred, Swiss-born bitch Ch. Fleetwing Opening Night was bred to a Samoem dog and produced the first multiple titled home-bred champions for the kennel. Mr. Münch has brought in several winning English dogs, of which Int. Ch. Hammonds Simple Simon must be considered as one of the most successful British whippets ever in Germany. He is sired by Ch. Hammond´s Sebastian out of a Hillsdown Fergal daughter.

Whippets are not a popular breed in Germany; less than 200 are usually registered each year—only a few dozen more than in neighboring Switzerland, which has less than one-tenth of Germany´s population! The German sighthound club has long campaigned for a strict size limit: dogs over 20 in. and bitches over 18.75 in. are not approved for breeding and racing remains extremely popular, sometimes to the extent that a different, pure racing type has been created. The newly formed Whippet Club Deutschland has generated much enthusiasm and is endeavoring to bring over primarily British breeder judges for its specialty shows.

In spite of a small population, Holland has some of the biggest and best dog shows in Europe; the autumn "Winner Show" in Amsterdam often attracts around 4,000 exhibits. Whippets are known to have been shown and raced as early as in the 1890s; Freeman Lloyd writes that the entries then consisted of half a dozen English dogs which had crossed the Channel with their owners for the show. (This was before the days of quarantine.) The Dutch liked the whippets so much that they bought them all and Holland has remained a stronghold for the breed ever since. The Dutch whippet club, for many years in the experienced hands of Mrs. Hugenholtz-van de Velde, holds an annual show which often attracts well over a hundred exhibits, and blood from the early Dutch kennels of Kafiristan, Nimblefooted and Getrouwen has been spread across Europe, to Scandinavia, England and even the U.S.

These kennels were all based on a number of imported Wingedfoot dogs from England, including at least three champions by Marksman and of course the famous Hildegarde. They provided the foundation for one of the most successful whippet breeding establishments anywhere in the world: the Samoem Kennel of Tim Teillers. The bloodlines from the 1950s were maintained intact into the 1980s, with the addition only of some closely related Shalfleet imports in later years, and with almost monotonous regularity the home-bred Samoem dogs have managed to stay on top wherever shown in Europe.

In type, bone and general soundness the Samoem dogs excel as much as the old Marksman stock did, and Tim Teillers seems to have added a few qualities of his own—notably a little more of the desired length of loin. Almost all his early dogs were fawn, with an occasional parti-color, but it was left to the brindle Ch. Samoems Silent Knight, in the ownership of the Shalfleet kennels, to make history by becoming the first imported English whippet champion. In the mid-1980s Samoem in a rather drastic turnaround added new blood by importing an American brood bitch, Plumcreek Morshor´s Jasmine, and also took over the much titled Canadian dog Eng. Am. Can. Ch. Lorricbrook Runaway at Shalfleet when Barbara Wilton-Clark closed down her kennels in England. The Samoem dogs added refinement and brighter colors but the winning has continued unabated.

Several other Dutch kennels bred along the same lines—e.g. Sylvan Dwelling and Longrove, the latter owned by expatriate Australian R.G. Fisher. In the late 1970s Frank Sampers imported dogs of different bloodlines; his mostly white Int. Ch. Statesman of Silkstone and parti-colored Int. Ch. Dondelayo Paint Tin both won well. Several other successful kennels emerged in the 1980s, notably Gullyridge and Herlaers Town.

Spain appears to be almost devoid of whippets, while in Portugal the internationally renowned all-rounder judge and sighthound specialist Carla Molinari developed an active whippet interest in the 1980s, showing dogs of French and Canadian breeding with great success. Italy has had some of the best whippets in the world for a long time. Since the 1960s many of the best British champions have been picked up by Italian exhibitors; the great Statue's dam Ch. Denhill's Delectabelle was exported by Mrs. Knight to Baron and Baroness Renai della Rena after winning her title at Crufts, and following her a whole series of the best British dogs emigrated south. Piero Renai della Rena is one of Italy's foremost Sighthound judges and with his American-born wife maintains the small but successful "di Farneto" kennel. Mauro Carpone's Almaglo kennel has housed such stars as English Champions Novacroft Starbright, Glenbervie White Frost, Savilepark Sweet Harmony and many others, including the American bitch Int. Ch. Gold Dust's Petite d'Or. With this background the home-bred Almaglos have won well all over central Europe. Among the newer Italian breeders the best known is Gaetano Turrini's Rivarco kennel, which owns the English stud dog Ch. Toffee Paper of Nevedith (by Eng. Am. Can. Ch. Nevedith Paper Weight).

As the borders to former communist countries opened, some breeders have established contact with whippet fanciers in the east. The long isolation from the rest of the world has caused an obvious discrepancy in type, but it is clear that whippets attract fans all across eastern Europe, and western judges in Russia have been seen sizeable entries of whippets. One whippet breeder in Poland wrote enthusiastically that photos of a current American Best in Show winner were the most beautiful he had ever seen, so obviously the modern western whippet can appeal even to an untrained eye.

The Dutch Samoems Kennel has experienced worldwide success since the early 1960s. In recent years outcross blood has been added: the Canadian dog Ch. Lorricbrook Runaway at Shalfleet came to Holland via England and is the only whippet with champion titles in England, USA, Canada and Europe. Owner Tim Teillers handles.

Latin America

Whippets are not among the most popular breeds in Central and South America, but the relatively small population is of a high international quality. Mexico appears to have no really active breeder since Christina Adenfors-Rodriguez disappeared from the show scene. Together with a renowned international judge and sighthound specialist, the late Robin Hernandez, she imported Ch. Bohem Flamous and

Ch. Seeberga Öroica from her native Sweden and produced a series of attractive champions from them. One of the few consistent exhibitors since then, Dr. Francisco Chapa, started with some of the Swedish-bred dogs but later imported dogs of American breeding. The few whippets seen at Mexican shows today are usually imports or are owned by exhibitors visiting from north of the border, however.

Most of the imports in South America come from the U.S. or Canada. Jacqueline Q. Kubat moved her successful Dragonfly kennel—based on British Wingedfoot and Anglo-American Pennyworth lines—from the U.S. to Argentina in the early 1970s and has provided foundation stock for many other breeders across the continent: one of her later additions from the USA is Ch. Moorland's Gainsborough of Dragonfly, sire of such winners as the multi-BIS Ch. Malro's Nouvelle Vague in Brazil.

Whippets were introduced to Brazil around 1945. For the first twenty-five years Mrs. Maria Lucia Kernke, of the Pirajense kennel near Campinas (São Paulo), was the driving force. Her foundation was the brother-and-sister pair Chs. Silver Dollar and Golden Guinea do Camandocaia Pirajense, of which the latter—in 1964 when eight years old—won BIS at the first Festival of Dogs show, one of the most prestigious canine events in South America. The American judge Mr. Louis Murr compared her to "the great Fleetfoot" himself! Mrs. Kernke's imports, Ch. Meander Traveller and Ch. Meander Passenger from the U.S., as well as Ch. Dragonfly's D'Argental from Argentina, all sired champions.

Of the current Brazilian fanciers the most important is José Mauricio Machline, whose large Roberjos establishment outside São Paulo has housed more American champions of different breeds than most kennels north of the border. In whippets, the background is thoroughly international; some Dragonfly champions from Argentina, the BIS winning Int. Am. Ch. Oldland's First Frost, born in the U.S. from an Anglo-African sire, and his son Int. Can. Ch. Lorricbrook Barnstormer who was one of the top dogs of all breeds in Brazil 1980. Another import from Max Magder's kennel in Canada did even better: Int. Can. Ch. Lorricbrook Winning Streak won 32 groups in 37 shows, BIS 18 times and runner-up for the Dog of the Year title in 1981. She later almost completed the circle by going north to gain her American title as well. Later additions include successful imports from Sporting Fields in the U.S. and a breeding to the English-born stud dog Am. Ch. Hardknott Maestro of Bohem which resulted in at least a couple of champions.

Several other American whippets have won well in Brazil. The showy black-and-white Int. Ch. PJ's Step Ahead was a champion in the U.S., Brazil and Uruguay as well as a multiple BIS winner. Registrations have increased drastically in recent years but remain under a hundred per year. Peru has only a tiny whippet population, but Colombia in fact produced one of the American champions in the 1980s, Ch. Eucaliptus Blue Tango, bred from Oldland and Karasar lines and shown to her title in the US by Mrs. Gordon-Creed.

Asia

Although Japan has experienced a dog-population explosion of sometimes worrying proportions beginning in the 1960s, this has hardly affected whippets at all. Only a dozen or so have been registered each year, sometimes even less. The first whippet was brought to Japan from the west in 1956, and during the next few years several imports from Waddellie and Rosiel in Australia, Meander in America, Jynx in Canada, Oakbark and Barnesmore in Britain all became Japanese champions. When Japan celebrated its entrance into the FCI by hosting the World Dog Show in 1982, the only whippet shown was the white bitch Ch. Barnesmore Koo Koo. A few other British dogs of Hillsdown and Charmoll breeding have been added later, but the Japanese have yet to discover the charms of the whippet; as a comparison, toy-dog breeds such as Maltese and Pomeranians register around 30,000 dogs per year.

China has almost no dog activities, while in Hong Kong there has been a small but top class population of English whippets, primarily of Dondelayo breeding. Asian interest in whippets may be growing, judging by a disturbing inquiry about bulk imports in 1994: twenty brood bitches, five stud dogs and an unspecified number of puppies were requested.

Jacqueline Quiros Kubat bred whippets in the U.S. during the 1960s but now lives in Argentina. One of her top winners in recent years was Ch. Dragonfly's Man O'War (Ch. Dragonfly's The Whistler - Pennyworth Shimmering Gold, imp. USA). Mrs. Kubat is an international judge and regularly travels across North and South America.

Africa

Through a string of top-quality British dogs, South Africa occupies a special place in whippet history. The first great import was the glamorous Ch. Wingedfoot Claire de Lune, imported in whelp by Gary and Anna Kartsounis in 1962 and the foundation for their famous Tula Kennel. Others to follow included Eng. Ch. Denorsi Moonduster of Glenbervie, who won his South African title with seventeen BIS and sired a long row of champions, and in 1976 the outstanding Ch. Beseeka Knight Errant of Silkstone, fresh from a brilliant career in Britain which included the Hound Group at Crufts. He won at least sixteen BIS in his new country and crossed well as a sire with the Moonduster daughters at Tula.

The FCI World Show is held once each year in a different country. Only once has a whippet won Best in Show — at the 1980 show, when Ch. Beseeka Knight Errant of Silkstone travelled half way across the world from South Africa to defeat 4,300 dogs in Italy. "Whiskey" was born in England and was a Crufts group winner in 1976. Owner Gary Kartsounis showed Whiskey to first place in the group under the author, en route to Best in Show.

Knight Errant—known as "Whiskey"—made history in 1980 when the Kartsounises traveled with him across half the globe to the World Dog Show in Italy. He won the Sighthound Group under the author and went on to BIS from 4,300 dogs under old-time Italian all-rounder Paolo Ciceri—one of the breed's most exciting international victories and the only time a whippet has won the World Show. Whiskey even has winning offspring in Italy; a breeder ambitiously sent a bitch all the way to South Africa to be mated to him, and was rewarded with a healthy top-quality litter of six.

The Kartsounises' homebred stock has had a strong influence in America. Mrs. Christy Gordon-Creed started her Oldlands Kennel in 1971 while living in South Africa, and when she moved back to her native U.S. she took with her two Moonduster sons, who then sired champions in both North and South America. At the 1983 specialty show of the American Whippet Club in California, the winner was the fawn bitch Ch. Oldland's Singing in the Rain, a daughter of the imported Ch. Tula's Duststorm of Oldlands. Mrs. Kartsounis died in 1984, but her daughter has retained most of the whippets.

Other breeders who have imported top-quality British dogs include Mr. and Mrs. Pretorius, whose most successful dogs have been the fawn-and-white Ch. Folkline Sticklepath Sailor Boy, the Crufts winner Ch. Porthurst Martini Sweet and Ch. Dondelayo Hijack. Obviously Jack Peden's Denorsi prefix, originally of England, has been a strong influence in South Africa, and so has another kennel which was started in Britain—Stan Kay's De Gratton. Mr. Kay's son Neil carried on the line through such champions as Oakbark Mastermark De Gratton and others.

The Whippet Club of South Africa was formed in the 1980s, but little has been heard of whippets in this part of the world over the past decade. Zambia, however, which until recently had no discernible whippet population, received a boost with the arrival of Jean-Pascal Botella and his Sol y Sombra whippets from Brazil in the early 1990s. Originating in Europe with a French bitch of Mme. Bourdin´s breeding, Mr. Botella bred some successful Brazilian champions by Am. Ch. Chelsea Drakkar of Oxford, and these have continued to win Best in Show while transplanted on African soil.

Ch. Sporting Fields Clansman (Eng. Am. Ch. Charmoll Clansman-Dadaelis Cerulea) won Best in Show 59 times in the late 1970s and early 1980s, at the time of writing still the all-time record in the U.S. "Buoy" is shown with his last Best in Show ribbon and owner Debbie Butt.

ENGLISH WHIPPET BREED STANDARD

Approved by The Kennel Club, London, in 1988 and also approved by the Fédération Cynologique Internationale, which incorporates most of Europe, Asia, South America and Australia.

GENERAL APPEARANCE Balanced combination of muscular power and strength with elegance and grace of outline. Built for speed and work. All forms of exaggeration should be avoided.

CHARACTERISTICS An ideal companion. Highly adaptable in domestic and sporting surroundings.

TEMPERAMENT Gentle, affectionate, even disposition.

HEAD & SKULL Long and lean, flat on the top tapering to muzzle with slight stop, rather wide between the eyes, jaws powerful and clean cut, nose black, in blues a bluish colour permitted, in livers a nose of the same colour, in whites or parti-colour a butterfly nose permissible.

EYES Oval, bright, expression very alert.

EARS Rose shaped, small, fine in texture.

MOUTH Jaws strong with a perfect, regular and compete scissor bite, i.e., the upper teeth closely overlapping the lower teeth and set square to the jaws.

NECK Long, muscular, elegantly arched.

FOREQUARTERS Shoulders oblique and muscular, blades carried up to top of spine, where they are clearly defined. Forelegs straight and upright, front not too wide, pasterns strong with slight spring, elbows set well under body.

BODY Chest very deep with plenty of heart room, brisket deep, well defined, broad back, firm, somewhat long, showing definite arch over lain but not humped. Loin giving impression of strength and power, ribs well sprung, muscled on back.

HINDQUARTERS Strong, broad across thighs, stifles well bent, hocks well let down, well developed second thighs, dog able to stand over a lot of ground and show great driving power.

FEET Very neat, well split up between toes, knuckles well arched, pads thick and strong.

TAIL No feathering. Long, tapering, when in action carried in a delicate curve upward but not over back.

GAIT/MOVEMENT Free, hindlegs coming well under body for propulsion. Forelegs thrown well forward low over the ground, true coming and going. General movement not to look stilted, high stepping, short or mincing.

COAT Fine, short, close in texture.

COLOUR Any colour or mixture of colours.

SIZE Height: Dogs 47-51 cm (18 1/2-20 ins). Bitches: 44-47 cm (17 1/2 - 18 1/2 ins).

FAULTS Any departure from the foregoing points should be considered a fault and the seriousness with which the fault should be regarded should be in exact proportion to its degree.

NOTE Male animals should have two apparently normal testicles fully descended into the scrotum.

AMERICAN WHIPPET STANDARD

Revised and approved by the American Kennel Club on
August 10, 1993.
Effective September 30, 1993.

General Appearance
A medium size sighthound giving the appearance of elegance and fitness, denoting great speed, power and balance without coarseness. A true sporting hound that covers a maximum of distance with a minimum of lost motion. should convey an impression of beautifully balanced muscular power and strength, combined with great elegance and grace of outline. Symmetry of outline, muscular development and powerful gait are the main considerations; the dog being built for speed and work, all forms of exaggeration should be avoided.

Size, Proportion, Substance
Ideal height for dogs, 19 to 20 inches; for bitches, 18 to 21 inches, measured at the highest point of the withers. More than one-half inch above or below the stated limits will disqualify. Length from forechest to buttocks equal to or slightly greater than height at the withers. Moderate bone throughout.

Head
Keen intelligent alert expression. *Eyes* large and dark. Both eyes must be of the same color. Yellow or light eyes should be strictly penalized. Blue or wall eyes shall disqualify. Fully pigmented eyelids are desirable.

Rose *ears*, small, fine in texture; in repose, thrown back and folded along neck. fold should be maintained when at attention. Erect ears should be severely penalized.

Skull long and lean, fairly wide between the ears, scarcely perceptible stop.

Muzzle should be long and powerful denoting great strength of bite, without coarseness. Lack of underjaw should be strictly penalized. Nose entirely black.

Teeth of upper jaw should fit closely over teeth of lower jaw creating a scissors bite. Teeth should be white and strong. Undershot shall disqualify. Overshot one-quarter inch or more shall disqualify.

Neck, Topline, Body
Neck long, clean and muscular, well arched with no suggestion of throatiness, widening gracefully into the top of the shoulder. A short thick neck, or a ewe neck, should be penalized.

The *back* is broad, firm and well muscled, having length over the loin. The backline runs smoothly from the withers with a graceful natural arch, not too accentuated, beginning over the loin and carrying through over the croup; the arch is continuous without flatness. A dip behind shoulder blades, wheelback, flat back, or a steep or flat croup should be penalized.

Brisket vary deep, reach as nearly as possible to the point of the elbow. *Ribs* well sprung but with no suggestion of barrel shape. The space between the forelegs is filled in so that there is no appearance of a hollow between them. There is a definite tuckup of the underline.

The *tail* long and tapering, reaching to the hipbone when drawn through between the hind legs. when the dog is in motion, the tail is carried low with only a gentle upward curve; tail should not be carried higher that the top of back.

Forequarters
Shoulder blade long, well laid back, with flat muscles, allowing for moderate space between shoulder blades at peak of withers. Upper arm of equal length, placed so that the elbow falls directly under the withers.

The points of the elbows should point neither in nor out, but straight back. A steep shoulder, short upper arm, a heavily muscled or loaded should, or a very narrow shoulder, all of which restrict low free movement, should be strictly penalized.

Forelegs straight, giving appearance of strength and substance of bone. Pasterns strong, slightly bent and flexible. Bowed legs, tied-in elbows, legs lacking substance, legs set far under the body so as to create an exaggerated forechest, weak or upright pasterns should be strictly penalized.

Both front and rear feet must be well formed with hard, thick pads. Feet more hare than cat, but both are acceptable. Flat, splayed or soft feet without thick hard pads should be strictly penalized. Toes should be long, close and well arched. Nails strong and naturally short or of moderate length. Dewclaws may be removed.

Hindquarters
Long and powerful. the thighs are broad and muscular, stifles well bent; muscles are long and flat and carry well down toward the hock. the hocks are well let down and close to the ground. Sickle or cow hocks should be sticky penalized.

Coat
Short, close, smooth and firm in texture. any other coat shall be a disqualification. Old scars and injuries, the result of work or accident, should not be allowed to prejudice the dog's chance in the show ring.

Color
Color immaterial

Gait
Low, free moving and smooth, with reach in the forequarters and strong drive in the hindquarters. The dog has great freedom of action when viewed from the side; the forelegs move forward close to the ground to give a long, low reach; the hind legs have strong propelling power. When moving and viewed from front or rear, legs should turn neither in nor out, nor should feet cross or interfere with each other. Lack of front reach or rear drive, or a short, hackney gait with high wrist action, should be strictly penalized. Crossing in front or moving too close should be strictly penalized.

Temperament
Amiable, friendly, gentle, but capable of great intensity during sporting pursuits.

Disqualifications
More than on-half inch above or below stated height limits.
Blue or wall eyes.
Undershot; overshot one-quarter inch or more.
Any coat other that short, close, smooth and firm in texture

RECORD BOOK

Top Whippet Breeders, Great Britain

Post-World War II through 1993, based on number of champions bred. Year of first champion in parenthesis. Minimum 5 champions.

Seagift, Mrs. D. Whitwell (1947)	8
Mrs. K. Chapman (1947)	10
Laguna, Mrs. D. McKay (1948)	11
Peppard, Mr. & Mrs. D. Gollan (1949)	8
Harque, Mrs. A. Argyle (1958)	9
Shalfleet, Mrs. B. Wilton-Clark (1961)	13
Deepridge, Miss E. M. Hawthorne	5
Glenbervie, Arthur B. Nicholson (1963)	15
Dondelayo, Mrs. A. R. Knight (1966)	12
Oakbark, Mr. & Mrs. D. Meakin (1968)	10
Samarkand, Robert M. James (1968)	5
Nevedith, Mr. N. Newton & family (1972)	6
Nimrodel, Mrs. I. H. Lowe (1970)	8
Allgarth, Mr. & Mrs. F. Moore (1975)	6
Hillsdown, Phil Moran-Healy (1975)	7
Savilepark, Mrs. B. Robinson (1979)	5
Barmoll , Mrs. B. M. McConkey (1981)	5

Top Whippet Sires, Great Britain

Based on number of English champions sired through 1993. Figure in parenthesis indicates year of first champion. Minimum 5 champions.

Watford Bon (1923)	5
Ch. Willesbeaux (1923)	5
Ch. Watford Brilliant (1927)	6
Sapperly Tiptree Pilot (1947)	6
Ch. Pilot Officer Prune (1949)	9
Ch. Sapperly Heralder (1950)	6
Ch. Wingedfoot Marksman of Allways (1954)	10
Ch. Fieldspring Bartsia of Allways (1955)	5
Ch. Evening Star of Allways (1958)	5
Ch. Bellavista Barry (1959)	7
Ch. Laguna Ligonier (1964)	11
Ch. Samarkand's Greenbrae Tarragon (1964)	5
Ch. Ravensdowne Bright Star (1966)	5
Ch. Cockrow Tarquogan of Glenbervie (1967)	9
Ch. Deepridge Mintmaster (1970)	5
Ch. Towercrest Flarepath Taurus (1971)	5
Ch. Baydale Cinnamon (1972)	5
Ch. Dondelayo Buckaroo (1972)	10

Ch. Lowglen Newbold Cavalier (1974)	9
Ch. Akeferry Jimmy (1975)	10
Ch. Charmoll Mactavish (1978)	7
Ch. Nimrodel Ruff (1981)	6

Top Whippet Dams, Great Britain

As above, but minimum 3 champions.

Ch. Manorley Mimosa (12)	4
Selina (1925)	3
Willesberyl (1930)	3
Ch. Seagift Seraph (1949)	3
Brekin Willow Pattern (1953)	3
Ch. Brekin Ballet Shoes (1954)	3
Rosaday of Knotnum (1963)	3
Ch. Hillgarth Sun Star of Glenbervie (1967)	3
White Gorse of Glenbervie (1969)	3
Ch. Dondelayo Rue (1969)	3
Ch. Dondelayo Ruanne of Charmoll (1969)	3
White Bridge of Glenbervie (1977)	4
Flarepath Aquaria (1977)	3
Ch. Samarkand's Subaru (1984)	3
Ch. Barmoll Beejapers (1991)	3

Top All-Time Whippets, Great Britain

Based on number of Challenge Certificates won through 1993. Year of title in parenthesis. Minimum 10 CCs.

Ch. Manorley Model (1898)	10
Ch. Manorley Maori (1906)	10
Ch. Manorley Moireen (1907)	18
Ch. Boy Scrounger (1934)	11
Ch. Wingedfoot Marksman of Allways (1951)	13
Eng. & Am. Ch. Allways Wingedfoot Running Fox (1954)	10
Ch. Wingedfoot Wild Goose (1954)	11
Ch. Lily of Laguna (1955)	11
Ch. Robmaywin Stargazer of Allways (1958)	17
Ch. Wingedfoot Claire de Lune (1958)	13
Ch. Teighways Tasmin (1960)	14
Ch. Samarkand's Greenbrae Tarragon (1963)	17
Ch. Hillgarth Sun Star of Glenbervie (1963)	10
Ch. Roanbar Star (1964)	10
Eng. & Int. Ch. Fleeting Flamboyant (1966)	11
Ch. Laguna Ravensdowne Astri (1966)	14
Ch. Deepridge Mintmaster (1967)	12
Ch. Harque The Lark (1968)	19
Ch. Dondelayo Roulette (1970)	20
Ch. Tweseldown Whinchat (1971)	10
Ch. Nimrodel Ruff (1972)	10

Ch. Sequence of Shalfleet (1973)	15
Eng. & S. Afr. Ch. Beseeka Knight Errant of Silkstone (1975)	13
Ch. Ambassador of Allgarth (1976)	13
Ch. Jubilant Lady of Tygreen and Lowerdon (1979)	12
Ch. Welstar Royal Mint (1979)	19
Ch. Novacroft Madrigal (1980)	14
Ch. Cottonmere Monty of Oakbark (1982)	13
Ch. Oakbark Middleman (1982)	10
Ch. Nevedith Paper Weight (1983)	12
Ch. Selinko Another Lady (1983)	25
Ch. Lowglen Magic Moments (1984)	12
Ch. Dyanne Dondelayo (1984)	12
Ch. Nimrodel Wanderer (1985)	22
Ch. Samarkand's Beau Ranger (1985)	12
Ch. Baldrey Limited Edition of Juneric (1987)	12
Ch. Tilegreen Tornado (1988)	24
Ch. Nutshell of Nevedith (1988)	44
Ch. Mithrandir Spider Orchid (1989)	10
Ch. Pencloe Dutch Gold (1991)	14

Top Coursing Whippets 1980s/1990s, Great Britain

Statistical compliation of top coursing whippets, based on percentage of wins per run. Years following names denote active coursing seasons.

Jimanica Jacinta, 1982/83 - 1989/90
Jimanica Jet Run, 1982/83 - 1990/91
Jimanica Jungle Bunny, 1982/83 - 1990/91
Ballagan Rouge Dragon, 1983/84 - 1989/90
Greywhip I'm Quickest Too, 1984/85 - 1988/89
Laguna Leader, 1984/85 - 1991/92
Summersway Lark of Stableyard, 1984/85-1990/91
Wirrawon Touch Toes, 1984/85 - 1992/93
June Honeymoon, 1985/86 - 1992/93
Laguna Black Larmite, 1985/86 - 1992/93
Nimrodel Pegasus, 1985/86 - 1992/93
Tamaline Tillia of Culverstreet, 1985/86 - 1990/91
Terichline Grenadier, 1985/86 - 1990/91
Jimanica Jaguar, 1986/87 - 1992/93
Jimanica Jensen, 1986/87 - 1992/93
Ashley Running Wild, 1988/89 - 1992/93
Chyton Bonne Chance, 1988/89 - 1992/93
Moviestar Madam, 1988/89 - 1992/93
Stableyard Boynton Bugler, 1988/89 -1992/93
Terichline Juno, 1989/90 - 1992/93
Hungry Hall Benjamin, 1989/90 - 1992/93

Top Whippet Kennels, USA

Based on number of AKC champions registered with the kennel's name through 1993. Minimum 50 AKC champions. Listed in approximate chronological order.

Meander, Misses Judith & Julia Shearer	92
Mardormere, Mrs. George Anderson	69
Stoney Meadows, Mrs. W. P. Wear	102
Pennyworth, Mrs. M. P. Newcombe	100
Appraxin, Calvin G. Perry	81
Morshor, Dianne T. Bleecker	97
Sporting Fields, Mr. & Mrs. James Butt, Dionne Butt Giles	125
Whippoorwill, Mrs. Barbara Henderson, DVM	66
Rafina, Barbara Pendergrass	58
Bo-Bett, Carol Harris	82

Top Whippet Sires, USA

Based on number of champions published by the American Kennel Club since 1952 through 1993. Minimum 25 AKC champions. Figure in parenthesis indicates year of birth.

Eng. & Am. Ch. Courtenay Fleetfoot of

Pennyworth, imp. UK (1960)	45
Ch. Greenbrae Barn Dance, imp. UK (1962)	63
Ch. Stoney Meadows Royal Fortune (1964)	34
Ch. Morshor's Whirlaway (1965)	57
Eng. & Am. Ch. Charmoll Clansman, imp. UK (1971)	25
Ch. Misty Moor's Chalmondoley (1971)	112
Ch. Fenwick of Whippoorwill (1974)	25
Ch. Khiva's Show Stopper (1976)	25
Ch. Plumcreek Chimney Swift (1977)	26
Ch. Rolling's Viktor (1979)	27
Ch. Runner's He's The Continental (1979)	28
Ch. Morshor's Majestic Dell (1980)	41
Ch. Plumcreek Chase Manhattan, CD (1980)	30
Ch. Plumcreek Walk On Water (1980)	45
Ch. Hardknott Maestro of Bohem, imp. UK (1981)	30
Ch. Saxon Shore Amber Waves (1981)	61
Ch. Sporting Fields Strider (1981)	33
Ch. Bo-Bett's Luke Skywalker, CD (1983)	27
Ch. Delacreme de la Renta (1983)	83
Ch. Surrey Hill's Houston (1983)	44
Ch. Morshor's Majestic Prince (1987)	27

Top Whippet Dams, USA

As above, but minimum 10 AKC champions.

Lorelei O´Lazeland (1957)11

Ch. Whipoo´s Tar Heel (1960)	11
Ch. Stoney Meadows Imp of Satan (1966)	15
Ch. Winterfold´s Bold Bid, imp. Canada (1967)	14
Ch. Unmitigated Gallway (1968)	11
Ch. Seven League Serenissima (1969)	10
Ch. Edenfield Flaming Rose (1972)	11
Ch. Kai Esa´s Southern Comfort-W (1972)	10
Ch. Westgate The Enchantress (1972)	11
Morshor´s Pillow Talk (1972)	12
Ch. Kai Esa´s Mood Indigo (1975)	10
Ch. Whippoorwill Precious Gem (1979)	12
Ch. Rafina Rhianda of Kamara (1979)	17
Ch. Misty Moor´s Divine Pleasure (1981)	24
Ch. Gold Dust´s Limited Edition (1982)	12

Top Whippets, USA 1961-1993

Based on number of dogs defeated at American Kennel Club shows each year as listed in the dog press.

1961 Ch. Bull o´the Woods of Blue Beaver
1962 Ch. Selbrook Highlight, imp. UK
1963 Eng. & Am. Ch. Courtenay Fleetfoot of Pennyworth, imp. UK
1964 Eng. & Am. Ch. Courtenay Fleetfoot of Pennyworth, imp. UK
1965 Ch. Greenbrae Barn Dance, imp. UK
1966 Ch. Greenbrae Barn Dance, imp. UK
1967 Ch. Morshor´s Whirlaway
1968 Ch. Leatty Court Marshall, imp. UK
1969 Ch. Winterfold´s Bold Bid, imp. Canada
1970 Ch. Hollypark Honey Bee
1971 Ch. Winterfold´s Bold Bid, imp. Canada
1972 Ch. Alpine Ski Bum
1973 Ch. Alpine Ski Bum/Ch. Winterfold´s Bold Bid, imp. Canada*
1974 Eng. & Am. Ch. Charmoll Clansman, imp. UK
1975 Eng. & Am. Ch. Charmoll Clansman, imp. UK
1976 Eng. & Am. Ch. Charmoll Clansman, imp. UK
1977 Ch. Sporting Fields Clansman
1978 Ch. Sporting Fields Clansman
1979 Ch. Sporting Fields Clansman
1980 Ch. Sporting Fields Clansman
1981 Ch. Sporting Fields Windjammer
1982 Ch. Delacreme Avant Garde
1983 Ch. Runner´s He´s The Continental
1984 Ch. Runner´s He´s The Continental
1985 Ch. Surrey Hill Golden Rod
1986 Ch. Surrey Hill Golden Rod
1987 Ch. Bo-Bett´s Wild Waylon
1988 Ch. Bo-Bett´s Wild Waylon/Ch. Bohem Delacreme Demoiselle*
1989 Ch. Bohem Delacreme Demoiselle
1990 Ch. Bo-Bett´s Snow Bunny
1991 Ch. Sporting Fields Kinsman
1992 Ch. Sporting Fields Kinsman
1993 Ch. Sporting Fields Kinsman

* Different winner according to different published systems

American Whippet Club National Specialty Show winners

Although AWC has held specialty shows since the 1930s, the first National Specialty Show was held in 1987.

1987 Ch. Morshor´s Majestic Ball O´Fire, judge Mrs. W.P. Wear
1988 Ch. Bohem Delacreme Demoiselle, judge Mrs. Isabell Speight
1989 Ch. Roving Roulette, judge Ms. Carol Curry
1990 Ch. Allerei´s Ain´t Misbehavin, judge Miss Carol Willumsen
1991 Ch. Sporting Fields Kinsman, judge Mrs. James E. Clark
1992 Ch. Sporting Fields Chosen One, judge Mrs. M.P. Newcombe
1993 Ch. Merci Isle Meridian, judge Mrs. Lorraine Groshans
1994 Ch. Starline´s Claim To Fame, judge Mrs. Joan Frailey

Top Open Field Coursing Whippets, USA

As published by the National Open Field Coursing Association. CC = Coursing Champion. CM = Courser of Merit.

1982 Silverado Flyaway Cooper, CC, CM
1983 Travlin Zazzarra Zazz, CC, CM
1984 WR´s Quantum Leap of Course, CC, CM
1985 WR´s Quantum Leap of Course, CC, CM
1986 Jandall´s Toby Tyler of Kent, ARM, ORC, CC, CM, LCM
1987 Winsome Gambit of Windyglen, CC, CM
1988 Lyth Ely, ARM, ORC, CC, CM, FCh
1989 Kentfield´s Kalypso, RCh, SORC, CC, CM
1990 Kentfield´s Kalypso, RCh, SORC, CC, CM
1991 Kentfield´s Karillon, CC, CM
1992 Kentfield´s Karillon, CC, CM
1993 Kentfield´s Zerlina, RCh, CC, CM

National Point Racing Champions 1959-1993

Winners from 1959 through 1966 are prior to the American Whippet Club's Award of Racing Merit program. ARM = Award of Racing Merit. CD = Companion Dog (obedience). PCC = Pacific Coursing Champion (obsolete). FCh. = Field Champion. ORC = Oval track Racing Champion.

1959 Ch. Whipoo's Whimsey, CD
1960 Eyleland Peppermint Boy
1961 Eyleland Peppermint Boy
1962 Ch. Eyleland Cinnamon Roll
1963 Ch. Eyleland Cinnamon Roll
1964 Eyleland Homer
1965 Eyleland Hannah
1966 Eyleland Homer
1967 Strathoak Spring Intrigue, ARM
1968 Totam Hobo, ARM
1969 Ch. Pinetop's Opening Knight, ARM
1970 Scram Whsiper, CD, ARM
1971 Ch. Pinetop's Opening Knight, ARM
1972 Epinard Shelby of Wyndsor, CD, ARM, PCC
1973 Volant Big Red Machine, ARM
1974 Volant Big Red Machine, ARM
1975 Volant Big Red Machine, ARM
1976 Van Oorschot's Roro, ARM
1977 Topper's Topping, ARM
1978 Knight Kap O'Lazebrook, ARM
1979 Ch. Marial's Padneyhill Illusion, CD, ARM
1980 Jandall's Formula One, ARM, ORC
1981 Regalstock Cimarron del Toro, ARM, ORC
1982 Regalstock Cimarron del Toro, ARM, ORC
1983 Trylson of Wyndsor, ARM, ORC
1984 Lyth Satus, ARM, ORC
1985 Lyth Satus, ARM, ORC
1986 Lyth Satus, ARM, ORC, F.Ch.
1987 Marial's Whitewater, ARM, ORC
1988 Lyth York, ARM, ORC
1989 Lyth Saturn, ARM, Can. F.Ch.
1990 Lyth Saturn, ARM, Can. F.Ch.
1991 Blarneystone's Shoreline Jet, ARM
1992 Windyglen's Tuff Enuff, ARM, ORC
1993 Windyglen's Tuff Enuff, ARM, ORC

Top Whippets in Canada

As listed in the Canadian Kennel Club's publication Dogs in Canada and based on number of defeated competitors.

1982 Ch. Alery Astrologer's Antares
1983 Ch. Sporting Fields Morgan Dollar
1984 Ch. Boarley Singing Hinny
1985 Ch. Ashgrove Aphrodite, CD
1986 Ch. Nineveh Royal Denby
1987 Ch. Woodsmoke's Share A Moment
1988 Ch. Mispickel's A Touch of Class
1989 Ch. Woodsmoke's Share A Moment
1990 Ch. Swiftsure Out Of Africa
1991 Ch. Sporting Fields Kinsman
1992 Ch. Sporting Fields Anecho of Promise
1993 Ch. Baccarat Bon Chance*

* Preliminary result

Photo Credits

iv: Laura Baker-Stanton
vi: Scott McClaine
x, 2, 4, 6, 9, 11, 12, 13, 14, 28, 29, 32 (top), 33 (below),
53, 70: Steve Eltinge
3, 24, 126, 152: courtesy of the American Whippet Club
7: Paul Lepiane
8: courtesy of Judy Marden
15, 18, 25, 37, 40, 71, 74, 75, 80, 95, 96, 98, 106, 107,
109, 118, 124, 133, 152, 169, 170, 174, 175, 179, 184,
186: author's collection
16: Bennett Associates
19, 113, 144: courtesy of D. Jay Hyman
20: Roberts Photo
21, 157: Fox & Cook
24: Klein Photo
26: courtesy of Carol Harris
32 (below): Phoebe Booth
33: courtesy of Mary Lowe
35: courtesy of Pip Campbell
36, 151: Martin Booth
47 (below), 159: Kim Booth
47 (top), 105: Fall Photo
48: courtesy of Linda Garwacki
50: Sundsvalls Tidning
54, 55: A.C.S. Howard
56: courtesy of Merril Woolf
57: Rodger Craig
59: courtesy of Sharon Sakson
60: courtesy of April Allaway
65, 131: courtesy of Christine Cormany
67: Dwight Ellefsen
68: Pam Mayberry
70: Eric Gilbert
72: courtesy of Kennel Review

74 (stamp): courtesy of Philip Senior
74 (painting): courtesy of the Dog Museum
76: Tunbridge Wells Advertiser
77: courtesy of Dan Lockhart
79, 134, 135, 136: Wm. Brown
86, 87, 88, 128: courtesy of Constance O. Miller
92, 118 (left), 167: Bo Bengtson
101, 192: courtesy of Magnus Hagstedt
107, 120 (left): H. Whimpanny
110, 115, 125: Diane Pearce
113, 114: Cooke & Son
120 (right): E.G. Walsh
132: courtesy of Nigel Aubrey-Jones
134: courtesy of Betty Stites
135: courtesy of Desmond Murphy, Jr.
140: courtesy of Carol H. Willumsen
142, 143 (lower), 166: Evelyn Shafer
143 (right): Joan Ludwig
146 (left): Richard Bergman
146: Janet Photo
155: C. Edwards
156 (left): Larry Photo
156 (right): courtesy of Deann Christianson
158: courtesy of Mary Dukes
162: Chuck Tatham
163: Earl Graham
176: courtesy of Patricia Miller
188: courtesy of Unto Timonen
189: courtesy of Nenne Runsten
191: courtesy of Espen Engh
192, 198: Gunnar Lindgren
195: courtesy of Marianne Kiack Knöfel
197: courtesy of Jacqueline Q. Kubat
200: John Ashbey

Index

Dogs are mainly listed under primary kennel reference. To find individual names not included below, please refer to kennel name.

210